CLASS, WHITENESS, AND SOUTHERN LITERATURE

Class, Whiteness, and Southern Literature explores the role that representations of poor white people play in shaping both middle-class American identity and major American literary movements and genres across the long twentieth century. Jolene Hubbs reveals that, more often than not, poor white characters imagined by middle-class writers embody what better-off people are anxious to distance themselves from in a given moment. Poor white southerners are cast as social climbers during the status-conscious Gilded Age, country rubes in the modern era, racist obstacles to progress during the civil rights struggle, and junk-food devotees in the health-conscious 1990s. Hubbs illuminates how Charles Chesnutt, William Faulkner, Flannery O'Connor, Dorothy Allison, and Barbara Robinette Moss swam against these tides, pioneering formal innovations with an eye to representing poor white characters in new ways.

JOLENE HUBBS is an associate professor of American Studies at the University of Alabama. She studies the literature and culture of the US South.

CAMBRIDGE STUDIES IN AMERICAN LITERATURE
AND CULTURE

Editor
Leonard Cassuto, *Fordham University*

Founding Editor
Albert Gelpi, *Stanford University*

Advisory Board
Robert Levine, *University of Maryland*
Ross Posnock, *Columbia University*
Branka Arsić, *Columbia University*
Wai Chee Dimock, *Yale University*
Tim Armstrong, *Royal Holloway, University of London*
Walter Benn Michaels, *University of Illinois, Chicago*
Kenneth Warren, *University of Chicago*

Recent books in this series

190. JOLENE HUBBS
   Class, Whiteness, and Southern Literature
189. RYAN M. BROOKS
   Liberalism and American Literature in the Clinton Era
188. JULIANA CHOW
   Nineteenth-Century American Literature and the Discourse of Natural History
187. JESSICA E. TEAGUE
   Sound Recording Technology and American Literature
186. BRYAN M. SANTIN
   Postwar American Fiction and the Rise of Modern Conservatism: A Literary History, 1945–2008
185. ALEXANDER MENRISKY
   Wild Abandon: American Literature and the Identity Politics of Ecology
184. HEIKE SCHAEFER
   American Literature and Immediacy: Literary Innovation and the Emergence of Photography, Film, and Television
183. DALE M. BAUER
   Nineteenth-Century American Women's Serial Novels
182. MARIANNE NOBLE
   Rethinking Sympathy and Human Contact in Nineteenth-Century American Literature

(Continued after Index)

CLASS, WHITENESS, AND SOUTHERN LITERATURE

JOLENE HUBBS
University of Alabama

Shaftesbury Road, Cambridge CB2 8EA, United Kingdom

One Liberty Plaza, 20th Floor, New York, NY 10006, USA

477 Williamstown Road, Port Melbourne, VIC 3207, Australia

314–321, 3rd Floor, Plot 3, Splendor Forum, Jasola District Centre, New Delhi – 110025, India

103 Penang Road, #05–06/07, Visioncrest Commercial, Singapore 238467

Cambridge University Press is part of Cambridge University Press & Assessment, a department of the University of Cambridge.

We share the University's mission to contribute to society through the pursuit of education, learning and research at the highest international levels of excellence.

www.cambridge.org
Information on this title: www.cambridge.org/9781009250641

DOI: 10.1017/9781009250627

© Jolene Hubbs 2023

This publication is in copyright. Subject to statutory exception and to the provisions of relevant collective licensing agreements, no reproduction of any part may take place without the written permission of Cambridge University Press & Assessment.

First published 2023
First paperback edition 2025

A catalogue record for this publication is available from the British Library

Library of Congress Cataloging-in-Publication data
NAMES: Hubbs, Jolene, author.
TITLE: Class, Whiteness, and Southern literature / Jolene Hubbs.
DESCRIPTION: Cambridge, United Kingdom ; New York : Cambridge University Press, 2023. | Series: Cambridge studies in American literature and culture | Includes bibliographical references and index.
IDENTIFIERS: LCCN 2022030487 (print) | LCCN 2022030488 (ebook) | ISBN 9781009250658 (hardback) | ISBN 9781009250641 (paperback) | ISBN 9781009250627 (epub)
SUBJECTS: LCSH: American literature–Southern States–History and criticism. | Authors, American–Southern States–History. | Poor white people in literature. | White people in literature. | Southern States–In literature. | Literature and society–United States–History. | American literature–20th century–History and criticism.
CLASSIFICATION: LCC PS261 .H7857 2023 (print) | LCC PS261 (ebook) | DDC 810.9/975–DC23/eng/20220718
LC record available at https://lccn.loc.gov/2022030487
LC ebook record available at https://lccn.loc.gov/2022030488

ISBN   978-1-009-25065-8   Hardback
ISBN   978-1-009-25064-1   Paperback

Cambridge University Press & Assessment has no responsibility for the persistence or accuracy of URLs for external or third-party internet websites referred to in this publication and does not guarantee that any content on such websites is, or will remain, accurate or appropriate.

Contents

List of Figures   *page* vi
Acknowledgments   vii

Introduction: Poor White Southerners in the American Imaginary   1

1. Riffraff and Half-Strainers: Charles W. Chesnutt and Regionalism   19

2. Slow, Sweating, Stinking Bumpkins: William Faulkner and Modernism   44

3. Civil Rights and Uncivil Whites: Flannery O'Connor and Southern Women's Midcentury Writing   68

4. Hungry Women and Horny Men: Dorothy Allison, Barbara Robinette Moss, and Grit Lit   94

Coda   123

Notes   134
Bibliography   166
Index   184

Figures

0.1	E. W. Kemble, "A Race Problem"	*page* 2
0.2	E. W. Kemble, "Poor White"	5
0.3	Walker Evans, "[Untitled photo, possibly related to: Dora Mae Tengle, Hale County, Alabama]"	14

Acknowledgments

It gives me great joy to thank the mentors, colleagues, friends, and family members who have supported me during the years I spent researching and writing this book.

I first explored questions of literary form and poor white identity in my doctoral dissertation. I am incredibly grateful to my dissertation directors for their advice and support during my time at Stanford and in the years since then. Ramón Saldívar, unstintingly generous with his time and enthusiasm, was the kind of mentor I try to be to my own students. Paula Moya asked questions that continue to shape my approaches to literature. Gavin Jones was instrumental in helping me formulate a method for analyzing how American authors represent poverty. At Stanford I also benefited from working with Andrea Lunsford, Scott Bukatman, Bryan Wolf, and Sianne Ngai. Numberless hours reading and writing in Green Library alongside Mark Vega made my solitary labors less solitary. Jenna Lay has been asking the important questions – whether "What's your argument here?" or "When did you last see your wallet?" – for the past two decades. Although I cannot reconcile myself to the fact that we are no longer roommates, I am happy to count her among my closest friends. A writing fellowship from Stanford's Center for Comparative Studies in Race and Ethnicity (CCSRE) provided me with essential support in finishing the dissertation as well as invaluable friendships with Matthew Daube, Jocelyn Lim Chua, and Doris Madrigal. The Mellon Foundation and Stanford's Diversity Dissertation Research Opportunity Grant also supported my work on the dissertation, and a second appointment as a visiting scholar at CCSRE in 2016–2017 supported my work on this book.

At the University of Alabama, my scholarly labors have been buoyed by wonderful colleagues and friends. Among my stellar colleagues in the American Studies department, Lynne Adrian, Stacy Morgan, and Edward Tang deserve particular thanks for offering advice and support throughout my years at UA. Historians Holly Grout and Jenny Shaw are savvy advisors and dear friends. Sharon O'Dair's feedback helped me become a better writer. Fred Whiting's kind invitations to many events made me feel like a member of a broader intellectual community at UA. I'm grateful, as well, for the Clarence Mondale Fellowship in American Studies and the Research Grants Committee Award, which funded my research for this book.

I owe a huge debt of gratitude to two anonymous readers for Cambridge University Press whose generous and constructive responses to this manuscript aided me in clarifying and bolstering my arguments. Publishing with CUP has also afforded me the privilege of working with Leonard Cassuto and Ray Ryan. I heartily thank them both for their interest in this project and their expert guidance on the road from manuscript to book. Thanks to Edgar Mendez for answering many questions while I readied the manuscript for delivery. Thanks, as well, to Sam Arnold-Boyd for preparing the index and to Dr. Mark Reynolds for defraying its cost. I am also grateful to Paula Dragosh for reviewing the page proofs and to the Clarence C. Mondale American Studies Fund for supporting that work. An earlier version of part of the second chapter appeared as "William Faulkner's Rural Modernism" in *Mississippi Quarterly* 61, no. 3 (2008): 461–75. Thanks to the copyright owner, Mississippi State University, for permission to reprint. A portion of Chapter 4 appeared, in a different form, in the *Southern Literary Journal* 47, no. 2 (2015): 1–19. It is reprinted by permission of the copyright owners, the *Southern Literary Journal* and the University of North Carolina at Chapel Hill Department of American Studies.

Thanks to Scotti Parrish for her feedback on my book proposal and to Sarah Allison, Chris Phillips, and Ellen Spears for showing me the ropes when it came time to reach out to presses. Countless conversations with Karen Maoki helped me refine my arguments and renew my excitement for this project. Han Yuan was an important part of my life from soon after this project began until shortly before I finished it, and I thank him for the ways he supported my scholarly work. I am grateful to Steve Tedeschi for coming into my life when the end of this book was in sight and cheering me across the finish line. Thanks to my parents, Jack and Jerrie Hubbs, and my siblings, Nancy, Jack, and Nadine, for their support. Nadine's comments on the introduction helped me better articulate the stakes of this project, and her encouragement and enthusiasm for my intellectual pursuits – from my first day of kindergarten to the present – mean a lot to me. Finally, thanks to Scripps College, my undergraduate alma mater, for awarding me the financial aid that made earning a bachelor's degree possible and for introducing me to an amazing mentor, Cheryl Walker, who first piqued my interest in southern literature.

Like Betsey Dole's poems in Mary E. Wilkins Freeman's story "A Poetess," which are "the love-letters that had passed between her and life," this book is a love letter to literary works that have uplifted me, caught me off guard, delighted me, puzzled me, and prompted me to read them again and again. It also conveys my deep regard for the cherished interlocutors whose responses to literature and life have informed, challenged, and enlivened my own.

Introduction
Poor White Southerners in the American Imaginary

In its February 1891 issue, the *Century Illustrated Monthly Magazine* laid before its readers "a race problem." Or, at least, so declared the caption for a pen-and-ink drawing of a man by E. W. Kemble, one of the magazine's staff illustrators. Reflecting on his career decades later, Kemble observed, "I was established as a delineator of the South, the Negro being my specialty," by working at the *Century* and illustrating stories by Mark Twain, George Washington Cable, Thomas Nelson Page, and other southern writers.[1] Racism and racial injustice were on the minds of many Americans at the end of the Gilded Age. The year before Kemble's "race problem" appeared in the *Century*, Frederick Douglass delivered a speech about southern efforts to curtail the civil rights of African Americans that he titled, simply, "The Race Problem." In 1892, the year after Kemble's illustration was published, activist and educator Anna Julia Cooper included a chapter called "Has America a Race Problem? If So, How Can it Best Be Solved?" in her book *A Voice from the South*. That same year, Marietta Holley – an American humorist sometimes referred to as the female Mark Twain – added to her popular book series featuring the wit and wisdom of an upstate New Yorker named Samantha by releasing a volume in which her eponymous heroine weighs in on race relations in the postbellum South. Its title? *Samantha on the Race Problem*.

Yet E. W. Kemble was not thinking about Jim Crow segregation, or disenfranchisement, or even lynching when he put pen to paper in 1890. Instead of addressing what W. E. B. Du Bois famously termed "the problem of the color-line," the artist took on an intraracial issue.[2] Kemble's "race problem" takes shape on the page as a poor white southerner (Figure 0.1). *Century* subscribers were primed to recognize the shabby, slouching figure before them as a familiar – and deeply problematic – poor white type. The magazine's readers had been looking at Kemble's pictures of poor whites in the South for six years – ever since his renderings of another fictional poor white southerner, Huckleberry Finn, captured the fancy of

A RACE PROBLEM.

Figure 0.1   A drawing by E. W. Kemble illustrating, according to the caption, "a race problem." Published in the February 1891 issue of the *Century Illustrated Monthly Magazine* as part of Clare de Graffenried's essay "The Georgia Cracker in the Cotton Mills."

editors at the *Century* and earned him a spot in the magazine's art department.³ In illustrations from his early days as a staff illustrator at the *Century*, Kemble's poor white southerners are Huck Finn's kissing cousins. For instance, a picture of a poor white Alabamian for "Hodson's Hide-Out," a local color story published in March 1885, closely resembles Kemble's frontispiece illustration of Huck Finn. Each figure stands at a forty-five-degree angle to the viewer with a rifle held vertically in his left hand and sports a battered hat, homespun shirt, and ragged pants.

As his work continued in this vein, Kemble developed a repertoire of visual signifiers of poor white identity that foregrounded characteristics regarded by some middle- and upper-class observers as markers of laziness, genetic inferiority, and ignorance. In his drawings, poor white men regularly have unkempt hair, scraggly beards, and worse-for-wear hats – attributes suggesting not only impoverishment but also slovenliness. Poor white southerners in the American imaginary routinely embrace anti-intellectualism, and Kemble's illustrations portray this by way of facial expressions that are sometimes perplexed, other times blank. The artist's poor white southern women are unfashionable from the tops of their slat bonnets to the bottoms of their ill-fitting brogans – or their bare feet. Their bodies are often distressingly gaunt, and occasionally impossibly fleshy, but rarely just like the physiques of more prosperous women in drawings by Kemble and other artists. In illustration after illustration, both sexes have their vice of choice – whiskey for men, tobacco for women – ready at hand.

Kemble's drawings jibe with local color writers' depictions of poor white southerners. In his stories about the denizens of Georgia's piney woods, Joel Chandler Harris portrays poor white people who are "steeped in poverty of the most desolate description."⁴ Again and again, local colorists attribute this destitution to individual rather than institutional factors, chalking up characters' privation to laziness. In one of Harry Stillwell Edwards's stories, an "air of listlessness" hangs around poor white people.⁵ In a tale by Mary Noailles Murfree, a poor white pair consists of a "slovenly, indolent woman" married to a "listless" man with "slow brains" and "dull," "listless" eyes.⁶ Third-person narrators and better-off characters frequently point to the sorry state of poor white southerners' homes and habiliments as evidence of their lassitude. As one middle-class white girl rather superciliously observes after successfully "mastering a natural repugnance to so much uncleanliness" in order to take on the task of reforming one of her poor white neighbors, "evidently cleanliness is not looked upon as next to godliness among the crackers."⁷

Local color stories are not the only late nineteenth-century literary works that treat poor white southern identity as a problem in need of a solution. Scholars have long recognized how *Adventures of Huckleberry Finn* speaks to its post-Reconstruction publication context by addressing racism and black disenfranchisement under the burgeoning Jim Crow system.[8] But the novel also engages with its era's classism by taking on the emerging American eugenics movement.[9] Eugenics offered "a way of reading the structure of social classes onto nature" by attributing differences in economic status to heredity rather than environment.[10] American eugenicists believed that poor white people living in rural areas represented a grave internal threat to the white race. As criminologist Nicole Hahn Rafter has observed, the social menace conjured by the bulk of late nineteenth- and early twentieth-century eugenic analyses is "the degenerate hillbilly family, dwelling in filthy shacks and spawning endless generations of paupers, criminals, and imbeciles."[11] Pap Finn's defining characteristics – intemperance, pauperism, vagabondage, and criminality ("take a chicken when you get a chance" is one of the few lessons Huck learns from his father) – represent the attributes that most fret eugenicists.[12] Yet Twain's novel defies eugenics, staging nurture's triumph over nature in Huck's maturation by making him more like Jim, his adoptive father, than Pap, his biological dad.

Even writers chiefly interested in African American life call attention to poor white southerners. In his 1890 speech to the Bethel Literary and Historical Association in Washington, DC, titled "The Race Problem," Frederick Douglass challenged the arguments against black citizenship and voting rights that some southern politicians and journalists were trumpeting. The southerners fulminating against less educated people's participation in the democratic process, Douglass observed, were the same ones who denied schooling to large swaths of the region's populace, because "it has been the policy of the ruling class there to oppose education not only for the blacks, but for the poor whites as well."[13] Humorist Marietta Holley also took up the issue of poor white southerners' voting rights in *Samantha on the Race Problem* (1892). Advocating for middle-class female suffrage, Holley's eponymous heroine argues that voting rights should be granted on the basis of education, not race or sex. Denying the vote to the "low, ignorant ones of the white people" would, Samantha explains, both protect society from that group's political will and inspire some poor white people to better themselves as a way to earn the right to vote.[14] The accompanying illustration, produced by Kemble, shows a poor white man who looks nearly identical to the fellow who incarnated the "race problem" in the *Century* the year before (Figure 0.2).

POOR WHITE.

Figure 0.2 E. W. Kemble's illustration of a "poor white." Published in *Samantha on the Race Problem* (1892), by Marietta Holley.

Foils and Forms

As the foregoing examples suggest, poor white southerners figure prominently in Gilded Age American literature. Yet literary criticism offers few ideas about how to make sense of late nineteenth-century writers' interest in poor white southerners. Historians have long studied the South's poor whites.[15] Social scientists frequently analyze poor white people.[16] The election of Donald Trump in 2016 prompted a flurry of interest in poor (and working-class) white Americans, including much-discussed books purporting to lay bare the mind of the poor white southerner.[17] These efforts to grasp poor white southerners' role in the American electorate have not been matched by attempts to understand their role in the American imaginary.

More often than not, literary scholars erase poor white literary characters and misread fictional treatments of cross-class conflicts among white people. In his field-defining work on American literary regionalism, Richard Brodhead accounts for the hordes of poor white southerners in local color stories by reading them as stand-ins for northern cities' new immigrant communities. In local color tales, Brodhead asserts, "Appalachian hillbillies [substitute] for Russian Jews and Chinese" people who had recently left their countries of origin and settled in the United States.[18] In a much-discussed book, Shelley Fisher Fishkin takes up Huckleberry Finn, arguably the most famous poor white southerner in American letters, and asks, *Was Huck Black?*[19] For his part, Twain suggested that he was not. In his autobiography, Twain wrote that "'Huckleberry Finn' was Tom Blankenship," an "ignorant, unwashed, insufficiently fed" poor white boy he knew as a child in Hannibal, Missouri.[20]

Reading poor white characters out of the works in which they appear is not confined to studies of late nineteenth-century literature. Nor is it unique to analyses of southern fiction. In 2000, a literary critic made a splash by arguing that Jazz Age literature's most celebrated social climber, who is born into a poor white family and raises himself up by his own bootlegging bootstraps, is black. Carlyle V. Thompson's take on Jay Gatsby stimulated a level of popular interest rare for literary scholars' arguments, garnering coverage by *The Guardian*, *Salon*, *Times Higher Education*, and other media outlets. But because the South is a hotbed for anxieties about impoverished white people, the region's literature teems with poor white characters.[21]

Although poverty is not unique to the South, poverty has long been viewed as a key part of what makes the South distinctive. In the middle of the twentieth century, C. Vann Woodward identified the South's "long and quite un-American experience with poverty" as a defining aspect of southern distinctiveness.[22] A half-century later, Jennifer Rae Greeson observed that "underdevelopment, poverty, [and] backwardness" are among the "enduring associations" that allow the region to serve as "an *internal other* for the nation."[23] Poverty in the South is often treated differently from poverty in other parts of the United States. At the end of the nineteenth century, works including Jacob Riis's *How the Other Half Lives* (1890) and Stephen Crane's *Maggie: A Girl of the Streets* (1893) shined a light on poor people in New York City. Local reformers embraced environmental strategies for alleviating poverty and its attendant ills during this era, advocating for boys' clubs offering "quiet and innocent amusement," city parks affording tenement residents an escape from their close living quarters, and homestays in the country for children from poor families.[24] Willard Parsons, whose Fresh-Air Fund sponsored two-week trips to the countryside for economically disadvantaged children, observed in an 1891 article for *Scribner's Monthly* that a fortnight on a farm could bring about a "complete transformation" in impoverished city kids, because countless recipients of his organization's aid returned to the Big Apple "with head and heart full of ... new ideas of decent living."[25]

By contrast, the very year that Parsons celebrated poor New Yorkers' transformative potential, an investigator with the US Bureau of Labor lamented that poor white Georgians were "less plastic to civilization than any other race in America."[26] In response to such ideas about their adamantine natures, some Americans endorsed sterilizing poor white southerners. When Indiana adopted the nation's first compulsory eugenic sterilization law in 1907, for instance, it did so in response to migrants from Kentucky and Tennessee. As historian Alexandra Minna Stern explains, "Hoosier eugenicists branded destitute white southerners as the state's most serious biological hazard."[27] Viewing poor white southerners' status as more or less immutable made poor white identity something one was unlikely to shed. Or to assume. In Charles Chesnutt's novel *The Colonel's Dream* (1905), young southerners who find themselves in reduced circumstances take comfort by insisting that being poor and white is different from being poor white: "We might be poor, but not poor-white! Our blood will still be of the best."[28] Regarded as unlikely to improve their situation by getting more fresh air or frequenting boys' clubs, poor white southerners have often been looked at differently from impecunious Americans in other parts of the country.

Some scholars view southern literature's poor white characters as proxies for other members of the social order. Others ignore them altogether. As a result, we have little sense of the cultural anxieties they embody or the textual effects they produce. Yet poor whites are important – and omnipresent – players in the southern literary landscape. They are southwestern humor's raison d'être. They populate the bayous, piney woods, and mountain hollers of late nineteenth-century local color fiction. They figure crucially in modernist literature, appearing as the protagonists of proletarian novels (*To Make My Bread*), experimental nonfiction (*Let Us Now Praise Famous Men*), novels admired in the modern era (*The Time of Man*), and novels well known today (*As I Lay Dying*). In postwar novels including *The Dollmaker* and *Seraph on the Suwanee*, poor white women seek out their places in the world. In works like *Deliverance* and *Ecology of a Cracker Childhood*, poor white southerners' experiences reveal the impact of ecological changes. Poor white southerners even have their own contemporary genre: grit lit.

This book analyzes the changes and constants in representations of poor white southerners across the long twentieth century to advance two major arguments. The first is that poor white literary characters are barometers of the cultural anxieties gripping middle-class white people in the periods in which they are produced. Throughout this study, I work to show how literary representations of poor white southerners divulge the aspirations and fears of the middle-class (and occasionally upper-class) writers and readers who create and consume them. Poor white southerners appear throughout US literature as embodiments of whatever wealthier white people are most eager to distance themselves from. My examples show the utility and malleability of southern poor white stereotypes during four different periods of social and economic upheaval: the late nineteenth-century Gilded Age, the Great Depression of the 1930s, the mid-twentieth-century civil rights era, and the economic boom of the 1990s.

This book's second major argument concerns the dynamic relationship between social structures and literary structures. I contend that writers' engagements with and investments in class distinctions manifest not only at the level of character and theme but also in the conventions that define major American literary movements and genres. Chapters focus on authors who push back on prevailing representations of poor white southerners, tracing out how social disruptions – depictions of poor white experience that challenge the status quo – take shape textually through formal disruptions. The middle class reproduces itself, I argue, through literary forms that have classist ideology baked into them. This makes it possible to represent poor white people as a problem, in terms that shift to fit each cultural moment under discussion. But this baked-in ideology also encumbers authors who wish to veer away from their periods' predominant portrayals of poor white identity. Thus, the five writers I concentrate on invent and adapt techniques in search of ways to contest negative representations of poor white southerners that buttress the major literary genres and movements of their eras. In highlighting these authors' counterdiscursive structural and stylistic innovations, I illuminate the ideological cast of not only dominant discourse but also, and more importantly, dominant literary forms.

Class, Whiteness, and Southern Literature is a study of traditions defined in the breach. Centering on writers who contest their eras' prevailing representations of poor white southerners, chapters examine the formal mechanisms for refiguring poverty these authors employ to write against the grain of their predecessors' and contemporaries' constructions of poor white identity. Because my foremost interest is in a two-way traffic in ideas – a classist tradition and a formally innovative countertradition – rather than in representations of poor white southerners per se, some genres that attend to poor white life in the South are peripheral to or even absent from this study. For instance, southwestern humor is an important part of the story this book tells insofar as the genre writes into literary history the contours of the poor white type. Southwestern humor stories' poor white raconteur, whose "barbarously authentic dialect" gave rise to a "linguistic revolution" in American literature, influenced almost all of the literary works addressed in this study.[29] Likewise, the "gaunt-looking specimen of freakish humanity" – Hardin E. Taliaferro's evocative description of southwestern humor's archetypal antihero – who speaks in dialect and dresses shabbily begets generations of imaginary poor white southerners.[30] But no southwestern humorist significantly reworked the form in order to rebut the stereotypes disseminated by his fellow humorists. Although southwestern humor's frame narrative structure evolved across the genre's three-decade run, sidelining the outer frame's gentlemanly speaker in order to cede more and more space to the vernacular-speaking frontiersman at the heart of the tale, this change happened progressively across numerous works in the tradition rather than solely in the writings of an iconoclast who sought to swim against the tide of his fellow southwestern humorists' depictions of poor white life. On the whole, George Washington Harris, Johnson Jones Hooper, Augustus Baldwin Longstreet, Thomas Bangs Thorpe, and other southwestern humorists seem pretty well aligned in terms of not only the forms they use but also the yarns they spin about rough-and-tumble dialect-speaking poor white southerners.

From the postbellum era to the present, "poor white" functions in some ways less as an economic designation than as an inflexible identity, because social status can prove surprisingly unresponsive to monetary ebbs and flows. In the Reconstruction and post-Reconstruction periods, southerners who had been affluent in the antebellum era forged new social categories that not only afforded them status despite their reduced circumstances but also undercut the prestige of arrivistes. Margaret Mitchell explored how antebellum elites denied prestige to postbellum upstarts in *Gone with the Wind* (1936). In Mitchell's work, the Civil War threatens to turn the social hierarchy of Clayton County, Georgia, on its head, because it leaves planters' daughters like Scarlett O'Hara penniless and allows poor white girls like Emmie Slattery to marry men flush with new money. But Mitchell's narrator makes clear that Emmie remains a "common, nasty piece of poor white trash" even after she is wealthy.[31] For one thing, the war revealed that social status amounted to more than one's clothes and cadences, because Scarlett and her sisters discovered while nursing wounded soldiers that they could discern the men's social stations "instinctively, as they knew thoroughbred horses from scrubs."[32] For another thing, Emmie's newfound prosperity demonstrates that money cannot buy taste. Emmie's pricey getup is so gauche – a dress "bright in color to the point of vulgarity," an "absurd" hat, and boots with red tops and tassels – that Scarlett simply scoffs at it.³³ Finally, even Emmie's whiteness is faulty. Taking her cues from myriad nineteenth-century forerunners, Mitchell gave poor white characters sickly yellow complexions.³⁴ Emmie's face, "caked with white powder," is a tragic burlesque of Scarlett's "magnolia-white skin."³⁵

This book delves into literature's role in class formation and cohesion by looking at literature as a domain of cultural capital in which middle-class producers use representations of poor white southerners in order to establish – by contrast – certain ideas about what middle-class white people are like. In identifying engagements with social class through textual elements fostering identifications and disavowals among readers, writers, narrators, and characters, I adapt historian E. P. Thompson's definition of class not as a structure or a category but as a "historical phenomenon" that *happens*: "Class happens when some men, as a result of common experiences (inherited or shared), feel and articulate the identity of their interests as between themselves, and as against other men whose interests are different from (and usually opposed to) theirs."³⁶ In turning from English history to American literature, my analysis takes up real and fictional experiences of affinity and discord that play powerful roles in the national imaginary. Some works establish a class-based us/them dichotomy, with both the syntax and the substance of the prose inscribing intraracial dividing lines. Lillian Smith's *Killers of the Dream* (1949), for example, forges a first-person plural collectivity out of common experiences imaginatively produced by depicting Smith and her readers as feeding on reading: "How can we who were fed so bountifully feel what it means to live with a mind emptied of words, bereft of ideas and facts, unknowing of books and man-made beauty?"³⁷ This rhetorical question aims to expose how far removed "we" are from the tripartite ignorance of poor white southerners.

Other works concentrate on the poor white southerner and depict him as aberrant, which encourages readers to conceive of themselves as his antithesis. Eudora Welty's short story "Where Is the Voice Coming From?" (1963) presents a first-person monologue by a poor white narrator whose racism, hostility, laziness, and vitiated language are calculated to repel and alienate readers. Class *happens* in response to such a text when middle-class readers become conscious of their superior social status by mentally cataloging the characteristics that differentiate them from poor white people. According to Pierre Bourdieu, "difference ... only becomes a visible, perceptible, non-indifferent, socially *pertinent* difference if it is perceived by someone who is capable of *making the distinction*."³⁸ Fiction affords a space for staging economic differences in ways that emphasize their social import. In Welty's story, the fictional narrator's ethical depravity and economic deprivation get tangled together in a mass of socially significant characteristics intended to distinguish him from Welty and her audience (in this case, readers of the *New Yorker*, which published the story in July 1963). Welty's work tells middle-class white people what they want to hear by promulgating what historian Joel Williamson identified as the "persisting myth ... that the lower classes were racial extremists while the upper classes were not."[39] Yet, in some sense, Welty's text does this surreptitiously. Structured as a first-person narrator's unselfconscious confessions, Welty's story befogs the answer to the question posed by its title: "Where Is the Voice Coming From?" Although the use of first-person point of view makes it seem as though the voice comes from the mouth of a poor white man, it actually arises from the mind – and the considered keystrokes – of a middle-class white woman.

This book offers an account of American literary history told through a series of struggles over how the poor white southerner would take shape in the national imaginary. Across the last century and a half of literary production, a multitude of writers have treated poor white identity as a foil for middle-class white people's desired self-presentations. But a few maverick authors pushed against these depictions, exerting enough force in the process to reshape the literary movements and genres in which they worked. By exploring these aesthetic and structural innovations, this study distinguishes itself from previous scholarship that analyzes authors' takes on how social class shapes American experience.[40] A few literary critics have published book-length treatments of southern literature's poor white characters; many more scholars have focused on literary depictions of working-class Americans.[41] Laura Hapke and Janet Zandy have considered the cultural work done by representations of working people.[42] Eric Schocket and Joe Shapiro have looked at working-class characters to understand how American writers treat economic inequality.[43] Barbara Foley and Paula Rabinowitz have investigated how literature from the 1930s engages with working-class life.[44] Michael Denning and Lori Merish have analyzed working-class readers' and writers' influences on US literature.[45]

A yawning chasm separates working-class whites from poor whites in the American imaginary. Working-class people are, as their name indicates, associated with labor, whereas poor white people have a longstanding reputation for laziness. Rick Bragg addresses this difference in his writings on blue-collar southerners. Bragg observes that although outsiders think of violence, or football, or NASCAR when they think of working-class people in the Deep South, in fact, "it is work that defines them."[46] Describing cotton mill workers in Alabama, Bragg suggests that industriousness underpins their identities: "You need not use foul language to damn a man here. Just say that a day's work would kill him, and you tore him down to the bald nothing."[47] Aware that some middle- and upper-class white people see poor white southerners as "the laziest two-legged animals that walk erect on the face of the Earth" (in the words of one classist chronicler), working-class white southerners distinguish themselves from the poor by insisting that they work hard.[48]

Working-class life also takes shape on the page differently from poor white life. Several scholars identify a worker-centered politics as working-class literature's animating impulse. For example, Janet Zandy identifies working-class texts by their empathetic approach to laborers, writing that such works "contest the dehumanization of the working mind/body," demonstrate "consciousness of class oppression," "give language to human suffering," and insist "on human dignity."[49] Zandy contends that working-class literature "centers the lived, material experiences of working-class people" and avoids "hegemonic ventriloquism."[50] By contrast, while poor white characters sometimes stand at the center of the texts in which they figure, other times they hover on the periphery, their textual marginality mirroring their social marginality. Moreover, hegemonic ventriloquism frequently occurs in fictional renderings of poor white people in the South – in fact, it figures in every chapter of this book. Throughout this study, I analyze how poor white puppets mouthing middle-class words expose the anxieties animating literary movements and shaping literary forms.

Class, Whiteness, and Southern Literature joins literary scholarship by Andrew Hoberek, Stephen Schryer, Robert Seguin, and Christopher Wilson in exploring how the middle class comes to understand itself through work.[51] Following philosopher Shannon Sullivan's definition of the term, I use *middle class* as "a broad rhetorical designation for the vast majority of Americans who see themselves as the moral norm: hard workers who deserve their success."[52] The chapters that follow look at a number of narrators and characters who shore up their hardworking, success-earning bona fides by tsk-tsking over lazy poor white people. When third-person narrators voice these reproaches, they often reinforce negative stereotypes about poor white southerners. For instance, Mary Noailles Murfree's local color stories about life in the Tennessee mountains make use of a third-person narrator who works to naturalize poor white stereotypes – in part, by making frequent, and ostensibly offhanded, comments about poor white Appalachians' slothfulness. Interestingly, though, shifting from classist narrators to classist characters can mean turning from bolstering poor white stereotypes to refuting them. Charles Chesnutt's local color tales set in North Carolina present a well-to-do white man named John who offers unflattering appraisals of poor people and their activity levels. Chesnutt's stories call into question this character's classism not only by introducing other characters who dispute his assertions but also by highlighting his hypocrisy: John scrutinizes others' exertions to help fill his days, which are largely unencumbered by work.

Chasing Shadows

In the preamble to his baroque meditation on white tenant farmers in the Depression-era South, James Agee pondered the nature of his artistic enterprise. Sent to Hale County, Alabama, by *Fortune* magazine in 1936 to document sharecroppers' lives, Agee worked to capture in prose what photographer Walker Evans, who accompanied him, caught on film. Agee opened *Let Us Now Praise Famous Men* – the book-length treatment of his ruminations that Houghton Mifflin published in 1941 (*Fortune* never ran the story) – by expressing what can only be described as qualms about his project:

> It seems to me curious, not to say obscene and thoroughly terrifying, ... to pry intimately into the lives of an undefended and appallingly damaged group of human beings, an ignorant and helpless rural family, for the purpose of parading the nakedness, disadvantage and humiliation of these lives before another group of human beings.[53]

Agee's words describe a broad swath of representations of poor white people in the rural South. This impulse "to pry intimately" into the lives of poor white southerners animates many of the works that figure in this study. Throughout this book, I attend to the "undefended and appallingly damaged" figures who populate American novels, essays, short stories, and memoirs. But rather than imagining that poor white southerners conceived in the minds of middle-class writers tell us something about poor white people, I treat them as windows onto their creators and consumers. By scrutinizing the functions that representations of poor white southerners serve in the cultural imaginary, I consider how the middle class comes to understand itself by dwelling on what it is not – how, in other words, the "disadvantage and humiliation" routinely depicted as pillars of poor white experience buttress the advantages and prideful self-conceptions of members of the middle class. For an illustration of the analytic method I use in this book, I turn to one of the photographs that Walker Evans, Agee's traveling companion and collaborator, took in Hale County (Figure 0.3).[54]

Figure 0.3 A photograph of Flora Tingle taken by Walker Evans in 1936.
Courtesy of the Library of Congress, Prints and Photographs Division, FSA/OWI Collection, LC-DIG-fsa-8a44590.

Evans's images have the potential to look different to different groups of spectators. Where many middle-class viewers see objectivity, some less prosperous onlookers see exploitation. Analyses of Evans's work often identify straightforwardness as a characteristic of his oeuvre. Lincoln Kirstein described his friend's work as "'straight' photography not only in technique but in the rigorous directness of its way of looking" and held that this two-part straightness gave the work a truth-telling power, asserting that "the facts pile up with the prints."[55] Scholars have often concurred, arguing that Evans valued the camera's ability to render life objectively and authoritatively.[56] By contrast, a member of one of the families shown in Evans's photographs turns attention from aesthetics to economics by observing, "Everyone gits rich offn us."[57] This comment refers to the high prices commanded by Evans's portraits of the speaker's relatives and neighbors. But this remark also works as shorthand for the phenomenon I track across this study, because it describes how class happens when better-off people, encountering Evans's images in galleries or publications, define themselves against the figures depicted. In doing so, they both exert and increase their cultural capital – another way the middle class "gits rich" off poor white southerners.[58]

What about this scene spoke to Evans? Why did he take nearly a dozen pictures of this young woman in this spot on this day? Part of the appeal, I suspect, was the ramshackle state of the barn behind her. Evans knew his large-format Deardorff camera would capture crisp shots of the rickety structure's weathered and fractured boards. The incongruity of the setting and the photographic genre – the weirdness of taking a portrait in a pigsty – also might have enticed Evans to capture this tableau. But this view's greatest draw was, I think, Flora Tingle's necklace. Middle-class chronicles of southern life present a rich record of contemptuous responses to poor white women's adornment practices. Some works call attention to the cheapness of poor white women's jewelry by, for example, depicting "dreadfully 'tacky'" country girls who dress up by donning "black gutta percha bracelets," which imitate finer bangles made of jet.[59] Other accounts underscore this shoddiness while also tut-tutting over poor people's profligacy. An 1891 article in the *Century*, for instance, makes a fuss about poor white southerners' embellishments by calling out women whose "funds are wasted on trumpery" including "pinchbeck jewelry," or baubles made of a form of brass that looks like gold.[60] The very same year Evans photographed Flora Tingle, William Faulkner published a novel pointing to the paltry social value accorded to poor white southerners. In *Absalom, Absalom!* (1936), an old man seduces a poor white teenager by proffering little more than "cheap ribbons and beads."⁶¹ Middle-class Americans bolster their confidence in their own tastefulness by recognizing and reproving poor white peoples' tawdriness. That all four of the foregoing examples come from periods of economic downturn (the economic depressions of the 1890s and 1930s) is no accident; poor white people come under particularly intense scrutiny amid social upheavals as the middle class tries to reestablish and reassert the terms of its distinction. Establishing their good taste by calling out someone else's tacky trinkets may have especially appealed to members of the middle and upper classes who, impacted by the financial panic of 1893 or the stock market crash in 1929, perhaps found it necessary to forgo new jewelry purchases or even sell some ornaments.

Evans's photograph explicitly reveals the hand of the middle-class maker at work in the aesthetic object. It is not simply that we can read the relevance of the necklace, but more dramatically, we can see Evans in this photograph. Shooting outdoors with his back to the sun, Evans cannot help but capture his own shadow.⁶² Like Athena springing fully formed from the head of Zeus, Flora Tingle almost seems to materialize out of the photographer's head.⁶³ And, in some sense, she does just that. In *Picture Theory*, W. J. T. Mitchell describes Evans's photography as a transfigurative process, observing that each of the "anonymous men and women captured by Evans's camera" morphs into "a pure aesthetic object."⁶⁴ Across this study, I scrutinize aesthetic objects offering pictures of poor white southerners in search of those shadows, because they reveal middle-class hands "twisting buttons" – Agee's description of Evans's labors⁶⁵ – hitting keys, and pushing pens as they give fictional life to ideas about worse-off white people.

In order to establish poor white southerners' importance to American literary history, this book's four chapters center on four distinct literary periods, bringing to light how the movements and genres of these eras engage with poor white life in the forms they take as well as the stories they tell. Each chapter explores texts that propagate negative ideas about poor white southerners, but each also concentrates on a writer (or, in the fourth chapter, a pair of writers) whose work contests stereotypical constructions of poor white identity. More often than not, poor white characters imagined by middle-class writers embody what better-off people are anxious to distance themselves from in a given moment. Thus poor white southerners are "half-strainers," or social climbers, in the status-anxious closing decades of the nineteenth century, country rubes in the modern era, racist impediments to change during the civil rights struggle, and devotees of unhealthy practices at the end of the twentieth century, when low-fat diets and high-intensity workouts were all the rage. But the authors at the heart of each chapter wrote against the grain, adapting narrative techniques, plot structures, rhetorical strategies, and other formal elements in an effort to challenge the classist (and, in the fourth chapter, sexist) ideas baked into the works of their contemporaries and predecessors.

Chapter 1 maps out a national conversation about poor white southerners that took shape in the pages of late nineteenth-century literary magazines. In this section, I argue that nonfiction essays in the Civil War and Reconstruction eras launched a lively debate about poor white southerners' roles in the nation that continued in the dialect fiction tales published by the august and influential *Atlantic* group of magazines during the 1880s and 1890s.[66] I analyze how classist portrayals of poor white southern identity shaped the work of local colorists and plantation fiction writers in order to set the backdrop for how Charles Chesnutt pioneered literary forms capable of representing poor white characters in new ways. Chesnutt adapted the frame narrative structure – the hallmark of plantation stories – with an eye toward challenging the denigrating representations of poor white southerners promulgated by writers including Joel Chandler Harris and Thomas Nelson Page.

The second chapter explores how middle-class Americans responded to the modernist battle cry "make it new!" not only by embracing new technologies, fashions, and aesthetic forms but also, and more simply, by representing poor white people as antiquated – a practice intended to throw into relief middle-class modernness. Focusing on *As I Lay Dying* (1930), I delve into how William Faulkner interrogated ideas about poor white southerners' backwardness set forth by eugenicists and other contemporaries. Faulkner deployed the structural forms and stylistic techniques that define modernism in response to the challenge of fictionally representing the ideas and experiences of rural poor white characters in new ways. Signal modernist devices like stream-of-consciousness narration allow poor white speakers to articulate sophisticated thoughts that their somewhat narrow lexicons would otherwise make it hard to voice.

Chapter 3 looks at works written during the civil rights era to understand how and why the poor white southerner entered the national spotlight as the face of racism in this era. In this part, I probe the disconnect between the period's activism and its literature – in other words, I work to make sense of why at the very moment that black civil rights activists were taking on the Board of Education of Topeka, Kansas, the public transit system of Montgomery, Alabama, and other discriminatory institutions, midcentury southern white women writers were depicting acts of racism perpetrated by isolated individuals located on the ragged margins of southern society. Using evidence from her fictional works as well as her letters to friends, I propose that Flannery O'Connor broke rank with some of her most celebrated contemporaries. In her short stories, O'Connor took up specific formal techniques that Harper Lee, Lillian Smith, and Eudora Welty had used to depict diabolical poor white men (Bob Ewell in *To Kill a Mockingbird*, Mr. Poor White in *Killers of the Dream*, and the unnamed assassin in "Where Is the Voice Coming From?") and repurposed them to expose the social blight her contemporaries were at pains to obscure: middle-class racism.

While the first three chapters focus on formal innovations developed by middle-class writers who strove to contest other middle-class writers' classist portrayals of poor white southerners, the fourth chapter considers techniques pioneered by authors who grew up poor, concentrating on literary devices designed to rebut deep-rooted narratives about poor white southerners' unhealthy appetites. Reading Dorothy Allison's *Bastard Out of Carolina* and Barbara Robinette Moss's *Change Me into Zeus's Daughter* in light of the rise of southern foodways – in 1999, the year Moss published her memoir, the Southern Foodways Alliance was founded and *USA Today* named Paula Deen's restaurant The Lady and Sons the International Meal of the Year – I show how hunger is written into the bodies of these texts. I also explore how Allison and Moss pushed back against male grit lit writers' depictions of delectable poor white women by crafting decidedly inedible female characters, as Allison's heroine's nickname – Bone – suggests.

The coda considers some of the classist ideas about poor white southerners that circulate in twenty-first-century America. Starting with *Strangers in Their Own Land* (2016) by Arlie Hochschild, I look at how this celebrated sociologist's account of her journey from her California home to her Louisiana fieldwork site turns the set-piece story of the well-to-do urbanite's visit to the rural South into a narrative of katabasis, or descent to the underworld, by playing up the contrast between middle-class white peoples' fixation on health and wellness and poor white southerners' unwholesome diets and polluted environments. J. D. Vance's bestselling *Hillbilly Elegy* (2016) continues in this vein, characterizing poor white people as unalive – that is, unconscious of what the text presents as their hazardous lifestyle practices and dangerously unwell as a result. The figure of the poor white, now banished to the world of the dead, continues to haunt the national imaginary as the nightmare vision in contrast to which the American dream often takes shape.

CHAPTER I

Riffraff and Half-Strainers
Charles W. Chesnutt and Regionalism

American fiction from the end of the nineteenth century is chockablock with poor white people. In this era, readers gobbled up local color stories featuring characters whose dialects, customs, and forms of labor and leisure brought to life distinctive pockets of the country. Writers eager to feed this appetite for internal exotics filled their tales with poor white types associated with the South, offering colorful renderings of Appalachian mountaineers, Carolina sandhillers, Georgia crackers, and Louisiana Cajuns. A remarkable number of southern regionalist texts portray pockets of poor white life – we might think of, for example, James Lane Allen's tales depicting communities in Kentucky's Cumberland Gap, Kate Chopin's sketches set in Louisiana bayous, Harry Stillwell Edwards's short stories picturing rural homesteads in middle Georgia, John Fox Jr.'s works that take shape in the mountains of southwestern Virginia and eastern Kentucky, Joel Chandler Harris's short fiction representing life in the woods of middle Georgia, and Mary Noailles Murfree's yarns about small settlements in the Tennessee mountains.

What have literary critics made of this groundswell of interest in poor white southerners at the end of the century? Rather than recognizing that native-born white poverty is a contemporaneous concern taken up by local colorists, scholars have read poor white characters out of these tales by seeing them as figures standing in for other populations. Amy Kaplan contends that regional writers, anxious about "immigrants whose foreignness lay too close for comfort in an urban context," rewrote differences in national origin as differences in region.[1] The rationale, according to Kaplan, is that "by rendering social difference in terms of region, anchored and bound by separate spaces, more explosive social conflicts of class, race, and gender made contiguous by urban life could be effaced."[2] Richard Brodhead agrees, affirming that regionalism's poor whites are "less 'different' native ethnicities [substituting] for the truly foreign ones of contemporary reality."[3] Stephanie Foote reinforces this idea, maintaining that regionalism "creates the folk as doubles of foreigners, or immigrants."[4]

What accounts for this failure to recognize that anxieties about poor white southerners are, in fact, the motivating forces behind these stories? In part, it arises from a widely held belief that regionalists are really writing about their readers' communities rather than their characters' localities. This idea buttresses Eric Sundquist's assertion that local color stories respond to "the nation's inexorable drive toward cohesion and standardization" at the end of the century.[5] The urban North, which published and consumed the lion's share of late nineteenth-century regionalist fiction, may have been driving toward cohesion and standardization, but the rural South was heading in the opposite direction. Jim Crow segregation, which emerged alongside local color fiction, was atomization incarnate, creating racially separate and wildly unequal Souths. Eugenics, which began its rise to prominence in the late nineteenth century, also supported fragmentation rather than cohesion, because it provided a pseudoscientific justification for writing purportedly degenerate poor white people living in rural areas out of the white body politic.

In line with Sundquist, Brodhead suggests that in the decades following the Civil War, the nation undertook "the forcible repression of sectional autonomy in favor of national union and the legal supplanting of the locally variant by national norms of citizenry rights."[6] But during the post-Reconstruction period, American regionalism's heyday, the South experienced the opposite of what Brodhead describes. Nationally mandated citizenship rights, including those granted by the Reconstruction Amendments, were flouted by local laws (vagrancy laws, in the case of the Thirteenth Amendment) and by local practices – grandfather clauses, literacy tests, white primaries, and the like – that contravened the Fifteenth Amendment. Continuing in the same vein, Brodhead contends that regionalism's reign coincided with the "reinsertion of agrarian and artisanal orders into a new web of national market relations."[7] While these orders' products and profits circulated nationally and even internationally, their southern workforces were barred from participating in this new web of market relations. Receiving their earnings as credit, in the case of many sharecroppers, or scrip, which is how a lot of cotton mill workers got their wages, these laborers were confined to hyper-local economies.

During the Civil War, the northern literary magazines that would later brim with regionalist tales began publishing articles discussing the South's poor white population. In what follows, I track the development of this dialogue over the ensuing quarter century to suggest that local color fiction took part in an evolving national conversation about poor white southerners. I focus on the *Atlantic Monthly* because, while the magazine's engagement with white poverty is typical, its influence on literary culture is unique. As Frank Luther Mott explains, the *Atlantic Monthly* "enjoyed a perpetual state of literary grace, so that for a large section of the American public, whatever the *Atlantic* printed was literature."[8]

In the last two decades of the nineteenth century, when literary regionalism reached the height of its popularity, eugenics-informed critiques of poor white people proliferated in the *Atlantic Monthly* and other high-culture magazines. Regionalist writers' depictions of poor white southerners often echo these classist claims. This is not surprising. For one thing, authors knew that their readers were "the bourgeoisie and its aspirants"[9] – so were most local color writers, for that matter – and so they crafted derogatory pictures of poor white southerners that could act as foils for more affluent white people's self-conceptions. For another thing, these writers made their tales au courant by engaging with ideas espoused in the nonfictional essays on labor, pauperism, and heredity that appeared alongside their stories in the magazines. But Charles Chesnutt, whose writerly career took off after he published three conjure tales in the *Atlantic Monthly* in the late 1880s, swam against this tide.[10]

Chesnutt's fiction lays bare anxieties about whiteness that shaped life and literature in late nineteenth-century America – concerns obscured by scholarship that reads poor white characters as ciphers. As historian Natalie J. Ring has observed about the era, "disease coupled with extreme poverty and illiteracy among lower-class whites nurtured social scientific anxieties about racial degeneration at the very moment the white South tried to delineate the boundaries of the color line through the codification of Jim Crow."[11] Chesnutt's short stories speak to their moment by exposing the ideological inconsistencies of a culture in which fears of white racial degeneration emerged hand in hand with increasingly virulent white supremacy. Written during the period historian Rayford Logan termed "the nadir" of African American experience in the United States,[12] Chesnutt's conjure tales underscore class divides among white people and emphasize cross-racial connections among poor people in order to chip away at the classist and racist representations of southern identity that were the bedrock of other literary regionalists' tales.

From Regional Resource to National Plague

At the end of the nineteenth century, high-toned readers relished low-down fictional characters. Stories focusing on poor white southerners were common features of the nation's most venerable magazines during the

Gilded Age, filling the pages of the *Atlantic Monthly*, *Century Illustrated Monthly Magazine*, and *Harper's New Monthly Magazine*, among others. The reason, as Richard Brodhead observes, is that "regionalism made the experience of the socially marginalized into a literary asset."[13] But when fiction writers began penning short stories emphasizing poor white characters' distinctive speech habits, customs, foodways, and habitations, they did not introduce poor white people into the nation's preeminent magazines. Instead, short story writers used an increasingly popular literary form to take part in a discussion about poor white people in the US South that had been going on for decades in these periodicals. The *Atlantic Monthly*, for example, had been hosting debates about poor white southerners since it came into being.

Founded in Boston in 1857, the *Atlantic Monthly* was soon covering nineteenth-century America's biggest story: the Civil War. In the conflict's early days, *Atlantic Monthly* contributors championed the northern cause by chronicling the many evils of slavery, including its negative effects on poor white southerners. One essayist bemoaned the state of poor white life in the South by observing that "it gives but a poor description of the 'poor-white trash' to say that they cannot read," because their "inconceivably wretched and degraded" condition encompassed debilities far beyond illiteracy.[14] Another author detailed these debilities, describing poor white people as "destitute of schools, churches, and newspapers, unable to read or write, without culture, generally steeped in whiskey, their sole property a cabin, and perhaps a few swine."[15]

While some writers described dark days before and during the Civil War, others prophesied brighter skies if the Union won. Several authors envisioned new employment opportunities for poor white southerners. "With Slavery removed ... the poor-white trash of the South would gather to be educated in the labor-system of the North," one essayist predicted, bringing prosperity and productivity to a population long associated with poverty and lassitude.[16] "Emancipation at one stroke elevates the poor white of the South," another writer declared, by opening more jobs to poor white workers.[17] Other essays campaigned for new educational opportunities, explaining why it served the plantocracy's interests to keep poor white people uneducated and speculating about how establishing free schools across the South could transform poor people's lives.[18] These *Atlantic Monthly* writers not only highlighted the many benefits of a Union victory but also challenged arguments that defended slavery by attributing poor white southerners' lowly status to hereditary – rather than social – disadvantages. Daniel R. Hundley's *Social Relations in Our*

Southern States (1860), which lays out the "natural causes" of poverty in the South, offers one such hereditarian take.[19] Proposing that the nineteenth-century South's poor white population descended from people plucked from "the poor-houses and prison-cells of Great Britain" and sold as indentured servants in the New World, Hundley maintained that "there is a great deal more in *blood* than people in the United States are generally inclined to believe."[20]

Reconstruction ushered in a new perspective on white poverty.[21] Although presented as an untapped regional resource in the *Atlantic Monthly*'s wartime commentary, poor white southerners were reframed as a national problem in the aftermath of the war. In contrast to earlier accounts predicting that ending enslavement would emancipate African Americans and poor whites, albeit in quite different ways, postwar reports from the South suggested that "the poor negroes were making much more earnest efforts to rise than the poor whites."[22] Journalist Sidney Andrews pointed out black southerners' advantages over poor white people, finding them "superior in force and intellect" and more capable of supporting themselves.[23] Andrews concluded that "time and effort will lead the negro up to intelligent manhood; but I almost doubt if they will be able to lead this 'white trash' even to respectability."[24] Such conclusions had negative consequences for poor people of both races. In discussing government rations, for example, travel writers cited statistics indicating that white people constituted the majority of aid recipients not only to pave the way for abandoning relief efforts (on the grounds that formerly enslaved people were rapidly adjusting to the free market labor system) but also to argue against offering material assistance to poor white people because, they claimed, it made them dissolute and dependent.[25]

In this period, white poverty came to be treated as a social and personal pathology. In some sense, this view was a predictable byproduct of wartime commentary, since the absence of dramatic postwar improvement in poor white southerners' lives seemed to some observers to corroborate biological explanations, validating Hundley's claim that "there is a great deal in *blood*."[26] An article called "Drawing Bureau Rations" that appeared in *Harper's New Monthly Magazine* in 1868, for example, describes the poor white population as "that tenth of humanity which the severe law of natural selection is perpetually punishing for the sin of shiftlessness."[27] Its author, J. W. De Forest, combined emerging scientific concepts – Charles Darwin's theory of natural selection from *The Origin of Species* (1859), for one – with old-fashioned moralizing by way of the well-worn notion that "the sin of shiftlessness" represents one of poor white peoples' principal transgressions.²⁸ De Forest also reworked the link between slavery and white poverty. Writing that "slavery was costly, with its breed of parasite poor whites," De Forest portrayed poor white southerners not as prey to others' greed but rather as leeches living at others' expense.²⁹ "Drawing Bureau Rations" presents poverty as a social ill by picturing poor white people as a malady infecting the body politic.

Writers continued to pathologize white poverty in the post-Reconstruction period, but they moved from treating it as a metaphorical affliction – a blight on the body politic – to a medical condition: an inheritable, incurable ailment infecting the poor white body. In 1877, as federal troops left the South and Reconstruction came to an end, Richard L. Dugdale published a book exploring how heredity and environment influence poverty. Dugdale, a volunteer prison inspector, researched inmates' family trees in search of the roots of their criminal behavior. The resulting analysis, published as *"The Jukes": A Study in Crime, Pauperism, Disease and Heredity*, examines "a strictly American family" of native-born poor whites whose members supposedly engaged in theft and prostitution and received charity at higher rates than the general citizenry.³⁰ Dugdale ultimately decided that environment was a greater influence than heredity on family members' criminality and poverty, but many readers took away a different message, led by his genealogy-based method and heredity-focused terms (jargon including "pauper stock" and "Juke blood") to conclude that heredity trumped environment.³¹

Atlantic Monthly readers encountered Dugdale's ideas first in a review of *"The Jukes"* that the magazine published in 1878 and then in an 1881–1882 series called "Origin of Crime in Society," in which Dugdale further theorized about the causes of criminal behavior. Dugdale's work launched a conversation about the links between genetics and poverty that continued for the next two decades in the *Atlantic Monthly* and other highbrow periodicals. Some later *Atlantic Monthly* articles directly engage with Dugdale's work. An 1883 essay called "The Pauper Question," for instance, cites *"The Jukes"* to support the claim that "pauperism involves a deeper incapacity to sustain social relations than crime," making it the "more incorrigible" of the two social issues.³² Other pieces published in the *Atlantic Monthly* advance ideas influenced by Dugdale's work without mentioning him by name. "The progress of civilization," an essay from 1883 (tellingly titled "Heredity") declares, "is not a question of education, but of stock."³³ These articles reveal a seismic shift in the *Atlantic Monthly*'s treatment of poor white people, exemplifying how the 1860s view of white poverty as a social ill that could be remedied by improving educational and employment opportunities gave way, beginning in the 1880s, to claims that social reform was futile because biological inferiority – bad stock – made poverty inevitable.

Looking for the Lazy South

Like essayists, fiction writers took up poverty's causes and consequences. In fact, some authors were penning both essays and stories. Although Alice French, who published under the pseudonym Octave Thanet, is today remembered (when at all) for her local color stories, she was also contributing nonfictional works to the magazines. French's 1881 *Atlantic Monthly* essay on pauperism, which proposes that the "vices and weaknesses" that doom people to almshouses are "tendencies which are to a greater or less degree hereditary," illustrates the kinds of eugenic claims that were becoming high-culture magazines' party-line stance.[34] Many fiction writers brought notions from the pseudoscience of pauperism into their tales about poor people. In a sketch about a middle-class white girl who teaches industry and thrift to her poor white "protégé," Harry Stillwell Edwards makes a point of establishing that the boy can learn to be self-supporting because he is from "good old English stock" and thus not "restricted by mental inaptitude" like southerners whose ancestors came from "the debtor prisons and the poorhouses" of England.[35] Even local colorists who steered clear of the era's eugenic buzzwords came into dialogue with arguments about heredity that appeared alongside their stories in monthly magazines. Mary Noailles Murfree, who published her regionalist tales under the name Charles Egbert Craddock, is a case in point.

Although Murfree's work first saw print in *Lippincott's Magazine*, which published a few of her satirical essays under the name R. Emmet Dembry in the mid-1870s, her career as a fiction writer took off in 1878 when the *Atlantic Monthly* published her story "Dancin' Party at Harrison's Cove." Murfree made a name for herself by spinning yarns about the poor white Appalachians whom she glimpsed during her family's summer vacations at Beersheba Springs, a fashionable resort in the Cumberland Mountains. For the past few decades, one of the central questions in studies of Murfree's work has been the writer's relation to Appalachian culture: Is she a sympathetic insider or an exploitative outsider?[36] Contextualizing Murfree in terms of the places her stories depict rather than the publications in which these tales appear, these critics have not considered how Murfree's local color fiction participated in a discussion about poor white southerners that took shape within and across issues of the *Atlantic Monthly*.

In the *Atlantic Monthly*'s December 1880 issue, a story by Murfree depicting how living among poor white Appalachians changes two middle-class men immediately precedes a report on child labor in New England factories. Both works express fears about racial degeneration. In Emma E. Brown's essay "Children's Labor: A Problem," one of the central evils of child labor is its ability to warp workers, producing "a deteriorated race." Brown's essay presents British mill workers – "an almost distinct class of English working people" who are "pale, sallow, and stunted both in physical and mental growth" – as harbingers of how New Englanders will degenerate unless the labor system is reformed.[37] Brown looks to England, the birthplace of eugenics, because in the late Victorian period "the 'condition of England question' was now centrally concerned with the condition of the English body."[38] But in the American imaginary during this era, the South also had the power to degrade outsiders who ventured into the region. In Murfree's tale, a doctor from a "good family" (John Cleaver) leaves the "Western city" of his birth and heads to East Tennessee, following in the footsteps of a friend who abandoned his legal career and moved to the mountains to become a sheep farmer.[39] At the story's outset, the narrator emphasizes the stark physical contrasts between a typical mountaineer – a "hairy animal, whose jeans suit proclaimed him man" – and Cleaver's friend Fred Trelawney, who is "a man of splendid proportions, [with] a fine, frank, intellectual face."[40] But Cleaver fears that dwelling in the mountains is taking a toll on Trelawney. The narrator bluntly observes that Cleaver "thought Trelawney was already degenerating," because his speech, actions, and ideas after spending just a short time in East Tennessee suggested "descent toward the level of its inhabitants."[41] Terrified of plummeting to the "lower social plane" of the "ignorant" and "uncivilized" poor white people among whom he lives, Cleaver decides that "he would not deteriorate" like Trelawney, and so he leaves Appalachia.[42]

The idea that the South harbored a unique race of degenerate poor white people was bandied about in a number of magazines' essays and stories in the last decades of the nineteenth century. As early as 1874, in his series for *Scribner's Monthly* called "The Great South," Edward King described the South's "poor white trash" as people with "counterparts nowhere among native Americans at the North."[43] By the end of the century, writers routinely treated poor white people in the South as a discrete racial group. For example, an investigator for the US Bureau of Labor launched her 1891 *Century* article about poor white mill workers in Georgia by declaring, "The race that tends the spindles of the cotton-growing states is altogether unique."[44] To explain this distinctiveness, the author served up a smorgasbord of ideas then in vogue, suggesting that these southerners' ancestors were "impecunious gentlemen brought by Oglethorpe to Georgia" whose "deterioration" was supercharged by "breeding in for generations," but also that this community suffered "race degeneration caused partly by climate, partly by caste prejudices."[45]

Some Americans considered laziness a hallmark of such degeneration, and in later issues of the *Atlantic Monthly*, contributions by Murfree and other writers attribute poor white peoples' difficulties to their indolence. In the magazine's June 1881 issue, Murfree's "Over on the T'other Mounting" appears immediately before Alice French's "The Indoor Pauper: A Study." Both authors insist upon poor people's slothfulness. In her report, French diagnoses laziness as a disorder that leads to the poorhouse, writing that "not one" almshouse resident was "decent, industrious, laboring." Instead, "idleness" beleaguers paupers.[46] In Murfree's short story, lethargy defines Appalachians. Across the tale, only a few exigencies have the power to spur mountain dwellers to action. For instance, when a fire threatens their homes, "the apathetic residents of old Rocky-Top were stirred into an activity very incongruous with their habits."[47] Otherwise, "the mountaineer seldom makes any exertion."[48]

Lassitude was one of the debilities that made poor people impediments, rather than contributors, to social progress in the eyes of late-century eugenicists and reformers. In 1883, Murfree published two stories about impoverished Appalachians in the *Atlantic Monthly* that jibe with social science–styled analyses of poverty printed in the same issues. May's issue featured an essay called "The Pauper Question" by D. O. Kellogg, a founding member of the Philadelphia Society for Organizing Charity. As Kellogg explained in an 1880 speech at the American Social Science Association, "poverty is weakness" born of being "inefficient, or useless."[49] Kellogg elaborated on these ideas in his contribution to the *Atlantic Monthly*, describing pauperism as a more "incorrigible" social issue than crime because an "abyss of physical and mental inaptitude" entrapped the poor.[50] Murfree's story from the same issue, "The 'Harnt' That Walks Chilhowee," buttresses these claims about poor people's inefficiency and inaptitude. Murfree's tale characterizes mountain dwellers thrice as "slow," twice as "listless," and also as "indolent."[51] Representing poor white southerners as "densely ignorant," "slovenly," and "uncouth" beings who act – on the rare occasions they do take action – in a "lacklustre manner," Murfree's story reinforces the classist claims made in Kellogg's essay.[52]

Five months later, Murfree's work appeared in the same issue as an essay endorsing eugenic theories of human advancement. Henry W. Holland's article declares that civilization will "move steadily forward" only if intelligent and industrious people are at its helm. As a result, "the progress of civilization" requires a concerted effort to "replace the feebler race by the better one" through selective breeding.⁵³ Murfree's tale, "A-Playin' of Old Sledge at the Settlemint," portrays poor whites as physically and mentally feeble people who cannot move civilization forward because they hardly move at all. The story opens with mountain dwellers "leaning lazily" on spades and hoes rather than using these tools – inactivity that demonstrates "sloth" and a "sluggish disinclination" toward work.⁵⁴ The tale's narrator repeatedly describes characters as slow: they "spoke slowly," are "slow" in their movements, and "slow" to take their turns in the card game – old sledge – at the center of the story.⁵⁵ Men are twice described as watching the events around them with "slow eyes."⁵⁶ Additionally, Murfree's narrator terms these poor white southerners "restful," "languid," and "ineffectual."⁵⁷

Charles W. Chesnutt's literary career began in much the same way as Murfree's. Placing sketches in the *Atlantic Monthly* launched each writer's career and led Houghton Mifflin, the magazine's parent company, to publish a collection featuring those stories as each author's first book. In addition, editors initially took both of them for white men; to correct these mistaken impressions, Murfree made a surprise visit to the *Atlantic Monthly*'s offices in 1885, and Chesnutt revealed his race in a letter to Houghton Mifflin in 1891. But these local colorists part ways when it comes to their treatments of labor and laziness in the South.

In his conjure stories set in North Carolina, Chesnutt troubles the time-honored tradition of depicting black and poor white southerners as lazy. While surveying the boundary between North Carolina and Virginia in 1728, planter and government functionary William Byrd also surveyed poor white North Carolinians, describing how their "slothfulness" and tendency to "loiter away their lives" made the area seem like "Lubberland," an imaginary place of luxury and ease.⁵⁸ The Sandhills region where Chesnutt's tales unfold gave rise to a distinctive pejorative term for poor white people: sandhiller. A few years before he helped design New York City's Central Park, Frederick Law Olmsted penned a southern travelogue in which he described sandhillers as people who subsist on stolen rice, milk, and meat because they are "incapable of applying themselves steadily to any labor."⁵⁹ Sidney Andrews offered up yet another regionally distinctive slur in his 1866 travel narrative: "I am certain that there can be no lower class of people than the North Carolina 'clay-eaters,' – this being the local name for the poor whites."⁶⁰

Black southerners fare worse. A contributor to the *Southern Agriculturist* in 1839 averred, "Laziness is one of the great characteristics of the negro."⁶¹ Edmund Ruffin, a member of the radical proslavery Fire-Eaters group, touted slavery's benefits by insisting that "free negroes ... are noted for ignorance, indolence, improvidence, and poverty."⁶² For Thomas Nelson Page, patrician par excellence – both his mother and father descended from First Families of Virginia – antebellum black southerners were not guilty of indolence because enslavement was a permanent vacation: Enslaved people "didn' hed nothin' 't all to do" before the Civil War according to his most famous formerly enslaved storyteller.⁶³ By contrast, Page found postbellum black southerners "lazy, thriftless, intemperate, insolent, dishonest."⁶⁴

Chesnutt kicked off his authorial career with a tale that lambastes such claims. In "The Goophered Grapevine," the first conjure story Chesnutt published (in the *Atlantic Monthly*'s August 1887 issue) that later appeared as the first tale in his 1899 conjure collection, the narrator of the frame story acknowledges that when he moved from Ohio to North Carolina, his "unaccustomed eyes" mistook Patesville for a sleepy little town enveloped in "a calm that seemed almost sabbatic in its restfulness."⁶⁵ This narrator, whose name is John, eventually "learned" to read his environs more accurately (80). Subsequent tales make clear that John's employee Julius directs his education, using stories about the consequences that befall other misperceiving elites to correct John's myopic views of the working poor. In "Mars Jeems's Nightmare," for instance, Julius uses a story about enslaver Jeems McLean's eye-opening education in slavery to offer John a different vantage point onto his own workers.

"Mars Jeems's Nightmare" begins with John judging potential employees by their looks. Evaluating Tom, Julius's grandson, John finds himself "not favorably impressed by the youth's appearance" (55–6). Ensuing experiences with the young man seem to validate his visual assessment: "My first impression of Tom proved to be correct. He turned out to be very trifling, and I was much annoyed by his laziness" (56). To unsettle John's faith in the power of his own perceptions, Julius tells John and his wife about Mars Jeems, an antebellum planter who deemed the people he enslaved "monst'us trifflin' en lazy" and compelled them to work even longer days than were the norm on neighboring plantations (60). Desperate for relief from this draconian regime, an enslaved man named Solomon sought out Aunt Peggy, the conjure woman, and procured a magical mixture "ter make Mars Jeems treat de darkies bettah" (59). The goopher gave Jeems a new line of sight onto his own management strategies by turning him into an enslaved person. As a recently acquired field hand, the "noo man" was subjected to merciless beatings at the hands of Jeems's overseer to punish him for his "laziness" (62). After being transformed back into an enslaver, Jeems was a changed man; as Julius explains, "Aun' Peggy's goopher had made a noo man un 'im enti'ely" (67). Returning to his plantation, Jeems fires his overseer and institutes a new labor system on his plantation – one with shorter workdays and fewer physical abuses. In its antebellum yarn and its postbellum frame story, Chesnutt's tale depicts patricians discovering and correcting their distorted perceptions of the energy and activity levels of people who work. Just as Jeems's experience of enslavement prompts him to tamp down some of the most glaring abuses on his plantation (without, however, inducing him to free the people he enslaves), Julius's story teaches John about the perils of harshly judging laborers, and so Tom remains in his employ.

Whereas Murfree's fiction treats indolence as a symptom of poor whites' degradation, Chesnutt's work explores how elite whites' indolence underscores and secures their social status. Like Thorstein Veblen, whose book *The Theory of the Leisure Class* was published in the same year as *The Conjure Woman*, Chesnutt considers the significance of "the nonproductive consumption of time" in affluent Americans' daily lives.[66] John supports himself by investing in agricultural and industrial ventures in the cash-strapped postbellum South; the only work-related activity he engages in across Chesnutt's fourteen conjure tales is making site visits, including touring vineyards in "The Goophered Grapevine" and surveying a clay bank as part of a brick-making scheme in "Lonesome Ben." Apart from these jaunts, John whiles away his days by reading, napping, taking carriage rides, entertaining friends and relatives, relaxing on his piazza, and smoking cigars. His wife, Annie, forgoes the cigars but otherwise spends her days in the same way. The tales' frame stories draw attention to the couple's concerted efforts to divert all productive endeavors to the people who work for them, bearing out Veblen's claim that "the characteristic feature of leisure-class life is a conspicuous exemption from all useful employment."[67]

In "A Deep Sleeper," John suggests to his wife that they "relieve the deadly dulness [sic] of the afternoon" by picking a watermelon (136). Annie "sleepily" asks questions forestalling the venture until John clarifies that he does not intend for them to do any harvesting or conveying of the garden truck (136). He delegates that work to Julius, who is described as "elderly" and depicted as suffering a painful flare-up of rheumatism en route to the melon patch – details emphasizing that social class, not physical condition, determines the distribution of labor (136). To pass the time while he waits for someone else to fetch the fruit he wants to eat,

John mentally decries lazy poor people, including "listless" poor whites (137) and Julius's "lubberly" grandson Tom (138). The latter critique, which invokes William Byrd's condemnations of poor white people in early eighteenth-century North Carolina, drives home how such classist appraisals endure across time and ensnare both black and white people.

John makes clear that he views deprivation as an individual failure rather than an institutional one by prescribing industry and thrift as the cure for what ails hungry poor people. Encountering poor white people gathering clay on his land in order to eat it – a nod to southerners' long history of using geophagy to suppress hunger – John laments that they have not learned "those habits of industry and thrift whereby they could get their living from the soil in a manner less direct but more commendable" (157). John neglects to mention that he bought all the land in the vicinity "for a mere song" after the Civil War, so all of the industrious and thrifty farmers eking out a living from the soil are also enriching him (31). Having detained a poor black man who tried to take a chicken from his henhouse, John contemplates punishments capable of teaching his hungry neighbors the importance of "industry and thrift" (173). But John's commentary in the frame stories also reveals that what he considers laziness when practiced by poor people is what he calls leisure when he himself does it. "The Marked Tree" begins with John waxing poetic over "the dignity of ease":

> The dignity of labor is a beautiful modern theory, in which no doubt many of the sterner virtues find their root, but the dignity of ease was celebrated at least as long ago as the days of Horace, a gentleman and philosopher, with some reputation as a poet. (194)

This tale, which first saw print in *The Crisis*, the official magazine of the NAACP, engages with ideas espoused by Booker T. Washington. Chesnutt enjoyed a cordial personal relationship with Washington but had some concerns about his political positions, so he may have submitted this story to *The Crisis* anticipating that its editor, W. E. B. Du Bois, would recognize and sympathize with the tale's critique of Washington's take on labor's power to improve race relations in the South.[68] A few years before he promoted teaching African American students about the "dignity of labour" in his bestselling autobiography *Up from Slavery* (1901), Washington published an *Atlantic Monthly* essay setting forth his reasons for uniting industrial and academic training at Tuskegee.[69] Washington described how his teacher-training program was reshaping the South by sending graduates trained in "economy, thrift, and the dignity of labor" into the region's new primary and secondary schools.[70] These lessons appealed to many ruling-class white people, who had "feared that the opening of the free schools to the freedmen and the poor whites ... would result merely in increasing the class who sought to escape labor."[71] Through John, Chesnutt's story highlights elites' self-serving double standard: they require industry and thrift from poor people precisely because a hardworking and frugal proletariat enables their ease and indulgence. Furthermore, Chesnutt's fiction questions longstanding conceptions of poor white people as uniquely (not to mention genetically) slothful by bringing to light the fact that, to better-off white people – from Murfree, Chesnutt's contemporary, to John, his creation – what seems a "sluggish disinclination"[72] toward work when practiced by the poor looks like the "dignity of ease" due to a "gentleman" when enjoyed among themselves (194).

Poverty in Plantation Fiction

Given the many styles and subgenres of local color fiction available to him, why did Chesnutt write plantation stories? We have long understood plantation fiction's raison d'être as celebrating the antebellum southern order by trotting out formerly enslaved people who spend their postbellum days reminiscing about the joys of life before the Civil War. For Gran'mammy, the "old colored mammy" whose nostalgic recollections make up a half-dozen of Sherwood Bonner's *Suwanee River Tales* (1884), life after the Civil War pales in comparison to the antebellum order: "Nothin' like dat beauty and gorgeousness in dese days!"[73] Sam, a formerly enslaved storyteller in one of Thomas Nelson Page's plantation stories, describes his antebellum experience in similar terms, insisting, "dem wuz good ole times, marster – de bes' Sam ever see!" (10). In light of these plantation fiction writers' celebrations of the antebellum order and concerns about postbellum life, a number of scholars have concluded that Chesnutt ventured into "unfavorable terrain" in writing plantation fiction, because the genre's "character types" and "social message" doomed him to literary failure by forcing him onto "his opponents' territory."[74] So, why did Chesnutt launch his authorial career by penning plantation tales?

Richard Brodhead reads Chesnutt's turn to plantation fiction as a pragmatic response to the literary marketplace. Observing that popular plantation fiction collections including Joel Chandler Harris's *Uncle Remus: His Songs and His Sayings* (1881) and Thomas Nelson Page's *In Ole Virginia* (1887) "established a new formula for the literary production of Southernness," Brodhead reasons that the form's critical and commercial success "formed the immediate occasion for Chesnutt's literary emergence."[75]

Kenneth Price also maintains that market forces compelled Chesnutt to adopt the plantation formula, asserting that "a framed tale making use of characters resembling minstrel types ... was the main avenue available" to the up-and-coming writer.[76] Yet Chesnutt saw that many authors outside of the plantation school found success writing fiction about the South. For instance, Chesnutt knew of Albion Tourgée, whose two novels about life in the Reconstruction South became bestsellers. He also was aware of the achievements of George Washington Cable, whose renderings of Creole New Orleans inspired Mark Twain to dub him "the South's finest literary genius."[77] Chesnutt not only read Cable's and Tourgée's popular works but also corresponded with both men starting in the late 1880s.[78]

Chesnutt adopted the plantation fiction format less to avail himself of its marketability than to prod its animating anxieties. Scholars have long recognized changing race relations as one of the genre's central concerns.[79] But another source of unease in these stories is economic mobility. Nostalgia for the antebellum racial hierarchy is tangled up with longing for rigid class stratification – a system that would indelibly mark out "the quality" from "the trash." The plantation form was well suited to Chesnutt's literary ends. Like Harris and Page, Chesnutt used stories of the antebellum past to address race and class relations during the post-Reconstruction period. But Chesnutt's stories part ways with his fellow plantation writers' tales by exposing, rather than inflaming, the social anxiety at the heart of the plantation genre.[80]

Across the nineteenth century, concerns about social change gave rise to plantation fiction. During the 1830s, planter elites in the South began to feel beleaguered by hostile forces. In 1831, William Lloyd Garrison launched *The Liberator*, a Boston-based abolitionist newspaper that became a powerful organ of antislavery advocacy. That same year saw Nat Turner's Rebellion, an uprising led by enslaved people in Virginia that left enslavers across the state, and across the South, terrified by the prospect of other revolts against slavery.[81] Tariffs enacted in 1828 and 1832 to protect northern industry infuriated southern states – South Carolina in particular – by reducing international demand for cotton exports and raising prices for imported finished goods. This atmosphere gave rise to John Pendleton Kennedy's *Swallow Barn* (1832), widely recognized as the first plantation novel, which presents an idealized vision of plantation life in Virginia. John Grammer contends that Kennedy took up his pen to limn a picture of patrician life in the Tidewater out of concern that "the social order represented by the plantation is marked as irrelevant to the bustling American world taking shape around it."[82] But in this era, many of the South's planters felt embattled, not irrelevant. Kennedy crafted his novel as a weapon to wield against social change, using it to defend the status quo first in 1832 and again in 1851, when he revised and reissued the text so that it might serve, in his words, as "an antidote to this abolition mischief."[83]

Historian Drew Gilpin Faust explains that "during the last three decades of the antebellum period ... the slavery controversy not only became a matter of survival for the southern way of life; it served for Americans as a means of reassessing the profoundest assumptions on which their world was built."[84] Across these decades, plantation fiction writers worked to show how the southern way of life, with slavery as its cornerstone, squared with Americans' "profoundest assumptions," which included notions about the pecking order among white people. As Susan J. Tracy observes in her study of antebellum southern literature, because poor white people "lived away from the plantation and were not under the planters' direct control," they represent "the gravest threat to peaceful social relations" in plantation novels.[85] Plantation fiction paints a rosy picture of cross-racial relations, evoking the myth of the plantation family to tie together the "mannered and attractive" planter and the "loyal and passive" enslaved person.[86] But intraracial relations are another story. Some works of plantation fiction give voice to "unabashed class hatred ... toward poor whites."[87] Others write poor white people out of the southern social order altogether. Caroline Lee Hentz's novel *The Planter's Northern Bride* (1854) lays the groundwork for one character's "irresistible conclusion" that enslaved people in the US South "were the happiest *subservient* race that were found on the face of the globe" by erasing poor white people from the southern landscape.[88] Contemplating the lives of working people, Hentz's hero – a planter named Russell Moreland – suggests that enslaved people were the antebellum South's only laboring population. To find white laborers, Moreland looks far beyond the region, evaluating the experiences of "the groaning serfs of Russia; the starving sons of Ireland; the squalid operatives of England," as well as "the free hirelings of the North, who, as a *class*, travail in discontent and repining."[89] Having fashioned her novel as a proslavery rebuttal to Harriet Beecher Stowe's *Uncle Tom's Cabin* (1852), Hentz misrepresented enslaved people's work and failed to represent poor white people's work in an effort to delude readers about the realities of laborers' lives in the antebellum South.

In the 1880s and 1890s as in the 1830s and 1850s, the plantation legend appealed to readers drawn to an "essentially antidemocratic and static ideal of a Good Society" during a period of significant social change.⁹⁰ Postbellum plantation fiction delivers this antidemocratic idyll through its two defining characteristics: the expression of nostalgia and the frame narrative structure. Plantation stories by Joel Chandler Harris and Thomas Nelson Page depict an Old South without social mobility and with stark social divisions among enslaved people of African descent, white planter aristocrats, and white trash. These imaginary visions of antebellum society offered their contemporary readers an escape from the post-Reconstruction present. The postbellum frames enclosing these antebellum tales critique the situation in the South in the decades after the Civil War – often by bemoaning the actions of poor white people who, whether clambering up the social ladder or remaining mired in poverty, cause trouble for the stories' upper-crust characters.

Taking shape as nostalgia-laden accounts of antebellum life told by formerly enslaved people, plantation stories demonstrate "the plantation's freedom from ideological division" by highlighting figures at the bottom of the southern hierarchy who identify with those at the top.⁹¹ Scholars including Robert Hemenway and Kenneth Warren have established how these nostalgic black narrators allay postbellum concerns about black social mobility and social unrest. But critics have been less attentive to how they also reinforce class divisions within whiteness. By identifying with ruling-class whites and disparaging poor whites, these narrators validate intraracial class divisions and quell fears of interracial alliances among poor southerners. Laying bare plantation fiction's class politics corrects the mistaken impression that the genre promotes broad-based unity, whether by promising a "clearly defined and harmonious relationship between the races" or by "defus[ing] class tensions in the white South."⁹² Instead, plantation fiction portrays alliances between formerly enslaved people and former enslavers forged by uniting against a common enemy: poor white people.

Menacing Social Mobility

A number of scholars have argued that postbellum plantation fiction worked to unify the country after the Civil War. For instance, Hemenway identifies Harris's storyteller Uncle Remus as "an image of black people around which Northern and Southern whites could unite," promoting sectional reconciliation by assuaging white guilt about the abuses of enslavement and the withdrawal of federal support for Reconstruction.⁹³ But these "Northern and Southern whites" are necessarily middle- and upper-class people. While Remus does indeed demonstrate "that black people would turn the other cheek, would continue to love" their former enslavers and other elites,[94] he also unleashes virulent tirades against white people whose material conditions resemble his own. In a similar way, Thomas Nelson Page's black storytellers proudly recount the exploits of the white families who claimed them as property while refusing to learn the names of the upstart white people on whose property they reside after the war. In "Marse Chan," Sam takes pains to establish that the present owner of the plantation he worked on while enslaved is a nobody: "Arfter de war some one or nurr bought our place, but his name done kind o' slipped me. I nuver hearn on 'im befo'; I think dey's half-strainers. I don' ax none on 'em no odds" (3). Remus, Sam, and other black storytellers created by white plantation fiction writers endeared themselves to middle- and upper-class white readers of the post-Reconstruction era by glorifying the antebellum aristocracy and insisting upon that class's enduring social superiority at a time when social upheaval seemed capable of weakening social divisions within whiteness.

In Harris's and Page's stories, social mobility represents one of the chief evils of the postbellum South. Harris's *Uncle Remus* counters this menace by romanticizing social continuities and rooting out social changes.[95] Remus's post-Emancipation life barely differs from his antebellum experience. After the war, he lives in a cabin on a plantation doing odd jobs and receiving privileged white people's "leavin's" as paltry payment for his labors.[96] Unfailingly supportive of the old order's white patricians, he remains in the employ of his former enslavers and, in the commentary that frames the folklore tales he tells, projects a fantasy of a stable caste system. In the opening of the story "Mr. Bear Catches Old Mr. Bull-Frog," for example, Remus ingratiates himself with elite white people by suggesting that the postbellum economy follows the antebellum order in excluding poor whites and African Americans:

> "Ef folks could make der livin' longer gittin' inter trubble," continued the old man, looking curiously at the little boy, "ole Miss Favers wouldn't be bodder'n yo' ma fer ter borry a cup full er sugar eve'y now en den; en it look like ter me dat I knows a nigger dat wouldn't be squattin' 'roun' yer makin' dese yer fish-baskits."[97]

Remus links himself with Miss Favers, a poor white mother who lives nearby, by suggesting that both are good at "gittin' inter trubble." However, while Remus manages to eke out a living on the fringe of the new economy, the postbellum order wholly excludes Miss Favers, who must "borry" sugar and other provisions to meet her needs. In Harris's imaginative vision, the antebellum order persists in the postbellum period:

white patricians occupy the top rung of the social ladder, African Americans work contentedly in their service – providing labor, culture, and love and expecting little in return – and poor white people struggle to maintain a foothold on the community's ragged edge.

Remus's role in the elite white household requires him not only to perform a certain racial identity but also to adopt a specific socioeconomic perspective. In "Why Mr. Possum Has No Hair on his Tail," Remus, "frowning," scolds the little boy for "playin' en makin' free" with Miss Favers's children.[98] The omniscient narrator explains that the little boy "knew that, in Uncle Remus's eyes, he had been guilty of a flagrant violation of the family code."[99] This passage underscores how the "racial utopia" that Robert Hemenway has identified in Harris's tales, in which "the confusing world of racial caste disappears at the slave cabin's door,"[100] hinges on indelibly inscribing socioeconomic caste. As Remus observes, finding the little boy "han'-in-glove" with the underprivileged Favers children is so terrible that it might well "fetch ole Miss right up out'n dat berryin'-groun'."[101] The southern past, which takes shape as "ole Miss," the little boy's grandmother, threatens to rise up in response to class infractions unthinkable in the antebellum order that Remus would like to make equally impossible in the postbellum world.

Harris's fiction offers readers an imaginative escape from the specter of social mobility by insisting on the unchangeable nature of poor white degeneracy. As Remus explains to the little boy, the antebellum aristocracy's heir apparent, "Dem Favers's wa'n't no 'count 'fo' de war, en dey wa'n't no 'count endurin' er de war, en dey ain't no 'count atterwards, en ... you ain't gwineter go mixin' up yo'se'f wid de riff-raff er creashun."[102] Asserting that members of the Favers family have been no-account people not only across southern history but also since the dawn of time, Remus pronounces them everlastingly debased. So, while Eric Sundquist is correct in contending that plantation fiction shows that "the forms and hierarchies of a clearly defined racial order ... could still be maintained" after the abolition of slavery, this is only half the story.[103] Remus reinforces racial divides by serving high-status whites and scorning poor whites (allaying fears of cross-racial alliances among working people), and shores up socioeconomic divides by insisting that, despite the upheavals wrought by the Civil War, people like the Favers would stay at the bottom of the social hierarchy and the little boy's family would remain at the top.

Page's stories romanticize the old order by contrasting a halcyon antebellum past with a hellish postbellum present. In the tale "Ole 'Stracted,"

Ephraim and his wife dream of owning the land they rent – a lofty ambition, because this young black couple can afford to pay just a few dollars over the rent each year. Their economic salvation comes with the revelation that Ole 'Stracted, the elderly formerly enslaved man who lived on the land when it boasted a grand plantation, is Ephraim's father, because the money the old man saved to buy his wife and son from their enslavers offers a way to buy the land. At first blush, the story might seem to leave Page hard-pressed to show antebellum aristocrats preferable, for black southerners, to postbellum socially aspirant whites. Before the Civil War, Ephraim's father is sold away from his wife and child and spends the rest of his life working to earn the money to purchase their freedom, whereas Ephraim lives and works with his wife and children while pursuing his dream of making it as a small farmer. Page's tale overcomes this ideological obstacle via its characterization of the two white landowners. Ole 'Stracted's enslaver is depicted as a benevolent patriarch who suffered economic ruin after a fire destroyed his mansion. "Dee" – an unnamed "they" – become the malevolent force to whose will "marster," like the people he claims as his property, must bend (158). "Marster sutny did cry" when Ole 'Stracted was sold, but the whole nasty business was out of his hands: "*dee* teck all he land an' all he niggers an' tu'n him out in de old fiel'" (158; emphasis mine). Unlike Ole 'Stracted's former enslaver, a paragon of paternalism to whom Ole 'Stracted maintains a "sublime devotion" (151), Ephraim's landlord is a skinflint parvenu: "a half-strainer" (147). Ephraim's wife reacts to her landlord with "an expression of mingled disgust and contempt" (146) because, as she explains, "he ain' nuttin but po' white trash!" (147). In Page's tales, the move from enslavement to freedom hurts black southerners because it replaces enslavers' benevolent paternalism with socially aspirant white people's rapacious greed. From Page's cockeyed perspective, social mobility, not slavery, introduces exploitation into the southern agricultural system.[104]

Whereas Harris's and Page's tales downplay antebellum social mobility, Chesnutt's stories underscore it. One of the conjure tales' antebellum arrivistes is Mars Donal' McDonal', "a monst'us rich w'ite gent'eman" who started off as an overseer, then farmed rented land, and finally bought a plantation (174). McDonal's story points to antebellum social climbing and to acquiring, rather than inheriting, aristocratic pretenses because, although born poor, McDonal' becomes a "gent'eman." Chesnutt's fiction also calls into question Harris's and Page's anxieties about social mobility during the Gilded Age by casting doubt on the notion that such movement was common or even feasible. In the conjure stories, Julius's life changes very little between the antebellum tales and the postbellum frame stories – in part, because moving from being enslaved by a southern planter to being employed by a northern capitalist barely alters Julius's material conditions. Like Harris's Remus, Julius lives on the land he worked while enslaved, supplementing insufficient wages with odds and ends earned by telling stories. The conjure tales show that postbellum agriculture – whether tenant farming or wage labor – affords working people a meager existence and few opportunities for advancement. The end of "The Goophered Grapevine" drives home this point. Despite hearing Julius's cautionary tale about the conjure spells that had been cast on the grapevines in a vineyard, John buys the property and later boasts that the "local press" refers to his viticultural enterprise as "a striking illustration of the opportunities open to Northern capital in the development of Southern industries" (43). John's neighborhood newspaper sounds a lot like the *Atlanta Constitution* under editor Henry Grady, who advocated for northern investment in southern industries. Grady, one of late nineteenth-century America's most prominent New South boosters, promoted new economic enterprises capable of preserving old social injustices. In a speech published posthumously – part of a memorial volume put together by none other than Joel Chandler Harris, who worked with Grady at the *Atlanta Constitution* – Grady asserted that "the supremacy of the white race of the South must be maintained forever, and the dominion of the negro race resisted at all points and at all hazards."[105] "The Goophered Grapevine" evokes Grady – and Harris – to demonstrate that John's opportunities and Julius's oppression are interconnected.

Polyvocality's Politics

Why did postbellum plantation fiction writers employ the story-within-a-story structure? In plantation tales, this framework consists of a white Standard English speaker who prompts a dialect-speaking formerly enslaved person to tell a story about life before the Civil War. A number of scholars read plantation fiction's frame narrative as a formal mechanism of racial control – an interpretation that puts Chesnutt's forms and themes at cross purposes. For instance, one critic contends that the story-within-a-story device "perpetuat[es] white authority because the white voice contains the black voice by framing it."[106] But this is an overly literal reading of the frame. The white speaker of the external frame, far from "contain[ing] the black voice," elicits it. The formerly enslaved storyteller, always a rhetorically savvy character, complains about poor white people to his elite white auditor to create common ground – a shared enemy –

and to craft a message that he knows will be music to his listener's ears: that poor whites are entirely unlike affluent whites and intensely unappealing allies to black people. By fortifying social divisions, such claims spoke to a late nineteenth-century white readership anxious about the southern social order's ostensible instability. According to Harris's Uncle Remus, the poor white Favers clan is "de riff-raff er creashun": a kind of taint sure to persist despite any change in material circumstances.[107] For Page's black storytellers, postbellum nouveaux riches are "po' white trash" despite their wealth (148), and former enslavers are "quality" regardless of reduced circumstances (125). Having formerly enslaved people voice such ideas not only lends them credence – black southerners, having just cause to condemn both former slaveholders and the poor white men who sometimes worked as patrollers and overseers, seem like evenhanded judges – but also allays fears of interracial alliances among working people in the post-Emancipation United States. Chesnutt adapted this form, introducing a polyvocal narrative structure in place of the customary dialogic formation, in order to confront the classism undergirding his fellow plantation fiction writers' stories.

Recognizing how the plantation tale's frame structure communicates class concerns offers us a fresh perspective on what Eric Sundquist has identified as the "seemingly polar contradictions in white racial attitudes" during the 1890s, when significant interest in African American folklife emerged alongside the Jim Crow system.[108] The white supremacist social order of the late nineteenth century made possible forms of intraracial cross-class cooperation with the power to destabilize caste divisions. With their stories, plantation fiction writers including Harris and Page let readers escape from the class anxieties of the postbellum present by losing themselves in fantasies of an antebellum past in which African Americans protected wealthy whites from poor whites. In the ruling-class white imagination, black people serve as physical and symbolic gatekeepers who maintain elites' material inviolability by, as Faulkner describes it in *Absalom, Absalom!*, working as the "butler [who] kept the [mansion's front] door barred with his body" as he told the poor white boy to go to the back door.[109] Likewise, the African American characters created by these writers react to poor white people in scornful and supercilious ways – responses intended to validate and reinforce socioeconomic divides.

Plantation fiction's racism – in particular, its paternalism and appropriation of black voices – buttresses the form's classism. African Americans shield affluent whites from poor whites in Harris's and Page's depictions of antebellum society. Furthermore, scenes of interracial cooperation fortify intraracial caste divisions in these writers' works. In Harris's fiction, Remus responds to his young white charge's fraternization with the poor white Favers children by assembling an interracial parental unit made up of "me en yo' ma" who "ain't gwineter stan'" any cross-class friendship.[110] In Page's tales, formerly enslaved people's fond reminiscences about the old order intertwine with their condemnations of socially aspirant white people. In "Meh Lady: A Story of the War," newly emancipated African Americans band together with the people who used to enslave them against a common enemy: "half-strainers," or poor white people striving to better their material conditions (3). Billy and his wife take pains to keep poor white people ignorant of the financial troubles that plague their "young mistis" (117). They also provide her with a patrician "pertector" (126) whom she eventually marries, thus forestalling the financial devastation that allows parvenus to take possession of plantations in other stories. Keeping poor whites powerless and penniless unites African Americans and ruling-class whites in Page's fiction. It also creates consistency between the antebellum and postbellum orders, allowing Page's formerly enslaved storyteller Billy to rejoice that sometimes it seems that "de ole times done come back ag'in" (138) as though "de ain' nuver been no war nor nuttin'" (79).

In Page's tales, black characters' hostility toward poor white people springs from their identification with elite whites. Billy and his wife identify with the planter class, using the collective pronouns "us" and "we" to refer to experiences that were in fact enslavers' alone. Fondly recalling antebellum life, Billy declares, "we wuz rich den," papering over the monstrous reality that he was construed as property, rather than propertied, under slavery (80). Reminiscing about leaner days, Billy laments that "de war dun git us so low, wid all dem niggers to feed" (108). Furthermore, Billy shows that he feels like a member of the family that enslaved him by proudly giving away his "young mistis," Meh Lady, at her wedding, and he exposes his internalized racism when he recoils at Meh Lady teaching at a school for African Americans (117).[111]

By reworking plantation fiction's narrative structure, Chesnutt reoriented the form's ideology. In Harris's and Page's stories, a white character in the postbellum frame tale prompts a black speaker to tell a story about antebellum life but then disappears from the narrative, reappearing at the conclusion (if at all) simply to signal the return to the postbellum present from which the story began. This narrative arrangement serves a didactic purpose by modeling how to read the story. In other words, the white auditor does not participate in the tale but simply receives it, allowing the story to speak for itself. At the end of Chesnutt's stories, by contrast, listeners John and Annie usually voice two different responses to the tale, and Julius sometimes offers a third interpretation.[112] Responding to this interpretative open-endedness, a number of literary scholars have worked to determine which character's response is the correct one. Some early critics argued that John represents Chesnutt, pointing out similarities between John's formal style and erudite diction and Chesnutt's own. However, subsequent scholars took issue with this interpretation, asserting, "it might be uncomfortable for the black writer to identify with his white narrator and condescend to his black storyteller."[113] Other critics decided that the frame invites "readers to choose Annie as our model for response."[114] To these scholars, Annie's "sentimental engagement" with Julius's tales offers the best way to respond to the horrors of enslavement.[115] But contending for one speaker over the others misses the function of polyvocality in Chesnutt's plantation stories. Chesnutt's tripartite narrative structure cleverly addressed his different audiences, with each speaker reflecting and thus potentially speaking to one set of late nineteenth-century readers: the erudite white male editors who reviewed Chesnutt's works, the upper-middle-class white women who constituted the principal readership of magazine fiction, and the African American bourgeoisie hungry for new, nuanced representations of black life.

Chesnutt's use of polyvocality reroutes plantation fiction's political possibilities. In Harris's and Page's tales, both form (the story-within-a-story structure) and content (the anecdote of amiable antebellum relations) emphasize accord between black laborers and white patricians. In Chesnutt's stories, multiple speakers articulate multiple social and political views. For example, although Julius voices derogatory views of poor white people akin to those articulated by the African American narrators of Harris's and Page's stories, John offers dissenting takes on poor white southerners. Polyvocality frustrates any attempt to draw a straight line from characters' utterances to textual or authorial politics.

Other scholars have seen the plantation formula as a limit on Chesnutt's work – a form adhered to because of its commercial viability that at best required Chesnutt to "buil[d] a duality into his early tales that virtually asked that he be 'misunderstood' by some readers"[116] and that at worst "constrained his work" to "feeding an [elite] appetite for consumable otherness" rather than "dismantling prejudice."[117] In fact, Chesnutt reworked plantation fiction's conventions to his own ends, disavowing nostalgia for the antebellum order by troubling the form's foundational premises and reworking the frame narrative structure to engage a diverse readership and support divergent interpretations of his tales.

* * *

A half-century after local color fiction reached the peak of its popularity, poor white people continued to vex well-off white southerners. In 1941, a scion of the Old South published a memoir expressing many of the same concerns that Thomas Nelson Page had voiced in his fiction. William Alexander Percy's *Lanterns on the Levee* – significantly subtitled *Recollections of a Planter's Son* – echoes Page's apprehensions about déclassé whites introducing exploitation into southern agriculture. Whereas the antebellum planter, descended from "an ancient lineage" that graced him with "ancestral hereditaments of virtue," lived and died by his sense of "noblesse oblige," the landowner of Percy's time, who was either "a little fellow operating ... 'on a shoe-string,' or a nouveau riche," exploited the African Americans who worked for him "because of the mortgage that makes his title and his morals insecure."[118] As his condescending comments make clear, Percy's disdain for "unworthy landlords" sprang less from concern over tenants' exploitation and more from self-interested anxiety that people like him might be deposed by upstarts motivated by "pathetic ambition" to "imitate what they do not understand."[119]

The intraracial class conflicts animating American literature have barely rippled the surface of literary criticism. Percy, who identified poor whites as "the most unprepossessing [people] on the broad face of the ill-populated earth,"[120] is characterized as "aristocratic in the best sense" in the back cover blurb of the edition of *Lanterns on the Levee* published by Louisiana State University Press. In the case of Page, some scholars read his poor white southerners as proxies for immigrants. Others look at his splenetic appraisals of poor white characters and somehow see "bucolic images of fundamental accord among white southern people."[121] By recognizing that Page's stories excoriate poor white people because they are poor and white – and that Page is just one of the many regionalist writers heaping contempt on this population – we begin to grapple with the central role that anxieties about white poverty play in shaping American literature and life at the end of the nineteenth century. This unease, stoked by national recessions in the 1880s and panics in the 1890s and by regional social and economic upheavals, flared up again on or about October 1929, when the stock market crashed and William Faulkner began writing *As I Lay Dying*.

CHAPTER 2

Slow, Sweating, Stinking Bumpkins
William Faulkner and Modernism

Toward the end of the funeral journey in William Faulkner's *As I Lay Dying*, when Addie Bundren has spent more than a week dead but unburied, the Bundren wagon-cum-hearse rolls past a trio of black pedestrians, ahead of whom a white man walks. The scene's narrator describes the walkers' response to the stench of the putrefying corpse and the reaction it elicits from Addie's favorite son:

> When we pass the negroes their heads turn suddenly with that expression of shock and instinctive outrage. "Great God," one says; "what they got in that wagon?"
>
> Jewel whirls. "Son of a bitches," he says. As he does so he is abreast of the white man, who has paused. It is as though Jewel had gone blind for the moment, for it is the white man toward whom he whirls.[1]

Darl, Jewel's brother and the chapter's narrator, suggests that Jewel must have "gone blind" in confronting the white man rather than the black man who spoke. Yet Jewel does not hesitate to identify the white pedestrian as his adversary, and he ties the man's offense to being a city slicker: "'Thinks because he's a goddamn town fellow,' Jewel says.... 'Son of a bitch'" (230). A verbal brawl ensues, culminating in an interruption-filled exchange:

> "I thought he said something," Jewel says. "Just because he's—"
> "Hush," I say. "Tell him you didn't mean it."
> "I didn't mean it," Jewel says.
> "He better not," the man says. "Calling me a—" (231)

We might expect the man to object to being called a "son of a bitch." However, Darl interrupts Jewel as he is repeating his initial dig – that "he's a goddamn town fellow" – and this is the pejorative moniker that Darl makes Jewel retract as he tries to de-escalate the situation. Jewel's attempt to use the man's urban origins to explain his behavior is one of the many times when characters invoke the country/town divide to situate themselves and others in the social hierarchy in *As I Lay Dying*. For instance, Darl's sister, Dewey Dell, suggests that living in town confers social status when she ruefully reflects, "we are country people, not as good as town people" (60). Vardaman, the youngest child in the Bundren family, has imbibed the idea that town dwellers enjoy greater affluence than their country counterparts, and so coveting a toy train that his family cannot afford causes him to lament being a country boy, asking, "Why aint I a town boy, pa?" (66). In the confrontation between Jewel and the man from town, the country/town difference threatens to erupt in physical violence, but the text contains this hazard formally through the use of dashes and narratively by hastily resolving the conflict.

Scholars have repeatedly misrepresented this episode. André Bleikasten and Michael Millgate both note that this incident is the only new plot element added to the story between the manuscript and the typescript – a striking detail about a novel written more quickly and with fewer revisions than Faulkner's other major works. Yet Bleikasten and Millgate miss how Jewel "go[es] blind," because each critic claims that Jewel fights with the man who comments on the smell.[2] Cleanth Brooks, despite offering a nearly line-by-line explication of this passage, also overlooks the surprising act of substitution that takes place and thus joins Bleikasten and Millgate in ignoring the scene's most intriguing element: a skirmish illustrating a significant rift between country- and town-dwelling white people.[3]

Tracking changes across early drafts of the novel reveals that Faulkner significantly enlarged this incident, reworking a brief cross-racial encounter into an extended intraracial conflict. In the manuscript, the confrontation spans four short paragraphs: the wagon passes three black pedestrians, one of whom wonders aloud about the contents of the wagon. In response, Jewel twice calls them "son of a bitches," Darl speaks to Jewel, Jewel glares at the black trio, and the wagon moves on.[4] In the typescript and in all published editions of the novel, by contrast, the altercation spans thirty paragraphs and takes shape as a clash prompted by the black man's question but pursued with a white town man. In its revised and published form, the episode stages an unexpected racial substitution, with the Bundrens flipping the script on a more common scene in southern literature and history that sees poor white people taking recourse to violence against black people either to express intraracial solidarity or as a proxy for intraracial conflict.[5] In the novel, however, the black man's comment sparks a confrontation with one of the white townspeople whose greater wealth, access to consumer goods, and disparaging opinions of rural whites dominate the Bundrens' thoughts and influence their actions throughout the journey.

With *As I Lay Dying*, Faulkner anticipates Fredric Jameson's influential observation that a "peculiar overlap of future and past" gave rise to modernism.[6] According to Jameson, "The keen sense of the New in the modern period was only possible because of the mixed, uneven, transitional nature of that period."[7] To illustrate such overlap, Jameson points to early twentieth-century Paris, where automobiles zoomed past medieval monuments and electric lights illuminated structures erected during the Renaissance. But *As I Lay Dying* makes clear that this generative unevenness takes shape not only in material reality but also in the social imaginary. Poor white people in the rural South, long viewed as backward, become the relics that bring into relief urbanites' modernity.

Interrogating the *sense* of the new in the early twentieth century – a sense that emerged from the dialectical relationship between material reality and the social imaginary – is one of Faulkner's central contributions to modernism. Some of the best recent studies of *As I Lay Dying* have explored the novel's engagement with modernity via characters' experiences with modern commodities including graphophones and contraceptives and with the modern era's signal events like the Great Mississippi Flood of 1927.[8] But such analyses, although at times sensitive to (returning to Jameson's phrasing) the "peculiar overlap of future and past" in the novel, treat it as a condition of, rather than as a catalyst to, the modern life Faulkner's fiction depicts. *As I Lay Dying* approaches the newness at the heart of the modern less as a tangible phenomenon – a novel set of consumer goods, historical experiences, or aesthetic forms – and more as a newly valuable form of cultural capital dependent upon longstanding fault lines between country and city, poor and rich, and backward and avant-garde. By engaging with eugenics, a movement that put old ideas about poor white people to new ends, *As I Lay Dying* lays bare how the figure of the poor white serves as a foil to Anglo-American modernity. Recognizing this, in turn, makes clear that Faulkner answered modernism's call to "make it new" by using new representational techniques to set forth new ideas about poor white people. For instance, he made use of stream-of-consciousness narration to explore not bourgeois interiority, as other modernist writers did, but poor white intellect, disputing the longstanding vilipending of poor white people as unintelligent. He eschewed linear narrative progression in favor of suspension – trapping readers in an event by offering several narrators' accounts of it rather than letting them forge ahead – in order to write the Bundrens' experience of social stagnation into the body of the text. And he represented sweat to make manifest poor white peoples' labor, troubling a three-century-long tradition of depicting them as lazy.

Sweat Economics

By shining a light on poor white farmers' problems and privations, Faulkner's fiction sets forth a more incisive critique of labor under American modes of agriculture than is offered in explicitly political works of the 1930s. Several of Faulkner's texts – including *As I Lay Dying* – use sweat to identify and measure labor veiled by the dominant economic order. By way of sweat, these works enter into dialogue with proletarianism and agrarianism, two influential early twentieth-century political and ideological movements Faulkner addressed in an introduction he drafted for a 1933 edition of *The Sound and the Fury*:

> We seem to try ... to draw a savage indictment of the contemporary scene or to escape from it into a makebelieve region of swords and magnolias and mockingbirds which perhaps never existed anywhere. Both of the courses are rooted in sentiment; perhaps the ones who write savagely and bitterly of the incest in clayfloored cabins are the most sentimental. Anyway, each course is a matter of violent partisanship.[9]

By drawing attention to clay-floored cabins used to forward "a savage indictment of the contemporary scene," this passage engages with proletarian fiction. Magnolias and mockingbirds, signature tropes of fiction nostalgic for an imaginary southern past, here seem to point to a contemporaneous incarnation of that stripe of historical revisionism: the Nashville Agrarians' 1930 manifesto *I'll Take My Stand*. Despite their ideological differences – proletarian literature looks ahead to a worker-centered world, whereas the Twelve Southerners' project gazes backward in search of a bourgeois pastoral utopia – both are propagandistic and reductively sociological. Both also inform readers' appraisals of *As I Lay Dying*. For one thing, the novel's departure from proletarian conventions is a recurring refrain in reviews from the 1930s. For another thing, the Nashville Agrarians' "retreat from social into aesthetic theory" gave rise to New Criticism, the predominant mode of mid-twentieth-century literary analysis.[10] The proletarian and Agrarian movements set the terms by which readers and reviewers would understand *As I Lay Dying*'s poor white characters for decades.

In his 1933 study of American literature from a Marxist perspective, Granville Hicks complained that Faulkner "will not write simply and realistically of southern life" or of "representative men and women" but instead tells the Bundrens' story "in a way that brings out all their eccentricities." Hicks suggested that Faulkner should "try to understand the world about him" by portraying more "representative" cases of suffering instead of reveling in "bitterness" and "violence" for their own sake.[11] In his assessment, Hicks voiced the party-line stance of Depression-era proletariat-oriented literary criticism. Writing in the leftist *New Masses* magazine the year *As I Lay Dying* was published, Mike Gold praised the then-emerging genre of "proletarian realism" – which "deals with the *real conflicts* of men and women who work for a living" and uses "as few words as possible" – as an antidote to stories about "bourgeois idleness" written by "verbal acrobats."[12] Hicks and Gold called for fiction that would deliver the "savage indictment of the contemporary scene" that Faulkner impugned in his 1933 introduction. However, in departing from this paradigm, *As I Lay Dying* evinces not apolitical detachment from its moment so much as politicized engagement with a broader swath of time. As John T. Matthews has suggested, "If more instrumental versions of proletarian literature sought a class revolution in no uncertain terms during this decade, perhaps Faulkner's texts kept alive another kind of spirit – a spirit devoted to the incessant questioning of history and social forms."[13]

Contrasting *As I Lay Dying* with more overtly political texts from the thirties bears out Matthews's claim. For example, several of Erskine Caldwell's 1930s publications join *As I Lay Dying* in depicting the lives of poor white farmers in the South. Caldwell's work, however, has an explicit political agenda. *Tobacco Road* (1932) and *You Have Seen Their Faces* (1937), which suggest that the sharecropping system is to blame for poor southerners' economic hardships, advocate for transforming the agricultural order via government intervention and tenant activism.[14] Starting in the late thirties, though, New Deal agricultural programs and modernized farming methods did lead to a decline in sharecropping. But instead of improving the lives of southern sharecroppers, these changes drove these workers into similarly exploitative wage labor on farms or in factories. In going against the precepts of proletarian fiction, Faulkner crafted a more enduring portrait of "the *real conflicts* of men and women who work," as Gold put it, because rather than offering solutions for ephemeral problems, Faulkner's fiction tackles broader questions about society and history.

Politically conservative and promulgating the "makebelieve region" that Faulkner's introduction to *The Sound and the Fury* critiques, the Nashville Agrarians and their 1930 manifesto represent the other side of the coin. The essays in *I'll Take My Stand* and Faulkner's works from the thirties that treat poor white life offer markedly different pictures of labor. According to the Twelve Southerners, industrialists in the North were addicted "to work and to gross material prosperity," while agrarians in the South devoted themselves to leisure.[15] Distinguishing southern farms from northern factories, Andrew Lytle asserted that devotees of the former preferred "the inertia of the fields to the acceleration of industry, and leisure to nervous prostration."[16] John Crowe Ransom insisted that the southerner "envelop[ed] both his work and his play with a leisure which permitted the activity of intelligence" and ludicrously maintained that in the antebellum era, "labor itself was leisurely."[17] Frank Lawrence Owsley's description of antebellum life continues in this vein: "The life of the South was leisurely and unhurried for the planter, the yeoman, or the landless tenant. It was a way of life, not a routine of planting and reaping merely for gain."[18] Such unrealistic portrayals of southern labor history whitewash the historical record, erasing antebellum agriculture's enslaved workforce. They also misrepresent the experiences of landless white southerners, whose struggles to eke out a living on the plantation system's ragged margins rarely yielded "leisurely and unhurried" lives.

Wishful thinking and willful ignorance account for the Twelve Southerners' specious claims about southern agricultural history. As historian Daniel J. Singal notes, "Ransom's Agrarianism was neither very agrarian nor very Southern."[19] Lytle was a farmer, but his line of sight onto early twentieth-century southern agriculture was atypical. Rather than the behind-the-mule perspective of most farmers, Lytle surveyed his farmlands from behind the wheel of his Mercedes. The Nashville Agrarians' South is, as Faulkner suggests, a "makebelieve region."

Faulkner's Depression-era fiction about poor white people counters this unrealistic representation of leisurely labor by taking recourse to a *sweat economy*: a system that staves off the dissociation of the laborer from the fruits of his or her labor by recognizing how work inheres in objects.[20] Sweat in *Absalom, Absalom!* (1936) exposes the underlying toil that upholds aristocratic privilege. Enslaved workers who "sweat in the fields" create patrician wealth.[21] Poor white sweat defines "the difference between white men and white men": while a planter leisurely reclines in a hammock, a poor white worker engages in labor "brutish and stupidly out of proportion to its reward."[22] In "Barn Burning" (1939), tenant farmer Ab Snopes sees the whiteness of Major de Spain's mansion as a product of "sweat. Nigger sweat. Maybe it ain't white enough yet to suit him. Maybe he wants to mix some white sweat with it."[23] The trope of sweat reveals whiteness founded on and sustained by African American workers, bearing witness to the antebellum labors of enslaved people and the postbellum industry of domestic workers and tenant farmers. "White sweat," the exertions of white tenant farmers including Snopes, also buttresses de Spain's whiteness, because poor white laborers work the farm and serve as foils for the respectability of planters like de Spain. In *Absalom, Absalom!* and "Barn Burning," the sweat economy reveals the labor that capitalism works to obfuscate: the exploited labor making possible the "intelligence and leisure" that, according to the Twelve Southerners, are hallmarks of agrarian society.[24]

Several characters in *As I Lay Dying* use sweat as a measure of labor. Farmer Vernon Tull describes looking at "the broad land and my house sweated outen it like it was the more the sweat, the broader the land; the more the sweat, the tighter the house" – a vision that renders his home and land as sweat-made possessions (139). Anse Bundren, father of the Bundren clan, reflects on the sweat economy in light of the country/town divide: "It's a hard country on man; it's hard. Eight miles of the sweat of his body washed up outen the Lord's earth, where the Lord Himself told him to put it. Nowhere in this sinful world can a honest, hardworking man profit. It takes them that runs the stores in the towns, doing no sweating, living off of them that sweats" (110). The incongruity between sentiment and speaker – the fact that Anse, physically and psychologically enervated from a labor-laden youth, manages to live off the sweat of his children and neighbors – does not make his observation any less accurate. In Faulkner's oeuvre, southern agriculture is an exploitative regime that benefits the few through the sweat of the many. Faulkner's sweat economy makes visible exploitative labor forms across southern history: enslaved people's labor in *Absalom, Absalom!*, tenant farmers' labor in "Barn Burning," and the labor of small farmers struggling in an agribusiness market dominated by large landholders in *As I Lay Dying*. Anse's observation begins to flesh out this third paradigm; his son Cash's narration elaborates on it.

Toward the end of the novel, Cash uses sweat to condemn his brother Darl for burning their neighbor Gillespie's barn, insisting that "there just aint nothing justifies the deliberate destruction of what a man has built with his own sweat and stored the fruit of his sweat into" (238). Here, sweat makes manifest the labor value of objects. As Calvin Bedient contends, "What Cash opposes is not simply the destruction of material property.... There is always the man *in* the property to take into account, the value it possesses from having absorbed part of the human life that shaped it."[25] Cash uses sweat to reckon the magnitude of Gillespie's loss, figuring the barn and its contents not in terms of dollars and cents but as extensions of Gillespie: as "the fruit of his sweat." Critics thus err when they view Cash's perspective as a commodifying vision. Dorothy Hale argues that Cash's statement illustrates his "materialism," because sweat imbues objects with value as private property.[26] According to Karl Marx, though, private property results from alienated labor, and Cash takes recourse to the sweat economy to show that Gillespie, far from estranged from the products of his labor, is embodied in them.[27] Cash's vision is materialistic only in the strictest sense: it works to materialize in concrete forms (a barn, animals, and crops) the labor of farming. Like Hale, John T. Matthews sees in Cash's statement "a conceptualization of labor and production that is fundamentally commodified" and that makes possible the reification of labor.[28] But Gillespie's barn and its contents are, from a Marxist perspective, use-values, or objects produced by Gillespie to satisfy his own wants, rather than commodities, which are articles intended for exchange.[29] Faulkner's sweat economy counters the Nashville Agrarians' "makebelieve" vision of the South and its dubious picture of leisurely labor.

Stasis and Status

In much of Faulkner's fiction, characters' travels up and down the social ladder map onto their progress through space and time. *Absalom, Absalom!* and the Snopes trilogy, for instance, center on the rise and fall of poor white protagonists Sutpen and Snopes. These two sagas, Faulknerian versions of the Franklinian Bildungsroman, begin with the youthful bumpkin's "education," which structures the novel's temporal and geographic planes insofar as each plot follows its protagonist from youth to death and changes setting in accordance with his travels. Sutpen's social status fluctuations in *Absalom, Absalom!* range across the text's broad temporal and spatial canvas, with the ebbs and flows of Sutpen's fortunes spanning nearly one hundred years and including treks through the South and into Haiti and (through Quentin and Shreve) Massachusetts.

As I Lay Dying differs from *Absalom, Absalom!* and other major works by depicting characters who are frozen rather than in flux. This novel describes neither ascent nor decline, neither progress nor regress, but rather spatial, temporal, and social stasis. Throughout the Bundrens' journey, Addie's rotting body offers the most vivid evidence that time is passing, because the stench from the coffin gets worse and the number of buzzards following the wagon steadily increases. Otherwise, frequent obstacles create a sense of arrested development. This seemingly immotile expedition fixes the Bundrens within a narrative of changelessness and suspension – a narrative that mirrors their social and economic immobility. Like its storyline, the novel's structure suggests fixity. In eschewing linear narrative progression by, for example, presenting several different narrators' accounts of the same scene, the text produces a sense of motionlessness – of circling around and around an event rather than plunging forward. Formal and thematic suspension and repetition forge a symbiotic relationship between the novel's form and content. In *As I Lay Dying*, the Bundrens' social stasis is transformed into and represented through physical and temporal stasis.[30]

During the Great Depression, a few southern writers experimented with new techniques for depicting the experiences of people who found themselves stuck on the social ladder's bottom rungs. Like Faulkner, Erskine Caldwell suggested characters' economic immobility by using repetition to produce a sense of narrative inertia. Jay Watson argues that Caldwell pioneered a form of "*discursive* poverty" – monotonous dialogue delivered as part of lifeless exchanges – to represent the spiritual and psychological effects of material deprivation.[31] Leigh Anne Duck analyzes how Caldwell's fiction offers a "spatializing account of white poverty" that employs repetitious dialogue and a reiterative storyline to situate poor white southerners in a place geographically removed and temporally distinct from the rest of the nation.[32] Sections of *Tobacco Road* that recount people's movements, as Duck shows, feature literary devices producing a sense of repetition. For instance, Caldwell's novel utilizes analepses, or accounts of events related after where they fit in the story's chronology, to recount how the protagonist's landlord and children move away from where he lives. In *Tobacco Road*, though, stagnation is neither absolute nor purely a result of class, because while the story's poor white patriarch, Jeeter Lester, is stuck, his children are not. In *As I Lay Dying*, by contrast, the novel's ending does not simply resituate all but one of the Bundren children back at their father's house, where the story's opening found them, but also roots them more firmly in place. In the closing pages of Faulkner's text, three of the Bundren boys have been stripped of the material or symbolic conveyances capable of carrying them away from their father's home: Jewel surrendered his horse, Cash lost part of his leg, and Vardaman did not get his dreamed-of toy train. The fourth, Darl, "in a cage in Jackson," is even more dramatically immobilized (254).

Recognizing the social salience of stasis offers a way to reconcile ostensibly opposed interpretations of *As I Lay Dying*, bridging debates about whether the novel is "an almost timeless fable" without political import or a timely social critique by an author as "class-conscious as any Marxist."[33] The novel's timelessness propels its class critique, because this temporal stasis mirrors the social stasis of the protagonists. However, not all readers consider the Bundrens socially immobile. Susan Willis sees the Bundrens' journey as "a historical metaphor ... for the migration of this country's agricultural work force to the cities."[34] John T. Matthews forwards a similar claim, reading the novel "as a fable of social upheaval ... with the modernization of the South implied both in the Bundrens' move to town and in their centrifugal impulses away from the broken forms of family and community."[35] But these readings posit a level of social change beyond what the Bundrens experience. Although family members acquire some sought-after consumer goods (a bag of bananas, a set of false teeth, and a graphophone) from their trip to town, the story's conclusion reveals no meaningful changes in their livelihood or standard of living.[36] Instead, the novel closes with the Bundrens back on the farm, listening to the graphophone "in the winter" (261). By indicating the season, the novel's last chapter drives home the fact that, far from metaphorical migration or social upheaval, the Bundrens' journey yields little more than a gizmo they find time to enjoy only in agriculturalists' off season.

Matthews's and Willis's arguments illustrate the challenges of connecting Faulkner's modernist fiction with reigning conceptions of modernism and modernity. Although Willis and Matthews cite different scholars – Walter Benjamin and Guy Debord on the one hand, Andreas Huyssen and Theodor Adorno on the other – both are drawing on works that theorize the modern as a largely urban phenomenon. This is why, for example, Willis and Matthews try to tie the Bundrens to the mass migration from farms to factories that produced significant demographic shifts in the first half of the twentieth century. But *As I Lay Dying* neither literally nor symbolically represents this migration; on the contrary, it depicts the effects of this exodus on people who stayed in rural areas and kept farming. Industrialization influences the novel not because Darl and Jewel Bundren leave the farm to seek employment in textile mills or sawmills – a familiar story in southern historical and literary accounts of the early twentieth century, when these mills were at the core of the region's industrial economy – but rather because they take a job transporting lumber to a mill. The novel illustrates the symbiosis between the country and the city, making clear how the Bundrens' rural labor (growing cotton and hauling lumber) serves the region's industrial markets (textile and lumber mills). Yet it also shows that rural modernization's central features – employment opportunities, roads, access to consumer goods – do not produce momentous changes in the lives of people like the Bundrens.

As I Lay Dying takes up not the archetypal modern – the neurasthenic, the blasé urban dweller[37] – but the seemingly anti-modern: the rural poor white. Through this personage, the novel explores the *creation* of the modern, laying bare the processes by which rural poor whites come to serve as foils for other people's modernness. Townsfolk in the novel read the Bundrens as out of step with the modern era. Literary critics, on the whole, have corroborated this view rather than questioning it. Sylvia Jenkins Cook, for instance, notes "a timeless quality" about the lives of Faulkner's rural-dwelling poor white people and writes of *As I Lay Dying* that "except for the few details that establish time, it might as easily be placed a century earlier."[38] In some ways, Cook is correct. True to the experiences of people living in poor and isolated rural communities, Faulkner's poor white characters lag behind the vanguard of progress. *As I Lay Dying* invokes longstanding ideas about poor white people as anachronisms – as vestigial organs of the white body politic – in order to probe the origins and functions of such notions, exposing them not simply as products of poor white people's old-fashioned practices and possessions but also as creations of middle-class, status-conscious commentators.

The turn of the twentieth century saw Americans starting to answer modernism's call to "make it new" by making poor whites seem old. Four years before German sociologist Georg Simmel published "The Metropolis and Mental Life," which explores how city dwellers were evolving in response to urban conditions, American sociologist William Goodell Frost published an essay discussing the opposite phenomenon: how mountain living stunted Appalachians' development. This 1899 *Atlantic Monthly* article, called "Our Contemporary Ancestors in the Southern Mountains," presents poor white Appalachians as "an anachronism" living in "the conditions of the colonial times" because "Rip Van Winkle sleep" had overtaken them.[39] Frost, then president of Berea College, hoped his essay would inspire northern donors to support his institution's efforts to make Appalachians "intelligent without making them sophisticated."[40] Accordingly, Frost was trying to put a positive spin on this poor white primitivism, portraying inhabitants' outdated employments, speech practices, and arts as "less a degradation than a survival" – in other words, as customs once common in English and Scottish settlements across the United States that persisted, by the dawn of the modern era, only in Appalachia.[41]

Such representations of poor white people as obsolete holdovers from earlier times found a ready audience. By the 1920s and 1930s, scholars were offering both genetic and cultural explanations for why poor white people were hopelessly out of step. Lothrop Stoddard, best known for *The Rising Tide of Color against White World-Supremacy* (1920), a racist manifesto about the threat that people of color purportedly posed to white imperial and colonial interests, also penned *The Revolt against Civilization:*

The Menace of the Under Man (1922), which identifies poor white people as a dire internal threat to the white race. Drawing on eugenic studies of poor white families, Stoddard suggested that "as a civilization advances it leaves behind multitudes of human beings who have not the capacity to keep pace." Among these outpaced multitudes are poor white people, whom Stoddard's book depicts as "melancholy waste-products which every living species excretes but which are promptly extirpated in the state of nature, whereas in human societies they are too often preserved."[42] Stoddard's description melds the idea of poor white people's obsolescence with the familiar derogation of them as trash, yielding a vision of poor whites as "waste-products" that would be "extirpated" by natural selection if not for philanthropic and medical intervention that "preserve[s]" them despite their inability "to keep pace." In his contribution to *Culture in the South* (1934), one of the seminal texts of southern studies, A. N. J. den Hollander used poor white peoples' obsolescence as a jumping-off point for his analysis, which works to pinpoint the causes of poor white southerners' "arrested cultural development" and "surprisingly primitive existences."[43]

Characters' observations about the Bundrens establish that poor white obsolescence is a matter both of reality and of perception, because family members and their possessions seem to degenerate as they move from descriptions offered by rural spectators to those tendered by urbanites. For example, the Bundrens' wagon, seen by Darl as merely "shabby" (157), is to town-dweller Moseley "ramshackle" (203). More dramatically, Addie's well-made coffin, admired in Frenchman's Bend as an example of Cash's carpentry skills and hailed by farmer Vernon Tull as "tight as a drum and neat as a sewing basket" (88), becomes to its town chronicler "that homemade box": one of several unfit objects that make the Bundrens' entrance into town comparable to "a piece of rotten cheese coming into an ant-hill" (203). These descriptions also extend to the Bundrens themselves. To Dewey Dell, time moves rapidly, and events occur "too soon" for her to handle them all (120). Yet when Moseley waits on her in his store, he tells Dewey Dell, "I'm pretty busy," explaining that "a man just hasn't got the time they have out there" (200). These examples bear out Evan Watkins's contention that obsolescence is "not at all a survival from the past" but rather something "produced by and integral to the conditions of dominance in the present."[44] Faulkner's townspeople establish their modern identities through their depictions of the Bundrens, spotlighting signs of obsolescence that throw into relief their own cutting-edge practices and possessions. The ramshackle wagon, the homemade coffin, and slow-moving country time are singled out because they contrast with hallmarks of the modern: the automobile, the mass-produced product, and fast-paced city life. By viewing poor whites as obsolete and alien, urban whites – in some cases neither wealthier nor better educated than their country counterparts – establish their cultural superiority.

As I Lay Dying features no Old South aristocrats or New South entrepreneurs. The novel's most prosperous character is probably either Dr. Peabody, whose dead accounts outnumber his viable ones, or the druggist Moseley. At the same time, the Bundrens are not destitute; after all, they own their land. Despite the relative economic uniformity of the portions of Yoknapatawpha County that the Bundrens traverse during their journey, though, the novel highlights two distinct social stratification schemas, one distinguishing the Bundrens from townsfolk in Mottson and Jefferson and another setting them apart from other farmers in Frenchman's Bend.

As Dewey Dell's experiences in town reveal, the country/city divide helps create social distinctions among white people. Dewey Dell and the city dwellers with whom she interacts recognize and reinforce the notion that city dwelling confers social capital. Dewey Dell thinks "we are country people, not as good as town people," and townsfolk agree with this judgment, viewing Dewey Dell by the light of stereotypes of country people as inarticulate, out of date, dawdling, and interchangeable (60). Moseley, a druggist in Mottson, says of Dewey Dell as she enters his store, "she kind of bumbled at the screen door a minute, *like they do*, and came in" (198; emphasis mine). With this opening gambit, Moseley launches a chapter in which, over the space of five pages, he offers nine observations about "them" (199): the class to which Dewey Dell belongs and with which Moseley considers himself quite familiar. And what Moseley knows about people like Dewey Dell is that they are bumbling, slow, eager to "poison themselves" with patent medicine, and that although they will take an inordinately long time spending very little money, "you have to humor them" (200). MacGowan, the next drugstore clerk Dewey Dell encounters, offers a faux ethnography of the "country woman" (241), classifying Dewey Dell as "one of them black eyed ones that look like she'd as soon put a knife in you as not if you two-timed her" (242) and explaining of country people that "half the time they dont know what they want, and the balance of the time they cant tell it to you" (243).[45] Moseley and MacGowan ultimately represent two different responses to rural people. Moseley comes to the sympathetic, if condescending, conclusion that "it's a hard life they have" (202), whereas MacGowan takes advantage of Dewey Dell's naiveté and desperation for the purpose of sexually exploiting her. Both, though, see Dewey Dell not as an individual but as an exemplar of a known and undeviating type: the anachronistic, inarticulate, and dim-witted country person.

The Bundrens' ontological reveries challenge these stereotypes about country people, shaping understandings of identity that dispute homogenizing treatments of poor white rural dwellers. In one of Darl's most opaque reveries, he considers his ambiguous economic and ontological position as a middleman in a lumber transaction by contemplating his relationship to the timber, positioning himself vis-à-vis "the load that is no longer theirs that felled and sawed it nor yet theirs that bought it and which is not ours either, lie on our wagon though it does" (80). In this passage, Darl's self-definition is tied to his socioeconomic status, because he links his place in the economic order – lacking the ability to buy or sell goods and instead equipped only with his labor-as-commodity, he takes piecemeal work ferrying others' goods – to the ontological questions that dominate his thoughts. Darl's ambiguous relationship to the lumber – he is the present *non*-owner, differentiated from the past owner and the future owner – kindles his crisis of being, reflected in his lament, "I dont know what I am. I dont know if I am or not" (80). Darl's inability to identify "what" he is, sparked by his in-between position in the economic exchange, devolves into questioning "if" he is. Thus while I agree with John T. Matthews's contention that "the Bundrens' function as 'middlemen' in this transaction becomes a metaphor for Darl's selfhood," I think this makes Darl not a representative *modern* man, as Matthews asserts, but paradigmatic *poor white* man.[46]

Like Darl, Vardaman and Addie define themselves in ways that conflict with townspeople's totalizing views of poor white countryfolk. Vardaman's most significant reverie of this sort takes shape when limited visibility in a dark barn prompts him to ponder the relationship between himself and Jewel's horse: "It is as though the dark were resolving him out of his integrity, into an unrelated scattering of components – snuffings and stampings; ... an illusion of a coordinated whole of splotched hide and strong bones within which, detached and secret and familiar, an *is* different from my *is*" (56).[47] By pondering his relationship to entities populating his world, Vardaman defines himself in a way that flies in the face of poor white stereotypes. Contemplating differences between himself and the horse, Vardaman dissects the "illusion of a coordinated whole" – the "them" to which urbanites relegate country people – and in this way defines his singularity: "an *is* different from my *is*." Addie, too, asserts a singular and self-defining poor white identity that opposes townspeople's view of poor white people living in rural areas as a homogeneous "them" when she declares, "I would be I" (174). In these instances, the Bundrens push back against efforts by Moseley, MacGowan, and other town dwellers to create a hierarchical system of intraracial social differentiation by using hyperbolic or fallacious contrasts between country backwardness and urban modernity.

The Bundrens are set apart not only from townsfolk but also from other farm families, because farmers in Frenchman's Bend portray Anse as an inept and lazy parasite who counts on their assistance. Tull, for example, says of Anse, "like most folks around here, I done help him so much already I cant quit now" (33). Farmers Uncle Billy and Quick express a similar sentiment, suggesting that Anse has "let everything slide all his life," but his fellow farmers have supported Anse for so long that they cannot stop (89). Samson stresses that Anse is "lazy" (114), while Armstid calls Anse "a durn fool" and laments, "be durn if there aint something about a durn fellow like Anse that seems to make a man have to help him, even when he knows he'll be wanting to kick himself next minute" (192). Literary scholars have often echoed these assessments. Cleanth Brooks deems Anse "one of Faulkner's most accomplished villains," possessing a "stubborn vitality which like that of some low order of organism allows him to fatten on what would starve nobler creatures."[48] Ted Atkinson writes that "Anse comes across as a shifty and acquisitive cracker."[49] But following the lead of Anse's fellow farmers neglects their reasons for emphasizing his shortcomings. As Julia Leyda notes, "Those who have the greatest stake in marking Anse as a white trash other are those who occupy positions closest to his, socioeconomically and geographically – farmers and townsfolk who want to be perceived as 'modern' and middle class and who see in the Bundrens' backwardness evidence of their own progress."[50] Frenchman's Bend farmers with middle-class aspirations elevate themselves above the Bundrens via ethics rather than economics because, in their largely homogeneous community, families' material conditions are more or less the same.[51]

Yet chapters narrated by three of Anse's fellow farmers call into question their critiques of him. Although the other farmers insist that they help Anse in innumerable ways, their interactions with him reveal his unwillingness to receive much assistance. Daniel J. Singal rightly observes that Anse accepts very little help or hospitality during his family's journey to Jefferson.

> When people outside the family offer help, Anse's standard response is "We wouldn't be beholden" or "We wouldn't discommode you." Critics have

assumed that these comments represent a shrewd tactic to weasel food and lodging out of his neighbors, but in fact he accepts the minimum amount of aid necessary to continue his trip under what can only be described as emergency conditions.[52]

Other farmers record their complaints about Anse alongside his refusals of their help, opening up a chasm between the narration and the action – between words and deeds, as Addie would phrase it. In his chapter, Armstid reflects on the assistance he routinely gives Anse and at the same time recounts how Anse refuses accommodation in the Armstids' home and tries to spare Mrs. Armstid the trouble of preparing meals for him and his family. Similarly, at Samson's, Anse politely refuses supper, but Samson will not take no for an answer, insisting that his "wife takes it as a insult" if guests do not join them for meals (116). Anse also declines beds in the house, instead sleeping with his family in the barn, and leaves before breakfast.

The narrative brings to light a system for establishing class distinctions among people on the same rung of the social ladder. The other farmers represent themselves as middle class – or, at least, as manifesting middle-class mores and values – by contrasting their self-reliance with Anse's dependence, which they have established as one of his defining characteristics through their frequent references to it. Perhaps Anse willingly participates in this process; after all, in exchange for serving as the community's social nadir, Anse assures himself of aid from the other farmers when he needs it, because it is by providing occasional help that the others achieve their social superiority. In any case, these instances depict how an otherwise homogeneous population creates social distinctions: Anse becomes the kind of person who needs help (whether or not he receives it) and the other farmers become the kind of people who are called upon to help him. By treating how urbanites understand country people as well as how other farmers perceive Anse, Faulkner's novel reveals how white people in similar material circumstances establish an intraracial pecking order.

Lazy Men and Lewd Women

In 1927, Oliver Wendell Holmes Jr. wrote the majority opinion for *Buck v. Bell*, a decision by the Supreme Court of the United States that upheld the state of Virginia's right to involuntarily sterilize the "feebleminded." Feeblemindedness was a catchall diagnosis – so much so that intelligence tests administered by the United States Army during World War I classified forty-seven percent of white recruits (and an even more absurd eighty-nine percent of black recruits) as feebleminded – but poverty (pauperism, in eugenic lingo) was one of the condition's telltale symptoms.[53] When applied to women, feeblemindedness "suggested weak intelligence, lack of inhibition, and a predisposition to sexual misbehavior."[54] The plaintiff in the case, Carrie Buck, was a poor white girl who, at seventeen years old, found herself committed to the Virginia State Colony for Epileptics and Feebleminded because she became pregnant after being raped. In the trial, Buck's social status was more text than subtext, with eugenic experts identifying her as part of "the shiftless, ignorant, and worthless class of anti-social whites of the South" in order to support the case for sterilization.[55] Holmes and his fellow justices were convinced, voting eight to one in support of Virginia's eugenic sterilization law, and Buck became one of the more than eight thousand people involuntarily sterilized in that state. These court proceedings, chockablock with eugenic jargon, ideas from the fledgling field of intelligence testing, and legalese, rendered poor white people mute. Three years later, Faulkner published a novel whose form gave poor white characters new ways to speak for themselves.

Around the time he was writing *As I Lay Dying*, Faulkner would have witnessed eugenicists scoring victories at the national level, in cases like *Buck v. Bell* (1927), and closer to home. In 1928, Mississippi passed a sterilization statute, making it the only Deep South state with such legislation before the Great Depression.[56] C. D. Mitchell, superintendent of what was then called the Mississippi State Insane Hospital in Jackson, went on record saying he hoped to sterilize every patient who came through the doors of his institution.[57] Because Mitchell headed Jackson's psychiatric facility at the time Darl would have been committed there, his eugenic ambitions add to readers' horror at finding Darl "in a cage in Jackson" at the close of the last – and most haunting – chapter he narrates (254). By midcentury, women of color were the principal victims of forced sterilization – a human rights issue that gained national attention thanks to civil rights leader Fannie Lou Hamer, who testified about her own experience with "Mississippi appendectomies," as black women's involuntary hysterectomies came to be known. But eugenicists in the twenties, concerned that "dominant whiteness was threatened with the spectre of inadequacy and fallibility within its own racial borders," focused their attention on poor white people.[58]

As I Lay Dying engages with early twentieth-century eugenic thinking through its characterizations of the Bundrens. As Jay Watson observes, the Bundrens are "a copious inventory of dysgenic traits."[59] Textbook examples of dysgenic progenitors, Anse and Addie seem like they sprang out of a eugenic family study and into fiction. Eugenic researchers considered women's "immorality and sexual degeneracy" and men's shiftlessness indicators of hereditary deficiency.[60] Accordingly, because of Addie's affair with Whitfield and Anse's reputation for laziness, each of them is "the probable potential parent of socially inadequate offspring" in the eyes of eugenicists.[61] But Faulkner used Anse's body and Addie's voice to contest such conclusions.

Environment, not heredity, accounts for Anse's broken body and browbeaten attitude. Bearing scars from his experiences as a worker engaged in small-scale unmechanized farming's backbreaking labor, Anse's body refutes the "powerful myth about the somatic nature of social problems" set forth by eugenics.[62] Darl observes that "Pa's feet are badly splayed, his toes cramped and bent and warped, with no toenail at all on his little toes, from working so hard in the wet in homemade shoes when he was a boy" (11). As a young man, Anse became seriously ill from working in the sun. In adulthood, Anse "laid sick" after a load of wood fell on him (15). These injuries testify to abiding labor in perilous conditions, and so does Anse's humped back, which may be the result of the painful posture the cotton farmer assumes while hoeing and picking. Anse's penchant for snuff – smokeless tobacco used by generations of poor southerners to stave off hunger – points to his inadequate diet. Nutritional deficiencies are probably also to blame for his many missing teeth. Anse says he wants false teeth so that he can again "eat God's own victuals as a man should" (37), which will allow him "to keep his strength up" (191), suggesting that what his neighbors call laziness might really be malnutrition-induced lethargy.

History rather than heredity explains Anse's poverty. As a young man, Anse was a "forehanded" farmer with "a house and a good farm" and "a good honest name" (171). How did this man devolve into a reputedly lazy and charity-dependent farmer who must take one son's money and another son's horse just to buy a mule team? Although the novel does not explicitly account for this reversal of fortune, situating Anse's career trajectory within the economic history of Mississippi does. Banner agricultural years in the early twentieth century, when Anse was a young farmer, gave way to farming crises in the 1910s and 1920s including boll weevil infestations, floods, and reduced demand in the aftermath of World War I. Anse might be right to call himself a "luckless man," because forces beyond his control conspired against his agricultural efforts for a sizable chunk of his working life (18).

Many scholars read Addie's chapter as a diatribe against language. Critics have written that Addie "despises words,"[63] expresses "frustration with the referentiality of all language,"[64] and advocates a "rejection of language"[65] and of "storytelling, which Faulkner ... regards in his major fiction as the only source of significant meaning."[66] But Addie embraces language "in which the words are the deeds," rejecting only language made up of "words that are not deeds, that are just the gaps in people's lacks" (174). Addie's neighbor Cora Tull employs this second linguistic system, drawing on eugenics-inflected ideas about morality and motherhood to critique Addie and distract from gaps in her own lacks, as Addie might put it.

In Cora's chapters and in Addie's, readers learn what Cora thinks of Addie's parenting; most revealingly, Addie relates that "Cora Tull would tell me I was not a true mother" (173). Cora's "true mother" evokes the cult of domesticity's "true woman." As historian Wendy Kline explains in her cultural history of eugenics in the United States, eugenicists' idealized "mother of tomorrow reaffirmed the nineteenth-century 'cult of true womanhood,' which positioned women as arbiters of morality within the home."[67] Cora fancies herself this sort of household moral authority, repeatedly referring to her Christian faith and her efforts "to live right in the sight of God and man" in the three chapters she narrates (23). By contrast, she has a laundry list of complaints against Addie, insisting that "the eternal and the everlasting salvation and grace is not upon her" (8) because she "had never been pure religious" (166) and had "closed her heart to God" (168) with her "blindness" (8), "pride" (22, 23), and "vanity" (166, 167, 168). Eugenics gauged not only a woman's moral fitness but also her fitness for motherhood. Battling what was termed "race suicide" at the start of the twentieth century and the "differential birthrate" by the 1930s, eugenicists encouraged middle-class women who were postponing having children or limiting the size of their families to have more babies at the same time that they were using institutionalization and sterilization to check poor women's reproductive capabilities. Viewing "rural folk who had more than two children and lived meagerly as harbingers of racial decline,"[68] eugenicists targeted women like Addie.

Addie rebuts Cora's eugenics-inspired critiques by emphasizing the chasm between words and actions: "And so when Cora Tull would tell me I was not a true mother, I would think how words go straight up in a thin line, quick and harmless, and how terribly doing goes along the earth, clinging to it, so that after a while the two lines are too far apart for the same person to straddle from one to the other" (173). Addie defines motherhood by "doing" – and she does it differently from Cora (172). For Cora, motherhood is a set of "duties" she performs even though her children can be "trials" (22). For Addie, motherhood remakes her understanding of herself. After giving birth to Cash and Darl, Addie thinks, "I was three now" (173). Having children forges bodily and sensory connections between Addie and the world around her. Describing her postpartum relationship to the earth, for example, Addie recounts "hearing the land that was now of my blood and flesh" (173).

Addie insists that "motherhood was invented by someone who had to have a word for it because the ones that had the children didn't care whether there was a word for it or not" (171–2). Addie critiques "motherhood" as a social construct rather than a biological experience – one describing "not the personal, individual act of bearing children, but its social, symbolic and public ramifications."[69] Rather than rejecting all language, then, Addie rebuffs a discourse invented by eugenicists and used to deny reproductive choice to women. That she forwards this critique in some of the most powerful and lyrical prose in all of Faulkner's fiction further testifies to Addie's faith in and fondness for language.

Addressing its profound influence on modern literature and culture, scholars have called eugenics "the paradigmatic modern American discourse"[70] and "the dark underbelly of much modernist writing and theorizing."[71] Faulkner engaged with this discourse in *As I Lay Dying* to expose its underbelly, bringing to light the flaws in pseudoscientific conceptions of motherhood at the very moment they were being codified and weaponized – used to thrust the "holy diadem of motherhood" onto the heads of middle-class women while putting it far out of poor women's reach.[72] In eugenic studies, "the 'defectives' lost their voice, as the authors assumed the ability to speak for (or, rather, against) them."[73] In *As I Lay Dying*, Addie uses her voice to contest eugenic characterizations of people like her.

Trashing Addie

In *Purity and Danger* (1966), anthropologist Mary Douglas famously defines dirt as "matter out of place."[74] For the Bundrens, journeying with Addie's unembalmed, putrefying body (with *mater* out of place, as it were) highlights their social out-of-placeness because Addie, literalizing the pejorative social status of poor white people, becomes trash. White trash is a slur that marks out "a certain form of racial detritus."[75] This disparaging term defines poor white people through their association with trash – defunct objects used despite their dilapidation or kept for parts or with plans for repair – and *as* trash: as social and cultural detritus. Addie's corpse fuses these two senses of trash, because the Bundrens' poverty leads to their prolonged contact with their matriarch's body. People more prosperous than the Bundrens would have had an embalmer prepare the body for burial and could have arranged for an undertaker to oversee interment. In addition, descriptions of Addie's body suggest refuse rather than human remains. Seeing Addie on her deathbed, other characters describe her body as rotten: Peabody calls it "a bundle of rotten sticks" (44) and Darl terms it a "handful of rotten bones" (49). Rottenness resurfaces during the funeral journey when Moseley likens the Bundrens' wagon arriving in Mottson to "a piece of rotten cheese coming into an ant-hill" (203). Moseley objectifies Addie, employing an object pronoun – "it had been dead eight days" he says – rather than a subject pronoun (203). Finally, after Darl, in an abortive attempt to cremate the body, sets fire to a barn that is sheltering the coffin, the box emits "a thin smell of scorching meat" (222). In each instance, Addie becomes not just an object but a ruined object – a form of refuse. Whether sticks, bones, or cheese, Addie's body is rotten, and even as meat she is scorched: burned, ruined.

By embodying the Bundrens' debased social status, Addie's corpse opens a vista onto the senses' role in social stratification. As trash and as reeking flesh, Addie's body gives grotesque life to the idea that poor people stink. In his 1907 essay "Sociology of the Senses," Georg Simmel wrote that body odor produces social divisions, observing that "if the other senses build a thousand bridges between human beings . . . then, by contrast, one can characterize the sense of smell as the dissociating sense."[76] In a collection of travel sketches published in 1922, W. Somerset Maugham asserted, "in the West we are divided from our fellows by our sense of smell" because the "stink" of working people "makes social intercourse difficult to persons of a sensitive nostril."[77] In his 1937 account of working-class life in northern England, George Orwell suggested that "the real secret of class distinctions in the West" is the bourgeois belief that "*the lower classes smell.*" Orwell insisted, "it may not greatly matter if the average middle-class person is brought up to believe that the working classes are ignorant, lazy, drunken, boorish, and dishonest; it is when he is brought up to believe that they are dirty that the harm is done."[78] Whereas Maugham's sketch presents a straightforward cause-and-effect scenario – people from the working class smell, and so upper-class individuals keep their distance from them – Orwell's account explores how associating working-class folks with dirt and unpleasant odors conditions middle-class people to shun interclass contact. For Orwell, "the essential thing is that middle-class people *believe* that the working class are dirty . . . and, what is worse, that they are somehow *inherently* dirty."[79] Filth morphs from a physical to a metaphysical blight that inheres in poor people, reinforcing and naturalizing the social order.

Addie's body incarnates negative stereotypes about poor white people. In their responses to her corpse, characters enact two socially salient responses to such stereotypes: her family members react with dissimulation, whereas outsiders respond with disgust. Although they spend more than a week in July aboard a wagon carrying a corpse that is not only drenched in river water but also burned in a fire, the Bundrens have little to say about the smell. Samson concludes "they was used to it" (114) after noticing that while fellow farmer Quick's "face looked funny, around the nostrils" after he approached the Bundren wagon, the Bundrens themselves "just sat there" (113). It seems unlikely that the Bundrens acclimated to the odor. For one thing, at the outset of the journey, family members do acknowledge the smell. Jewel's face changes from "greenish" (97) to "completely green" (98) when he moves Addie's coffin from the house to the wagon, and Darl recounts that he, Jewel, and Cash carry the coffin with "faces averted, breathing through our teeth to keep our nostrils closed" (98). A few pages later, Cash observes, "in a couple of days now it'll be smelling" – that is, the smell will be noticeable even at a distance (108). Addie has been dead for just three days at this point; the stench will get worse before they finally get her buried, and yet Vardaman is the only Bundren who will again acknowledge the smell.[80]

What explains the family's silence? Darl's description of moving the coffin to the wagon offers some insight, because it depicts using "a sort of modesty" to manage a stigmatizing experience (98). To account for what prevented Jewel from upending the coffin when he went at it with too much force, Darl imaginatively reanimates Addie's body: "For an instant it resists, as though volitional, as though within [the coffin] her pole-thin body clings furiously, even though dead, to a sort of modesty, as she would have tried to conceal a soiled garment that she could not prevent her body soiling" (97–8). Darl's imaginative account of his mother's body's resistance speaks to his family members' feigned immunity to the odor emanating from the coffin. Encumbered with something "soiled" – not only the dead body but also the social stigma of trash – the Bundrens respond to a state of affairs they feel powerless to change by concealing from outsiders, each other, and themselves their emotional and sensory responses to the situation. After they begin encountering neighbors and townspeople, the Bundrens adopt a strategy of dissimulation. Only Vardaman breaks the family's code of silence.

By acknowledging the smell, Vardaman confirms that his siblings' apparent lack of awareness of the odor is a defense mechanism. On one occasion, Vardaman says to his sister, "I can smell her," and asks, "Can you smell her too?" (216). But Dewey Dell only responds, "hush" (217). A generous reading might suggest that Dewey Dell is trying to teach her brother to use silence defensively – although the fact that she tells Vardaman to hush on a number of unrelated occasions might undermine this interpretation. In any event, it is clear that Vardaman, the youngest child, has not yet embraced silence as a tool for navigating the public sphere. Vardaman also tries to dissociate Addie from the stench of putrefaction, saying, "*my mother does not smell like that*" (196; emphasis original). In some sense, Vardaman is correct. In a perfectly Faulknerian turn of logic, the corpse is Addie and not-Addie. The body cannot be identified as anyone other than Addie, and yet by Addie's own reasoning, which insists on linking words with deeds, the body is not Vardaman's mother because the body cannot mother Vardaman. As a metaphor for the poor white body, the corpse points to the fraught relationship between poor white people and poor white stereotypes, with the smell making manifest the stigma of white trash. Whereas his siblings cope by dissimulating, Vardaman handles it using denial.

In contrast to the Bundrens, farmers and townsfolk react to the reeking coffin with disgust. Samson experiences the smell as an imagined residue of the Bundrens that lingers on his farm even after they leave, observing, "It was like I [was] ... smelling it even when I knew I couldn't" (118). Armstid perceives the odor while the Bundrens are present and imagines it after they depart, because seeing the buzzards that follow the coffin makes it seem as though he could still smell the stench: "Soon as I see [the buzzards] it was like I could smell it in the field a mile away from just watching them, and them circling and circling for everybody in the county to see what was in my barn" (186–7). Armstid finds the odor physically disgusting as well as embarrassing, because he feels chagrined that the buzzards reveal to "everybody in the county" that his barn shelters the coffin. Moseley reports that when the Bundrens arrived in town, women scattered while "hard-nosed men and boys" surrounded the wagon until the marshal told the Bundrens they had to leave because "folks couldn't stand it" (203).

Disgust reinforces boundaries.[81] In his study of disgust, William Ian Miller explains that disgust draws on the senses but is not simply a sensory response; rather, disgust has an "intensely political significance."[82] The "stench of the low," Miller observes, "bear[s] a direct relation to the anxiety they generate in the high. When out of place they smell; when safely in place they do not."[83] In *As I Lay Dying*, the smell from Addie's coffin arouses other peoples' disgust with the Bundrens. Disgust makes manifest others' views of the family as geographically out of place during the funeral journey and socially out of place as whites marked by their poverty within a social hierarchy that maintains the supremacy of whiteness by construing it as unmarked.[84]

The Bundrens' ostensible immunity to the smell – the fact that they seem "used to it" – gives the lie to the apparent naturalness and neutrality of others' reactions, laying bare socially significant responses to feeling or being perceived as out of place. Addie's two-part trashiness – her body's status as what must be disposed of and her debased class identity – prompts disgust, and this response shores up social, geographic, and even ontological boundaries. Addie's body embodies her family's social status and exposes intraracial social differentiation, revealing how the epithet "white trash" cordons off poor white people within the white body politic.

* * *

In the 1920s, Mississippi was the most rural state in the nation.[85] This setting, the backdrop for the composition of *As I Lay Dying* and for the story that unfolds across the text, serves as a laboratory for exploring the creation of the modern. By way of its slow-moving wagons, sweating farmers, and stinking corpses, the novel treats the modern as a form of cultural capital wielded by better-off people against the poor. When the Great Depression put conspicuous consumption out of reach for all but the richest of the rich, middle-class white people took recourse to symbolic forms of capital, associating poor white people with the outmoded to make themselves seem up to date. When the economically unprecedented gave way, a quarter-century later, to the socially unprecedented, middle-class white people used the same strategy in a different arena. To distance themselves from the racial discrimination and disenfranchisement for which civil rights protesters were taking to task not simply the South but the United States as a whole, middle-class white southerners started writing novels and stories about poor white racists.

CHAPTER 3

Civil Rights and Uncivil Whites
Flannery O'Connor and Southern Women's Midcentury Writing

A headline-grabbing hubbub in 2015 reminded us that some of the most beloved heroes of the civil rights movement are fictional characters. Fifty-five years after he was introduced to the world by the novel that made him famous, Atticus Finch was again making news. With the publication of *Go Set a Watchman*, Atticus's character did an about-face. And readers were up in arms. Instead of the Depression-era crusader for racial justice they knew and loved from *To Kill a Mockingbird*, readers encountered an older Atticus who, against the backdrop of the burgeoning civil rights struggle, attends a Klan meeting, disparages African Americans, and lauds segregation. Readers who adored *To Kill a Mockingbird* in their early years declared their childhoods retroactively ruined.[1] Parents who named their children after Atticus considered changing those names, and some even did so. *People* ran a story about a Colorado couple who rechristened their son in response to *Go Set a Watchman*. Originally named Atticus, the boy became Lucas.[2]

These responses to *Go Set a Watchman* bring into focus a key question about southern white women's celebrated texts from the civil rights era: Why do these works spotlight individual anti-racist heroes – and, just as significantly, individual racist villains – during a period of institutional change? Midcentury civil rights activists were taking on unjust institutions: the Board of Education of Topeka, Kansas; the bus system in Montgomery, Alabama; Central High School in Little Rock, Arkansas; and the Woolworth store in Greensboro, North Carolina, to name just a few. Yet works by several famed white women writers depict solitary villains located on the ragged margins of southern society. In Harper Lee's *To Kill a Mockingbird*, Bob Ewell lives in squalor behind the town dump. The unnamed narrator of Eudora Welty's short story "Where Is the Voice Coming From?" assassinates a civil rights worker not at the behest of any white supremacist organization but rather "for [his] own pure-D satisfaction."[3] In Lillian Smith's essay collection *Killers of the Dream*, a bedraggled figure named Mr. Poor White – a wretch "eaten up with malaria and hookworm" (164) who is "fed little except scraps of 'skin color' and 'white supremacy'" (171) – is singularly invested in upholding the unjust southern social order.

These works by Lee, Welty, and Smith represent racism as personal prejudices blighting poor white people rather than as policies and practices architected, in no small part, by middle- and upper-class white people.[4] Yet scholars have credited these authors with articulating a broad-reaching social critique, bearing out Lora Romero's observation that literary critics seem "unable to entertain the possibility that traditions, or even individual texts, could be radical on some issues ... and reactionary on others."[5] Radical and reactionary are inextricably linked in these writers' works, which use reactionary class positions as the bedrock of racial radicalism.

Unlike her contemporaries, Flannery O'Connor is often read as divorced from her social context, with scholars describing her as "silent toward the events of the civil rights movement" and "aloof from the politics" that galvanized the era.[6] But in her personal correspondence as well as in her short stories, O'Connor engaged with how the civil rights struggle was taking shape in her fellow white women writers' works. O'Connor's letters include criticisms of Lee's novel, Welty's story, and Smith herself. Her stories take up defining forms from these writers' texts and put them to fresh ends, exposing racism across the white socioeconomic spectrum and critiquing intraracial classism.

Locating the Voice

Just after midnight on June 12, 1963, civil rights activist Medgar Evers was shot dead in the driveway of his Jackson, Mississippi, home. As soon as she learned of this murder in her hometown, and before the police or the public knew the gunman's identity, Eudora Welty wrote a story about the assassination from the killer's point of view. Her motivation, as she explained decades later, was "the necessity I felt for entering into the mind and inside the skin of a character who could hardly have been more alien or repugnant to me."[7] One of her only topical tales, "Where Is the Voice Coming From?" paints a striking picture of the speaker and his hateful act. Despite its brevity – the story fills just two pages of the *New Yorker*'s July 6, 1963, issue – the narrator's language unambiguously establishes his social location, as the opening lines make clear:

> I says to my wife, "You can reach and turn it off. You don't have to set and look at a black nigger face no longer than you want to.... It's still a free country."
>
> I reckon that's how I give myself the idea.
>
> I says, I could find right exactly where in Thermopylae that nigger's living that's asking for equal time. And without a bit of trouble to me.[8]

The speaker's ungrammatical colloquialisms ("no longer" for "any longer," "set" for "sit"), use of present-tense verbs for past actions ("I says," "I give"), and regionalisms ("reckon") – identify him as a poor white southerner. His prejudices, too, conform to those stereotypically attributed to poor white people. His bald racism – most glaringly, his nonchalant use of the n-word – jars us just as it jarred *New Yorker* readers in 1963, and his racist rhetoric grows even more repulsive with the coining of "black nigger," a phrase hideous for its overwrought redundancy, beastly in its neurotic attention to race. By declaring that "it's still a free country," the unnamed narrator also identifies himself as a poor white person. American literature teems with poor white people spouting self-serving ideas about democracy – think of Pap's "call this a govment" speech in *Adventures of Huckleberry Finn*.[9] Finally, in noting that he could locate his victim "without a bit of trouble to me," the speaker reveals his laziness. Ruling-class writers have depicted poor white southerners as lazy for at least three hundred years, deeming them "indolent wretches" in the eighteenth century,[10] insisting that their "chief characteristic ... is laziness" in the nineteenth,[11] accusing them of "mainly pass[ing] their time on their backsides in the shade" in the twentieth,[12] and finding them "immune to hard work" in the twenty-first.[13]

Welty's story presents a killer driven by jealousy and a wide-ranging inferiority complex. We see both forces in action when the narrator dilates on how his material circumstances differ from his victim's. Whereas Roland Summers, Welty's fictionalized Medgar Evers, has a paved driveway, a garage, a grassy lawn, and a new car, the speaker parks a borrowed truck in his barren front yard. The narrator's inferiority complex kindles his antagonism toward not only his victim but also wealthy people – including "dern teen-ager[s]" who own cars and the "rich-bitch" women at his wife's workplace – and powerful entities like the police and the media.[14] In the killer's warped psyche, the murder offers an escape from a sense of abasement, making him feel "on top of the world myself. For once."[15] Confident that she "knew what was in that man's mind," Welty fashioned her tale as a psychological study of poor white depravity.[16]

But this story, written immediately after Medgar Evers was assassinated (and before the murderer had been identified), misapprehends the killer in one important respect. As Welty explained in a 1972 interview, "[I] thought it was a Snopes and it was a Compson."[17] Welty acknowledged that she "went a bit wide of the mark in placing the social background of the person arrested for it," imagining as poor white a man who was instead "a Southern-type gentleman," a member of blue-blood organizations including the Sons of Confederate Veterans and Sons of the American Revolution who was quick to "boast of his proud lineage or recount his ancestors' many noble deeds."[18] Despite this blunder, Welty insisted that she captured the "mind" and "*nature*" of the character, explaining, "I knew what was in that man's mind because I'd lived all my life where it happened."[19] What Welty likely meant is that, as a lifelong resident of Jackson, she had special insight into the murderer's ways of thinking. But what really explains her confidence in knowing "that man's mind" is her class status, not her hometown.

Welty was a member of what Nadine Hubbs calls the "narrating class," or the professional middle class, which tasks itself with "interpreting and narrating all levels of American life – including working-class existence."[20] Welty's membership in the narrating class may explain her confidence in her ability to intuit and narrate the racist words, thoughts, and deeds of a poor white man. As John Hartigan observes, "A comfortable conviction holds sway among middle-class whites that racism is concentrated in the lower classes – that it is certainly present in working-class whites, but bubbles up most vigorously from the hearts of poor whites," and this conviction may have motivated Welty to depict her killer as a poor white.[21] Her faith in her ability to, in her words, get "into the mind and inside the skin of a character who could hardly have been more alien or repugnant to me" also points to how Welty's class status informed her fiction.[22] Steph Lawler finds that working-class people "are assumed to be easily 'readable' to middle-class observers, although, interestingly, unable to know or understand *themselves* at all."[23] These intertwined assumptions structure Welty's text, which takes shape as a poor white narrator's internal monologue precisely so that Welty and her audience could *read* the speaker, coming to understand him better than he understands himself. So, where *is* the voice coming from? The narrating class. Rather than poor white racism, Welty's story exposes bourgeois white classism.

Welty's claim that she "knew ... what the murderer must be saying and why" is false.[24] Her narrator's life of penury and social marginality – "hocked" guitars and hackneyed paeans to freedom, "Surplus & Salvage" stores and nonstandard syntax – affords no glimpse into the racism of the South's decayed gentility.[25] While Welty's tale depicts a recognizable poor white literary type – a figure who, as Huck Finn says of his father, "warn't no more quality than a mud-cat" – Byron De La Beckwith, Medgar Evers's assassin, bragged about "a proud ancestry on both parents' sides."[26] Far from an unknown loner who felt alienated from and oppressed by the establishment like Welty's speaker, who fears that those in control will "find *some* way I don't get the credit," Beckwith was "aligned ... with the most powerful men in [his town's] small business community" through his participation in White Citizens' Councils.[27] As historian Pete Daniel explains, White Citizens' Councils "recruited upstanding citizens" and "distanced themselves from ... poor southern whites."[28] Defending white supremacy by subjecting civil rights supporters to economic, political, and social reprisals, the Councils carried out "the agenda of the Klan with the demeanor of the Rotary."[29] Finally, whereas Welty's character marvels at his anonymity after the murder, noting that "they know who Roland Summers was without knowing who I am," Beckwith "*loved* publicity, *loved* getting his name in the paper," and used his social position and understanding of media to garner publicity for himself.[30]

Writing about "Where Is the Voice Coming From?" in 1980, Welty observed that her certainty about the killer's point of view inspired her to use first-person narration: "I wrote his story – my fiction – in the first person: about that character's point of view, I felt, through my shock and revolt, I could make no mistake."[31] Might Welty's hedging language and bumpy syntax – her disruptive recharacterization of "his story" as "my fiction" and her insertion of "I felt" to temper the claim that she "could make no mistake" – signal that, at some level, she did recognize and wish to acknowledge her error? Whatever Welty's intentions, we need to reckon with her inaccurate representation of the killer's class because, for one thing, it makes her story less exposé than false alibi. As journalist Adam Nossiter notes, "Beckwith's kin could have rubbed shoulders with Welty's," and so trying to distance herself from the assassin by making him poor white is "wishful thinking."[32] For another thing, we need to underscore Welty's errors because readers continue to gloss over them. The author of a 2013 article in the *New Yorker* commemorating the publication of the story a half-century earlier applauds Welty for making "her characterization of the murderer so precise."[33] A contributor to *The Cambridge Companion to American Civil Rights Literature* (2015) asserts that Welty, "with surprising accuracy, profiled Medgar Evers's assassin long before Byron de la Beckwith was arrested."[34] But her characterization is inaccurate, and by misidentifying the murderer's social status, Welty distorts not only civil rights history but also the workings of racial inequality. John Hartigan contends that poor white stereotypes perform a "critical function in the maintenance of whiteness, for these are the figures whites use to delimit an attention to the subject of racism." In other words, overemphasizing poor white racists obscures the white-collar bigots who enact and sustain institutional racism:

> Poor whites are not the bank officers who deny mortgages and other loans to African-Americans of all classes at rates two to three times that of their white counterparts; poor whites are not among the landlords who refuse housing to African-Americans, nor are they the human resources managers who are racially influenced in their hiring and firing decisions.[35]

And poor whites are not the only white people who used violence to intimidate, injure, and end the lives of civil rights activists.

O'Connor rendered judgment on "Where Is the Voice Coming From?" in a September 1963 letter to her friend Betty Hester. With characteristic acerbity, O'Connor described Welty's tale as "the kind of story that the more you think about it the less satisfactory it gets."[36] The year after Welty's story appeared in the *New Yorker*, O'Connor published "Revelation" in the *Sewanee Review*. Whereas Welty's tale fictionally forays into the poor white mind, O'Connor's story explores the middle-class psyche. Bucking the trend of depicting poor whites as racism's agents and middle-class whites as its adversaries, O'Connor's tale reveals white racism across the socioeconomic spectrum. Her story also exposes intraracial classism, drawing attention to the strategies middle-class white people use to distinguish and distance themselves from poor white people.

Point of view in "Revelation" illustrates what Dorothy Hale has called the "representational economy" of third-person narration, because "exposition ... unites form and content by carrying the added value of character revelation."[37] Focal character Ruby Turpin is introduced to the story when, on the hunt for an empty seat in a doctor's waiting room, she scrutinizes "a place on the sofa occupied by a blond child in a dirty blue romper who should have been told to move over and make room for the lady."[38] Turpin's thoughts about the child reveal her own character, because by zealously identifying what "should have been" done for a "lady," Turpin lays bare her investment in southern social mores and gender constructs.

Beginning with the child on the sofa, Turpin points out what she sees as the social, physical, and hygienic shortcomings of the poor white people in the waiting room. Turpin establishes the child's class status by describing him in terms that jibe with the archetypal image of the poor white: "He was slumped down in the seat, his arms idle at his sides and his eyes idle in his head; his nose ran unchecked" (191). This brief description is brimming with longstanding poor white stereotypes, including the boy's "slumped" posture, an infantile version of the stoop-shouldered stance often attributed to the adult poor white male; his "idle" arms and eyes, evoking centuries of representations of poor white peoples' physical and intellectual lassitude; and his "unchecked" runny nose, suggesting insufficient parental oversight and a disease-ridden body.[39] Turpin reads class as character, and the text draws attention to the sweeping conclusions she comes to using scant evidence. Consider, for instance, the line "Mrs. Turpin saw at once that no one was going to tell him to move over" (191). What is it that Turpin "saw" that allowed her to foretell this social faux pas? Nothing more than the child in the "dirty blue romper" (191). By using what narratology terms internal focalization, or perspective constrained to a single character's (Turpin's) point of view, O'Connor depicts the narrowness of Turpin's line of sight.

Turpin looks for physical differences between her and the poor white family because she construes such variances as character differences. For example, the child and his family members are described as "dirty" four times (191, 194, 198, 204), and dirtiness signifies laziness to Turpin. Seeing "rusty" hands (192) and "gritty-looking" clothes (194), Turpin decides that these people's idleness knows no bounds. Another conclusion one might draw is that this family makes its living from farming, just as Turpin and her husband do. Calling herself a "hard-working" woman (210) and declaring "[I] break my back to the bone every day working" (215), Turpin characterizes herself as the polar opposite of poor white people, whom she thinks of as lazy.

Turpin takes material markers of poverty as indicators of personal failings. In introducing the matriarch of the waiting room's poor white family, Turpin describes little except her "cotton print dress," noting that "she and Claud had three sacks of chicken feed in their pump house that was in the same print" (194). Turpin calls attention to what she thinks most dramatically distinguishes her from these poor white people – in this instance, fashioning feed sacks into items of clothing rather than into curtains or towels, which is how people like the Turpins usually made use of the bright cotton print fabrics in which animal feed companies packaged their product. Turpin holds the poor white woman up for ridicule with what she says and how she says it, because Turpin's syntax equates person and provender, rendering both without volition in the matter of their enrobing via parallel prepositional phrases: "in a cotton print dress" and "in the same print." This projected passivity begins with clothing but then moves to character, with Turpin observing that the old woman and child look "vacant and white-trashy, as if they would sit there until Doomsday if nobody called and told them to get up" (194). Turpin looks at tangible evidence of industriousness – homemade clothes fashioned out of materials at hand and a "thin leathery old" body indicating a lifetime of hard outdoor work – and sees inaction (194).

While Turpin's candid assessment of the scene creates the sense of unmediated access to the middle-class mind's class-conscious cogitations, the lack of buttressing commentary from either an omniscient narrator or another character calls into question her assertions. Turpin insists upon her keen vision and accurate conclusions, averring that "she had seen from the first" that the old woman and child were related, because "she could tell by the way they sat" (194). Likewise, she saw that another woman "was certainly the child's mother" (194). Yet the wider narrative framework establishes that Turpin knows nothing about these people beyond what she observes, because she is not personally acquainted with this family and none of its members has even spoken yet. Furthermore, as the story progresses, Turpin increasingly relies on tautological claims that undermine her credibility. For instance, in surveying the shoes of the waiting room's occupants, Turpin notes that "the white-trashy mother had on what appeared to be bedroom slippers, black straw with gold braid threaded through them – exactly what you would have expected her to have on" (195). Given that Turpin knows little about the woman *except* what she is wearing, her claim is tautological: seeing that she wears what appear to be bedroom slippers, one recognizes her as the type of woman who wears slipper-like footwear.

"Revelation" casts doubt on what middle-class white people think they know about poor white people. Welty's sense of knowing Medgar Evers's killer is what drove her to write "Where Is the Voice Coming From?," and this same sense of certainty shaped how she talked about the story. When asked about the tale in a 1972 *Paris Review* interview, for example, Welty took recourse to forms of the verb "to know" three times: "I knew what was in that man's mind"; "I ... knew, was in a position to know."[40] In O'Connor's text, Turpin echoes Welty by insisting that, when it comes to poor white people, she is a domain expert: "There was nothing you could tell her about people like them that she didn't know already" (203). By ascribing this assertion to a character with bad judgment, O'Connor's story calls into question such feelings of certainty.

"Revelation" also reveals how classism can work in tandem with racism. To describe poor white peoples' debasement, Turpin declares them "worse than niggers any day" (194). Musing on whom she would be if forced to "either be a nigger or white-trash," Turpin imagines that, having "wiggled and squirmed and begged and pleaded" for another option, she would begrudgingly consent to be "a neat clean respectable Negro woman" (195). In another instance, Turpin diagrams the social hierarchy, situating poor white people next to – "not above, just away from" – "most colored people" (195). In each case, racism symbiotically supports classism insofar as Turpin denigrates poor whites by locating them at or below the social nadir to which she relegates African Americans. To be sure, Turpin's racism in these examples is more virulent than her classism. For one thing, her casual, repeated use of the n-word makes her bigotry startlingly venomous and vile. For another thing, Turpin puts "most colored people" on "the bottom of the heap" in her social ranking, while among whites only poor people occupy that position. Her social judgments, while uneven, are imbricated: racism and classism work together in Turpin's social economy.

"Where Is the Voice Coming From?" depicts poor whites enacting racism and puts middle-class whites – Welty and her readers – in the position of exposing and condemning that racism. By contrast, "Revelation" shows the cross-class nature of racism by representing white women across the social spectrum voicing differently worded versions of the same bigoted sentiments. When a young black man enters the doctor's waiting room to deliver an order from the drugstore, three female characters – representing poor, rich, and middle-class perspectives – respond to him in ways that seem, at first blush, quite different:

> "They ought to send all them niggers back to Africa," the white-trash woman said. . . .
>
> "Oh, I couldn't do without my good colored friends," the pleasant lady said.
>
> "There's a heap of things worse than a nigger," Mrs. Turpin agreed. "It's all kinds of them just like it's all kinds of us." (200–1)

The poor white woman uses repulsive language to express a repulsive idea.[41] But her words also underscore her social marginality. Unlike the other two women, who use first-person pronouns in their responses – the prosperous women referred to as the "pleasant lady" speaks of herself with "I" and "my," while Turpin refers to white people as a collective "us" – the poor white woman cedes power to an unnamed third-person entity, describing not what she thinks or wishes but rather what "they ought to" do. By voicing her racism alongside her sense of its social and structural insignificance, the poor white woman links her poverty and her prejudice. Turpin's comments, like so many of her declarations, intertwine racism and classism.[42] Using virulently racist language to refer to African Americans and dehumanizing poor whites as "things," Turpin aims to elevate herself by pushing others down.

The upper-crust lady gives voice to a polite euphemism that masks a cruel reality. Few affluent white women in the 1960s South had "good colored friends." The black women she "couldn't do without" are more likely to be domestic workers, including cooks and housekeepers whose labor supports her household. While couched in agreeable terms, this speaker's statement may represent the unkindest cut of all, because she mislabels as "friends" women who could be required to enter and exit through her home's back door,[43] eat meals on dishes kept separate from her own family's dinnerware,[44] sleep on cots in the kitchen when required to say overnight,[45] and accept leftovers in lieu of fair pay.[46]

O'Connor's waiting room is awash in hostilities. While Turpin antagonizes the poor white family, a "big fat girl with her face all broke out" named Mary Grace antagonizes Turpin (212). As Turpin describes it, the "ugly girl" directs "ugly looks" (197) and "loud ugly noise[s]" at her (205). Finding the situation inexplicable – "I haven't done a thing to you!" Turpin thinks in response to the girl's "urgent" hostility (203) – Turpin is taken aback when first a book, then Mary Grace herself, comes "crashing across the table toward her" (206), the latter howling, scratching, and demanding "go back to hell where you came from, you old wart hog" (207).

The attack enrages Turpin, who believes that her social status should shield her from such experiences. Turpin is incredulous that "she had been singled out for the message, though there was trash in the room to whom it might justly have been applied" (210). Interpreting the experience as a misdirected message from heaven, Turpin shouts at the sky, "There was plenty of trash there. It didn't have to be me" (216). Flabbergasted that God – the target of her angry monologue – could "like trash better" (216) than "respectable" (210) people like her, she insists upon her charitable works: "It's no trash around here, black or white, that I haven't given to" (215). As her fixation on "trash" makes clear, Turpin equates socioeconomic standing and spiritual standing, imagining that her middle-class social status puts her above poor people not simply monetarily but also morally.

"Revelation" ends with a celestial vision showing Turpin that she was wrong to conflate social condition and spiritual condition. When "a vast horde of souls [who] were rumbling toward heaven" appears in the sky, Turpin is shocked to see that the heavenly hierarchy inverts the social hierarchy, because at the front of the procession march "whole companies of white-trash, clean for the first time in their lives" and "bands" of African Americans (217). People like the Turpins "were marching behind the others with great dignity, accountable as they had always been for good order and common sense and respectable behavior.... Yet she could see by their shocked and altered faces that even their virtues were being burned away" (218). This scene turns Turpin's world on its head by situating black and poor white people at the head of the procession when the everyday practices of racism and classism in the South routinely enacted social subjugation through spatial subjugation, including making black riders sit in the back of the bus and making most black visitors and some poor white ones call at the back doors of homes and businesses.[47] Furthermore, seeing the "virtues" of the white middle class "being burned away" reveals that these qualities were social rather than moral merits. As Ralph C. Wood argues, with this conclusion O'Connor "does not romantically exalt the poor and the outcast as intrinsically righteous. The down and out are God's favorites, compared to the clean and dignified Turpins of this world, simply because they are less bent on their own justification."[48] "Revelation" explodes the bourgeois self-satisfaction seen in "Where Is the Voice Coming From?" not by raising up poor whites but by taking middle-class whites down a few pegs.

Mute Inglorious Mill Hands

In 1965, two years after Welty published "Where Is the Voice Coming From?," civil rights activist and writer Lillian Smith found herself musing about authoring a text a lot like Welty's: "I would like to do a collection of monologues in the voices of the 'poor whites....' I'd like to let them tell (through me) their thoughts, their bewilderments, their angers and resentments, the dark welling-up of their hate."[49] Smith envisioned a work similar to Welty's in form and function, because her project would take shape as a poor white speaker's first-person narrative and would channel poor whites' innermost thoughts, feelings, and perplexities. Like Welty, Smith was born into an upper-middle-class family – both women's fathers were businessmen – but she expressed confidence in her ability to serve as a mouthpiece for poor white people. Just as Welty believed that she was in a position to "know" her protagonist's experience ("his story – my fiction") so well that she "could make no mistake" about his drives and dissatisfactions,⁵⁰ Smith imagined that she had access to poor white peoples' "angers and resentments, the dark welling-up of their hate," which she would "let them tell (through me)." Yet punctuation registers unease in both writers' prose. While Welty's dash in "his story – my fiction" typographically enacts the distance between the two narratives, Smith's anxious parenthetical phrase "(through me)" and her scare-quoted reference to "the voices of the 'poor whites'" underscore the fact that these monologues would be messages conceived and conveyed by a member of the middle class.

Instead of following Welty's lead by fictionally rendering a poor white man speaking for himself, though, Smith's magnum opus *Killers of the Dream* scrutinizes poor white southerners from a middle-class vantage point. Both writers spoke for poor white people, but whereas Welty donned a poor white mask by narratively assuming a lower-class persona, Smith affixed a muzzle on the poor white mouth when she spoke from her middle-class social location on behalf of poor white people. Both gestures downplay middle-class whites' role in constructing and maintaining Jim Crow by placing responsibility squarely on the shoulders of poor whites.

Smith wrote that poor white southerners possess "mind[s] emptied of words, bereft of ideas and facts" (163). Because of this "terrifying ignorance" and "mental emptiness," poor white people prove incomprehensible to people like her and her readers, "whose minds have been nourished well since they were born" (163). With these assertions, Smith strove to justify her project, making clear both why poor white people are not speaking for themselves and how important it is for someone like her – a member of "the dominant class" whose members "are today determining the future of the world" (128) – to speak for them. This reasoning gives rise to a class-conscious single-speaker format that I call the middle-class monologic. Quashing dissent by prohibiting dialogue, the middle-class monologic is a misinformational mode in *Killers of the Dream*.⁵¹

Killers of the Dream describes white supremacy as the opiate of the masses. According to Smith, white supremacy made poor white people "forget that you were eaten up with malaria and hookworm; made you forget that you lived in a shanty and ate pot-likker and corn bread, and worked long hours for nothing" (164). Smith's argument builds on W. E. B. Du Bois's analysis of how poor white workers in the Jim Crow South "were compensated in part by a sort of public and psychological wage" in *Black Reconstruction* (1935).⁵² But whereas Du Bois dilated on the public privileges that white laborers enjoyed in place of higher pay – unrestricted access to civic spaces, voting rights, municipal job opportunities, and other remunerations – Smith emphasized the high costs of these compensations by pointing to underprivileged white southerners' poor health and poor diets. Focusing on how "the drug of white supremacy" fed poor white peoples' "starved minds and bodies," *Killers of the Dream* addresses white supremacy principally in terms of its appeal to impoverished whites by treating it as a balm that soothed their "spiritual bruises and material deprivations" (165). By contrast, Smith insisted that middle-class whites' "more informed minds could not wholly approve" and "never more than half believed" cant about Anglo-Saxon superiority (164).

Smith's analysis does not accord with what historians and sociologists tell us about the workings of white supremacy in twentieth-century America. Manning Marable argues that "beginning with the Great Depression, and especially after 1945, white racists began to rely almost exclusively on the state apparatus to carry out the battle for white supremacy."[53] Whereas Smith's account treats white supremacy as a set of ideas that fuels individual racists, Marable's scholarly work examines it as a set of practices – including governmental surveillance, capital punishment, and police brutality – that sustains institutional racism. As Eduardo Bonilla-Silva observes, "The United States does not depend on Archie Bunkers to defend white supremacy."[54] Although Smith may be correct that "white skin ... became the poor white's most precious possession," it was no less valuable to middle-class whites (165). White supremacy eased the pain of poor white people's economic, political, and educational disadvantages at the same time that it facilitated middle-class white people's accumulation of economic, political, and educational advantages.

In *Killers of the Dream*, Smith both inhabits the middle-class monologic by speaking for poor white people and enacts the middle-class monologic via the text's imaginary speakers. The latter monologic is at work in a chapter called "Two Men and a Bargain," in which a figure called Mr. Poor White stays silent while Mr. Rich White tells about the deal the two of them struck. The bargain the men negotiate – "you boss the nigger, and I'll boss the money," as Mr. Rich White phrases it (176) – points to how *Killers of the Dream* employs the middle-class monologic to exculpate better-off white people from the dirty work of Jim Crow by suggesting that rich whites ceded social power to poor whites in exchange for maintaining their financial hold on the South. According to Smith's narrator, although wealthy whites architected the southern system of racial apartheid, they turned it over to poor whites: "Jim Crow was Mr. Rich White's idea but Mr. Poor White made it work" (181). The poor white man "made it work" largely through extralegal violence, including acts like lynching. Smith's narrative depicts lynching as a socioeconomically segregated enterprise, proposing that ruling-class whites "gave the privilege of lynching to rural whites as a ritualistic reward for accepting so meekly their design for living," but then absented themselves (163); Mr. Rich White pointedly tells Mr. Poor White, "*don't expect me to come to the lynching, for I won't be there*" (177). In his study of lynching, however, historian William Fitzhugh Brundage observes that we have "no reason to question contemporary news accounts that describe many mass mobs as including 'the best citizens' of the community."[55] Far from ad hoc vigilantism enacted by a few outcasts, lynchings were orchestrated public spectacles that took advantage of modern modes of transportation including automobiles and chartered trains to bring together white racial terrorists across the social spectrum.[56]

Lillian Smith and Flannery O'Connor met on December 1, 1955, at a luncheon hosted by the Georgia Writers' Association. The next day, both women served up tidbits about their encounter in letters to friends. Smith merits only a passing glance in O'Connor's correspondence. Squeezed between inquiries about her friends' holiday in Rome and a colorful account of tenant farmers her mother had recently hired, O'Connor noted that Smith "asked me to visit her on her mountain top" – Smith lived on Screamer Mountain near Clayton, Georgia – but she declined the invitation.[57] In her letter, Smith played up the differences between them. Whereas Smith reported that the luncheon's organizers gushed over how "nice" she was and how she "dressed like Park Avenue," she pronounced O'Connor "a little on the grim side in personality and not personally very attractive," although she did acknowledge that her fellow Georgian gave "a hell of a good speech."[58]

Although O'Connor passed up the chance to further engage with Smith in person, she did go on to engage with her in print. O'Connor's short stories shine a light on the middle-class monologic's inner workings. By depicting middle-class speech alongside contradictory poor white thought, O'Connor's fiction suggests that the middle-class monologic goes unchallenged because the speaker is in a position of authority, not because the speaker's statements are accurate. In addition, by illustrating the dangers of talking without listening, O'Connor's tales suggest that middle-class monologues may take a toll not only on those who are silenced but also on those who voice them.

Whereas Smith's *Killers of the Dream* depicts poor people with "mind[s] emptied of words, bereft of ideas and facts" (163), O'Connor's fiction represents poor people with active intellects who are reluctant to speak when what they have to say might not be well received by middle-class people in positions of authority. In a story called "Greenleaf," an African American worker who needs to point out a mistake made by his employer does so by stating his disagreement obliquely and then "looking away as if this insolence were addressed to some one else" (43). "The Displaced Person" pairs middle-class speech with poor white thought to reveal how class impacts communication. As farm owner Mrs. McIntyre delivers what the story pointedly terms a "monologue" about her constrained position, farmworker Mrs. Shortley mentally frames a rejoinder: "You hire and fire, Mrs. Shortley thought, but she didn't always say what she thought. She stood by and let Mrs. McIntyre say it all out to the end."[59] Mrs. McIntyre's middle-class monologue goes unchallenged because of its social, rather than epistemic, force. Although Mrs. Shortley "thought" about the power Mrs. McIntyre wielded over her employees – agency McIntyre failed to acknowledge while lamenting her powerlessness – she kept her own council on that front. But while Shortley stays quiet within the plot, the text itself gives voice to her realization and in this way challenges the middle-class monologic.

"A Circle in the Fire" critiques the middle-class monologic by representing the dangers of talking without listening. This story opens with a poor white woman named Mrs. Pritchard trying to tell Mrs. Cope, her boss, about "that woman that had that baby in that iron lung" (130). The third-person narrator economically tenders Cope's response: "She was used to these calamitous stories; she said they wore her to a frazzle" (131). With the qualifying phrase "she said," the text launches its critique of its middle-class protagonist, because while Cope *says* she is frazzled by Pritchard's storytelling, the narrative *shows* that she is in truth oblivious to it. Cope's inattention takes shape as interruptions and non sequiturs that make the women's exchange humorous and help flesh out both characters:

> "I don't see myself how she had [a baby] *in* [an iron lung]," she went on. . . .
>
> Mrs. Cope was bent over, digging fiercely at the nut grass again. "We have a lot to be thankful for," she said. "Every day you should say a prayer of thanksgiving. Do you do that?"
>
> "Yes'm," Mrs. Pritchard said. "See she was in it four months before she even got thataway. Look like to me if I was in one of them, I would leave off . . . how you reckon they . . . ?"

"Every day I say a prayer of thanksgiving," Mrs. Cope said. "Think of all we have. Lord," she said and sighed, "we have everything," and she looked around at her rich pastures and hills heavy with timber. . . .

Mrs. Pritchard studied the woods. "All I got is four abscess teeth," she remarked.

"Well, be thankful you don't have five," Mrs. Cope snapped. . . . I can always find something to be thankful for."

. . . "I reckon *you* can," [Mrs. Pritchard] said, her voice a little more nasal than usual with contempt. (133)

Although these two might simply seem to be talking at cross-purposes, in fact they are talking in different ways, because while Mrs. Pritchard is aiming to have a dialogue, Mrs. Cope is delivering a monologue. Whereas Pritchard asks a real question about how Cope surmises a woman in an iron lung became pregnant, Cope asks a rhetorical question about thankfulness. Nonetheless, Pritchard answers "yes'm" before returning to her own train of thought. Cope, by contrast, ignores Pritchard's subsequent query and plows ahead with her reflections on thankfulness. Cope's meditations on gratitude culminate with "we have everything," a cruelly inappropriate use of first-person plural that fails to register that while Cope may have everything, Pritchard is probably telling the truth when she says that she has precious little beyond abscessed teeth. While Pritchard contemplates the lives of others by wondering about the experience of a pregnant woman in an iron lung, Cope spouts a self-involved harangue. Signaling that she is more familiar with commanding others than conversing with them, Cope issues three orders across the eight sentences she utters in this exchange, instructing Pritchard to say a prayer of thanksgiving, think of her many blessings, and be grateful. Immune even to direct address, Cope does not heed Pritchard's pointed rejoinder conveying "contempt" for her oblivious monologue and instead simply "went on" with her reflections on thankfulness (133).

Intoning monologues rather than engaging in dialogues proves to have dire repercussions. When Powell, the child of one of her former employees, returns to the farm with two friends, Cope listens neither to the boys nor to Pritchard, who, Cassandra-like, stands unheeded as she tries to warn Cope about what the boys are up to. The text underscores the divide between Powell's bucolic longings, rooted in his memories of life on the Cope farm, and Cope's matter-of-fact materialism. Learning from one of his companions that Powell "said he had the best time of his entire life right here on this here place," Cope worries about liability, fearing that "someone would get hurt on her place and sue her for everything she had" (136). Hearing her farm described as poor white Valhalla – Powell "said when he died he wanted to come here!" his friend exclaims – Cope first "looked blank," then "blushed," and finally looked "pain[ed]" as she decided that "these children were hungry" (137). Here O'Connor skewers Cope by acerbically reworking a passage in the Gospel according to John (6:48–58) in which Jesus encouraged those looking to satisfy their physical hungers to secure eternal life through the bread and wine of the Eucharist. For her part, Cope tries to satisfy the boys' spiritual hungers with crackers and Cokes. Finally, when Powell's friend quotes Powell as saying, "'Goddam, it was a horse down there name Gene and if I had him here I'd bust this concrete to hell riding him!'" Cope's concern is the profanity that punctuates this barbaric yawp. "I'm sure Powell doesn't use words like that," she responds (139).

Holding fast to her myopic monologue, Cope disregards what the boys tell her about themselves and what Pritchard observes about them. Although Pritchard deduces that the boys intend to spend the night after she sees that they are traveling with a suitcase, Cope erroneously insists "they'll go when I feed them" (138). While Pritchard surmises that "it ain't any telling what they'll do" after Cope makes the boys angry, Cope mistakenly decides that they will simply leave (148). Cleaving to her own narrative – founded on wishful thinking and at odds with what the boys say and do as well as with what Pritchard thinks – Cope illustrates the middle-class monologic at work. Poor white characters' broken language (fractured syntax, irregular grammar) describing injured bodies (pregnant women in iron lungs, abscessed teeth in sore mouths) may be messy, but it is meaningful. But, unable to recognize that Pritchard's judgments are sound, Cope reckons her employee's conclusions "figments of imagination" and "pride[s] herself on the way she handled the type of mind that Mrs. Pritchard had" (149). Handling Pritchard's mind means mishandling the boys, and at the story's conclusion, one of Cope's greatest fears is realized, and a fire consumes her woods. In this tale, as in "Greenleaf" and "The Displaced Person," O'Connor depicted the middle-class monologic as dishonest and, ultimately, dangerous.

Can the Subaltern Bible Salesman Speak?

It would be hard to overstate the impact of Harper Lee's *To Kill a Mockingbird* (1960) on visions of childhood, race, justice, and social class in America. In a survey asking people what book had made the greatest difference in their lives, *To Kill a Mockingbird* came in second, topped only by the Bible.[60] In 2003, the American Film Institute honored the tale's 1962 cinematic treatment by naming Atticus Finch (memorably played by Gregory Peck) the greatest movie hero of all time.[61] In 2004, the name Atticus entered the Social Security Administration's list of the 1,000 most popular names for boys and for a decade it trended upward, moving from spot 793 in 2005 to position 348 in 2015. Across this same ten-year span, the name Harper experienced a meteoric rise from number 742 to number 10 on the list of female names. And Harper continues to be a hit. More than eight thousand American girls born in 2020 were christened with the name.[62]

Change was in the air in the US South when Lee was writing her novel. In *The Burden of Southern History*, published in the same year as *To Kill a Mockingbird*, historian C. Vann Woodward observed about this era that "among all the many periods of change in the history of the South it is impossible to find one of such concentration and such substantive impact."[63] Woodward focused on the "Bulldozer Revolution," or postwar suburbanization, but by the late 1950s the civil rights revolution was also well underway.[64] Writing in the aftermath of the *Brown v. Board* decision, Emmett Till's murder and his killers' acquittals, the Montgomery bus boycott, and the integration of Central High School in Little Rock, Lee lionized the Finches by making them agents of change. By setting her story in the 1930s, Lee imaginatively rewrote the prehistory of the civil rights struggle as an intraracial fight pitting the radical Finches, middle-class change makers, against the racist Ewells, socially and intellectually immobile poor white people.

A restive inmate inside "the starched walls of a pink cotton penitentiary," Scout regularly clashes with expectations for women of her station, and the novel presents her as a beacon of change in part by accentuating how she differs from her Aunt Alexandra.[65] Scout, who narrates the story as an adult, pointedly calls Alexandra "one of the last of her kind," describing her "river-boat, boarding-school manners" and practice of "point[ing] out the shortcomings of other tribal groups to the greater glory of [her] own" as outmoded (139). How Scout deviates from her aunt's racial attitudes is well recognized, but Scout's conceptions of class break rank with Alexandra's, too. Scout divides what Alexandra sees as a single social stratum – poor whites – in two, distinguishing redeemable common whites from irremediable white trash. While Alexandra classifies the Cunningham family euphemistically as "not our kind of folks" (236) and more candidly as "trash" (237), Scout distinguishes "the Cunninghams out in the woods" (239) from "the Ewells down at the dump" (239), insisting that only those living among trash are trash. According to John Hartigan, the pejorative term "white trash" marks out "whites who, through their poverty and ungainliness, fit insecurely within the hegemonic order of white political power and social privilege."[66] The Cunninghams situate themselves more securely within this hegemonic order by accepting middle-class beliefs, values, and practices. Young Walter Cunningham, Scout's classmate, accepts Scout's negative judgment of his etiquette and appetites and responds with shame as soon as he is called out for deviating from middle-class norms. When he joins Scout for a meal at her house, Walter asks for molasses and then "drown[s] his dinner in syrup" (30). Generations of poor people in the South ate molasses, meat (fatback), and meal (cornmeal) – the three-M diet – at almost every meal, and so Walter is probably working to bring his dinner in line with the flavor preferences he has developed from his own family's fare.[67] But when Scout derides his actions, Walter does not defend himself; instead, he "put his hands in his lap" and "ducked his head" (30).

Like his son, Walter Cunningham père proves an apt pupil under Scout's tutelage; while the child learns culinary mores, the father acquires a moral compass. *To Kill a Mockingbird* joins *Killers of the Dream* in locating race-based violence in the lower classes, pitting Atticus against a mob of men stinking of "stale whiskey and pigpen" who try to wrest Tom Robinson, a black client whom Atticus is defending against false charges, from jail (163). Cunningham is a member of this mob, which suggests that nothing in his own milieu has caused him to question racist atrocities like lynching – no sermon at his church, no personal experience with his black neighbors, no experience with an interracial labor organization.[68] Yet Scout's attempt to engage Cunningham in polite conversation after she recognizes him among the massed men weakens his murderous resolve, and he commands the lynch mob to disband. Explaining the confrontation to his confused children the next day, Atticus suggests that empathy overcame enmity, telling them, "you children last night made Walter Cunningham stand in my shoes for a minute" (168).[69]

Ironically, this footwear-focused idiom about empathy represents one of the novel's gravest failures of empathy. Amid the financial hardships of the Great Depression, many Americans struggled to afford new shoes, wearing worn-out ones, donning their shoes sparingly to extend their life span, or forgoing them altogether.[70] Lee was aware of this fact and dilated on footwear – its presence or absence as well as its quality – in establishing class divides among the text's main characters. For example, Scout's classmate Walter Cunningham is introduced to the narrative through a detailed discussion of his shoeless state and its consequences:

> Walter Cunningham's face told everybody in the first grade he had hookworms. His absence of shoes told us how he got them. People caught hookworms going barefooted in barnyards and hog wallows. If Walter had owned any shoes he would have worn them the first day of school and then discarded them until mid-winter. (25)

Even as a child just starting elementary school, Scout can pinpoint Walter's social class simply by looking at his bare feet, because they tell her both the source of his hookworm – a disease associated with poor white southerners in early twentieth-century America[71] – and the depths of his family's poverty, given her knowledge that any kid who owns shoes wears them on the first day of school.

Shoes feature in many of the novel's climactic scenes. Surveying the lynch mob assembled at the jail, Scout observes that Walter Cunningham wore heavy work shoes. Under cross-examination during Tom Robinson's trial, Mayella Ewell describes how she makes shoes from strips of old tires. On the night Bob Ewell tries to kill them, Scout and Jem figure out that they are being pursued after discerning the sound of footfalls in heavy shoes. Footwear also figures in the Finches' efforts to concretize their social status. Explaining to Scout why the Cunninghams are "not our kind of folks" (236), Alexandra says of young Walter, "you can put him in shoes and a new suit, but he'll never be like Jem" (237). Alexandra's barb is doubly venomous, managing both to point out that Walter's family is too poor to provide shoes for him and to insist that he would be inferior to the Finches even if rigged out in finer attire. When Atticus speaks of Mr. Cunningham standing in his shoes, then, the expression takes a classist jab at the man, because it proposes that slipping out of his brogans and into Atticus's oxfords would afford Cunningham a more enlightened perspective on the social order, but it would not grant him social parity. By declaring in the novel's closing pages that "Atticus was right" when he insisted that "you never really know a man until you stand in his shoes," Scout proves that she has learned the importance of exclusions, not empathy (294). In a novel chock-full of shoeless Ewells and Cunninghams, Atticus's footwear-focused idiom indicates that poor white people may not be worth knowing.

Whereas the Finches and the Cunninghams are families in flux, the Ewells are not changing, and this stasis produces their degraded social status:

> Every town the size of Maycomb had families like the Ewells. No economic fluctuations changed their status – people like the Ewells lived as guests of

the county in prosperity as well as in the depths of a depression. No truant officers could keep their numerous offspring in school; no public health officer could free them from congenital defects, various worms, and the diseases indigenous to filthy surroundings. (181)

The repetition of the phrase "like the Ewells" – along with the claim that "every town" boasts a representative specimen – depicts members of the family as types rather than individuals. Unmoved by financial currents, poor white people are always impoverished, living "as guests of the county" while economic ebbs and flows impact those around them. Their condition not ameliorated by social services – whether administered by "truant officers" or "public health officer[s]" – poor white people make neither educational nor sanitary gains. While the Finches move in line with each era's Zeitgeist, the Ewells are freighted by nature ("congenital defects") and nurture ("filthy surroundings") with impediments to growth, and so they remain the same throughout their lives and across generations. Divorced from the novel's nesting-doll structure in which the individual, the family, and the community (Scout, the Finch family, and Maycomb) mature thanks to life-changing lessons about morality and justice, the Ewells do not learn and do not change.

O'Connor read *To Kill a Mockingbird* soon after it came out, having received it from a friend who "insisted" (O'Connor's word) on sending it to her.[72] Offering her take on the book in an October 1960 letter to Betty Hester, O'Connor pulled no punches. She marveled at the acclaim being heaped on Lee's novel because, as she observed three times in a single paragraph, it is "a child's book."[73] She compared the story to *Miss Minerva and William Green Hill*,[74] a bestselling children's book from 1909 that chronicles Minerva's efforts to educate – read: appropriately racialize – her little orphaned nephew Billy, who had enjoyed a "care-free existence on the plantation" among "idle, happy negro companions" before moving in with his uptight aunt.[75] While we cannot know for sure what prompted her to make this comparison, it is tempting to think that O'Connor associated these works because of their shared concern with how wellborn white kids learn their social roles. Taking charge of Billy's social education, Minerva requires him to renounce lessons learned from his African American playmates and caregivers, commanding him to "not talk so much like a negro" and to disavow superstition by relinquishing his rabbit's foot – a lucky charm he had worn since babyhood, when the black woman who cared for him put it around his neck.[76] Scout and Jem's lessons impart information about racial distinctions as well as socioeconomic divides. The little Finches learn that, as "the product of several generations' gentle breeding," they are constitutionally unlike "run-of-the-mill" people: those unfortunates in Maycomb who, on a par with unsorted goods made in Alabama's steel, textile, and lumber mills, are average and unremarkable (143). Although published a half-century apart, these books concern themselves with the cultivation of genteel southern children, and this shared interest may have linked them in O'Connor's mind.

Like Lee's novel, O'Connor's "Good Country People" features a young southerner who considers herself radically unlike her female forebears. Just as Jean Louise, who likes to be called Scout, thinks she is nothing like her aunt, Joy, who likes to be called Hulga, considers herself diametrically opposed to her mother. In O'Connor's story, though, this generation gap is illusory. Whereas *To Kill a Mockingbird* affirms Scout's effort to differentiate herself from Alexandra in terms of her ideas about poor white people, "Good Country People" explodes Joy/Hulga's sense that her class attitudes diverge from her mother's.

O'Connor's tale flips the script on Lee's novel's kinetic logics of class. *To Kill a Mockingbird* represents poor whites stuck in poverty, ignorance, and poor health, while "Good Country People" portrays poor whites in motion. The story opens by describing tenant farmer Mrs. Freeman's "two [expressions], forward and reverse, that she used for all her human dealings" (169). Although "she seldom used" reverse, she often employed her forward expression, which is "steady and driving like the advance of a heavy truck" (169). Freeman is a vehicle not just in the story but also for the story: O'Connor's tale opens with Freeman's itinerant expressions and concludes by giving her the last word. Manley Pointer, the story's other poor white character, is malleability incarnate, because he is a confidence man who routinely changes his affect, speech, and even his name. "Good Country People" also disavows the association between movement and the middle class seen in *To Kill a Mockingbird*. While Lee's novel underscores how Scout differs from her aunt in order to chart patrician change over time, O'Connor's short story uses two generations of Hopewells, her middle-class whites, to illustrate that superficial markers of progress mask an unchanging core.

To Kill a Mockingbird and "Good Country People" depict middle-class white women mischaracterizing as differences in social status what are in fact variances in poor white peoples' receptivity to middle-class mores and preferences. Scout uses this system to distinguish between the Cunninghams in the woods and the Ewells at the dump, while

Mrs. Hopewell employs it to separate tenant farmers who were "a godsend to her" from those who proved unsatisfactory (170). In both texts, middle-class characters mark out preferred poor white people as "not trash": Scout deems Walter Cunningham "not trash" (239), while Mrs. Hopewell terms her current tenant farmers, the Freemans, "not trash" but rather "good country people" (170). Yet O'Connor's story shows that distinguishing between good country people and trash represents a way of *not* knowing poor white people. Hopewell's hackneyed ideas about her employees make this apparent: "She realized that . . . in the Freemans she had good country people and that if, in this day and age, you get good country people, you had better hang onto them" (172). Repetition exposes this formulation as nonsense. Because "good country people" lacks a synonym or even a real definition, the narrator simply repeats the term to complete Hopewell's thought.

Mumbo jumbo takes the place of meaning in part because middle-class white people struggle to tell poor white people apart. Mrs. Hopewell treats Mrs. Freeman's daughters, Glynese and Carramae, in tandem: "'Glynese is a fine girl,' Mrs. Hopewell said. 'Glynese and Carramae are both fine girls'" (183); "Mrs. Hopewell said there were not many girls with Glynese's common sense. She said what she admired in those girls was their common sense" (184). Although Mrs. Hopewell offers generic platitudes about Mrs. Freeman's daughters as "fine girls" with "common sense," the narrator suggests that their differences outweigh their similarities, noting that "Glynese, a redhead, was eighteen and had many admirers; Carramae, a blonde, was only fifteen but already married and pregnant" (170). In *To Kill a Mockingbird*, narrator Scout unselfconsciously enacts the homogenizing gaze that O'Connor's narrator challenges. According to Scout, the Ewells are the same across generations, because "three generations" of the family "had lived . . . behind the Maycomb dump, and had thrived on county welfare money" (140).[77] Family members are also indistinguishable within each generation: "Nobody was quite sure how many children were on the place. Some people said six, others said nine; there were always several dirty-faced ones at the windows when anyone passed by" (182). In truth, though, at least one "nobody" was quite sure how many children were on the place: Mayella Ewell testifies at Tom Robinson's trial that she has seven siblings.

Through the Hopewells' reactions to Manley Pointer, a traveling Bible salesman, O'Connor's story suggests how middle-class whites at times misread poor whites by projecting onto them thoughts and ideas that, in fact, originate from and serve the interests of the middle-class observers.

O'Connor's language draws attention to this projection, emphasizing that what readers learn about Pointer comes from Hopewell. For example, after Mrs. Hopewell invited Pointer into her parlor, the narrator reports that "she decided he had never been in a room as elegant as this" (178). For his part, Pointer seems aware of her assumptions and tries to use them to his advantage. For example, when Hopewell rebuffs his wares, Pointer attempts to guilt her into making a purchase by suggesting that people like her value neither Bibles nor bumpkins: "Well lady . . . not many people want to buy [a Bible] nowadays and besides, I know I'm real simple. . . . I'm just a country boy. . . . People like you don't like to fool with country people like me!" (179).[78] Finding herself on the defensive, Hopewell starts spouting banalities, insisting that "good country people are the salt of the earth!" (179) and "real genuine folks!" (180). Punctuation registers Hopewell's unease, drawing attention to her effort to refute Pointer's pronouncements with little more than overreaching exuberance.

Hearing her mother utter the words "real genuine folks," Joy/Hulga signals her disapproval by emitting a "groan" (180). Joy/Hulga styles herself a "true genius" and regularly reflects on her radical estrangement from her mother's ways of thinking (186). Yet her interactions with Pointer make clear that she and her mother perceive poor white people in similar ways. Joy/Hulga recognizes the "profound implications" of an outing with Pointer that she has arranged by picturing "dialogues . . . that reached below to depths that no Bible salesman would be aware of" (184). Both women feel confident in their ability to gauge the limits of Pointer's knowledge; just as Mrs. Hopewell decides that he has never seen a space as elegant as her parlor, Joy/Hulga concludes that her conversation will be too deep for him. Like her mother, Joy/Hulga approaches Pointer not as an individual but as a type: a representative "Bible salesman," as she terms him. Joy/Hulga goes a step further than her mom, though, because her visions of debasing condescension evolve into fantasies of ethical violation. Joy/Hulga concocts a plan for seducing Pointer – one that she expects will provoke "shame" and "remorse" in a highly religious man (186). Deciding that Pointer's "inferior mind" can neither conceive of nor consent to her scheme (186), she tells him, "'You poor baby. . . . It's just as well you don't understand'" (191).

Pointer gains Joy/Hulga's trust by fulfilling her expectations, playing the part of the simpleminded and sincere bumpkin awed by her uniqueness and intelligence. Telling her "you ain't like anybody else," Pointer indulges Joy/Hulga's sense of her singularity (192). Of course, this declaration is patently false; it is precisely because Joy/Hulga cleaves to the same shopworn stereotypes about poor white people as her mother that Pointer is able to dupe her. Hoodwink her he does, though, and Joy/Hulga decides that through "instinct that came from beyond wisdom," Pointer "had touched the truth about her" (192). Having gained her trust, Pointer then seizes the trophy he has been after all along: her wooden leg. Then, abandoning his aw-shucks earnestness for "a lofty indignant tone," Pointer blows up middle-class constructions of poor white identity and asserts his equality (194). To Joy/Hulga's incredulous query, "aren't you just good country people?," Pointer responds, "Yeah ... but it ain't held me back none. I'm as good as you any day in the week" (194).

Reading *To Kill a Mockingbird* alongside "Good Country People" makes clear how O'Connor's work interrogates the social stigma that poor white characters internalize in Lee's novel. Poor white characters respond to their marginalization with a genuine sense of inferiority in *To Kill a Mockingbird*. Mayella Ewell feels shame as a result of believing herself "mock[ed]" (193) by Atticus Finch and other "fine fancy gentlemen" (200). Walter Cunningham escapes his degradation only by escaping his identity: during a fleeting moment of apparent social equality with the Finches, Scout says that Walter had "forgotten he was a Cunningham" (30). Whereas Lee's Ewells and Cunninghams naturalize the stigma of white poverty, O'Connor's Pointer rejects it, using "I'm just a country boy" to explode a threadbare type rather than to embrace subordinate status (179).

* * *

"I say a plague on everybody's house as far as the race business goes."[79] This reworking of Mercutio's dying curse appears in the 1963 letter that conveys O'Connor's withering assessment of "Where Is the Voice Coming From?" While other scholars have seen this malediction as evidence of O'Connor's "ironic detachment from social issues,"[80] I read it as a statement about how she engaged with her era's urgent social concerns. Aiming to expose racial prejudice and discrimination as a plague on everyone's house, O'Connor used her stories to unmask middle-class white southerners' racism.

The stories of poor white people who fought Jim Crow remain overshadowed by the fictional pictures of monstrous poor white racists drawn by Lee, Smith, and Welty. In thinking about poor white people's activities during the civil rights era, most Americans call to mind imaginary villains like Bob Ewell rather than people like Sputnik Monroe, a professional wrestler credited with integrating Ellis Auditorium in Memphis. Loved by scores of black wrestling fans and loathed by many whites (who considered him white trash), Monroe pressured Ellis's management to accommodate the many African American wrestling enthusiasts who wished to attend his matches by allowing them to sit outside of the tiny top balcony to which they were relegated in the segregated auditorium.[81] Likewise, figures like Bob Ewell overshadow Richard Loving, a "redneck" (in the words of his own lawyer) whose fight to live lawfully with his wife, a multiracial woman named Mildred, in their home state of Virginia led to the 1967 United States Supreme Court decision *Loving v. Virginia*, which overrode laws prohibiting interracial marriage.[82]

O'Connor, "distrust[ing] many of her own generation's enthusiasms" as well as its bugbears, responded to her contemporaries by unmasking middle-class southerners' class-based prejudices and exposing racism across the white socioeconomic spectrum.[83] The next generation of southern writers saw a new group begin to tell stories about poor white southerners: poor white southerners themselves. Dorothy Allison and Barbara Robinette Moss, key members of this cadre, followed in O'Connor's footsteps by challenging classist depictions of poor white people set forth by middle-class authors. But they also charted a new path with their works, mounting a critique of sexist treatments of poor white women in novels by their fellow poor white southern writers.

CHAPTER 4

Hungry Women and Horny Men
Dorothy Allison, Barbara Robinette Moss, and Grit Lit

In his celebrated meditations on gastronomy, French epicure Jean Anthelme Brillat-Savarin wrote, "Tell me what you eat, and I shall tell you what you are."[1] For poor white people, outsiders' efforts to link their diets and identities often turn out badly. For instance, in 1889, three years before Stanford University hired him to head its brand-new Department of Economics and Social Science, Amos G. Warner published an article suggesting that eating unhealthy fare was not simply an effect of poverty but also one of its root causes. According to Warner, whose claim to fame is the system he developed for statistically analyzing social welfare issues, destitution and diet were tangled together: unhealthy appetites plagued poor people, and unwholesome diets both brought about and resulted from these insalubrious cravings.[2]

A century later, poor white people continued to be identified with their purportedly diseased appetites. The title of Ernest Matthew Mickler's runaway bestseller *White Trash Cooking* (1986) blurs the line between poor white people and their cookery. Will the book depict the kinds of dishes often prepared by people identified (by themselves or others) as white trash? Will it show white trash individuals in the act of cooking? The book's cover art makes hay of this ambiguity. Familiar logos for packaged foods including margarine, pancake mix, processed cheese, rice, mayonnaise, oats, and crackers encircle a portrait of a woman selling watermelons from the back of a pickup truck. Mickler's introduction celebrates the "deliciousness" of the recipes he collected from "old family cookbooks, yellowed letters, whispered secrets, and a lot of good hints straight from the kitchens of longtime southern cooks."[3] Yet recipes for entrees like Aunt Donnah's roast possum or the kiss-me-not sandwich – onions and mustard on bread – seem sure to repulse the book's middle-class readership.[4] Poor white foodways serve the same purpose on *Here Comes Honey Boo Boo*, a hit show on the TLC television network during the early 2010s reign of so-called redneck reality television. Many episodes focus on food, depicting the show's stars – members of a poor white family in Georgia – eating meals including roadkill (a hog hit by a vehicle) and sketti, which is ketchup and margarine on noodles. By expressing shock and disgust at a recipe for roast possum or a close-up shot of sketti, audiences underscore the cultural and economic disparities between themselves and poor white southerners by instantiating those distinctions in foodways.

Whereas the preceding chapters focus on middle-class writers' strategies for contesting other middle-class writers' classist portrayals of poor white southerners, this chapter considers formal innovations pioneered by authors who grew up poor, concentrating on literary devices intended to rebut enduring narratives about poor white southerners' unhealthy appetites. In the 1990s, Dorothy Allison and Barbara Robinette Moss published books that grapple with "the inescapable impact of being born in a condition of poverty that this society finds shameful, contemptible, and somehow deserved," as Allison described "the central fact of [her] life" in an essay published a few years after her novel *Bastard Out of Carolina* came out.[5] Faced with a long history of reading empty cupboards and emaciated bodies as symptoms of unnatural appetites – as evidence not of starvation but of unwholesome cravings given free rein – Allison and Moss strove to make hunger visible. To this end, their best-known works, *Bastard Out of Carolina* and *Change Me into Zeus's Daughter*, employ a set of literary techniques that I term famineways, which stick in the craw. Knowing that affluent writers' representations of poor white people's unhealthy appetites go down easy, because readers have consumed these images for generations, Allison and Moss used literary devices that readers need to chew on.

In this chapter's first section, I plot a three-hundred-year history of downplaying poor white southerners' dietary insufficiencies and nutritional deficiencies by ascribing them to unhealthy diets that slake disordered appetites. The second and third sections explore how, in *Change Me into Zeus's Daughter* and *Bastard Out of Carolina*, famineways take shape as intertextual references that both represent poor white southerners' experiences with hunger and gainsay depictions of their ignorance. By engaging with a wealth of literary works, these texts show that their protagonists (and authors) read voraciously and think dynamically. By putting patrician words to poor white ends – specifically, by using intertextual references not only to map trajectories for awakening into class consciousness but also to fashion fresh strategies for representing food scarcity – these writers developed new ways to represent hunger. The fourth and final section shifts focus from classism to sexism, analyzing how Allison's novel and Moss's memoir push back against male grit lit writers' depictions of delectable poor white women by crafting decidedly inedible female figures, as Allison's heroine's nickname – Bone – suggests.

Unnatural Appetites

While surveying the boundary between North Carolina and Virginia in 1728, William Byrd inscribed dividing lines not only between states of the future United States but also between states of whiteness by distinguishing the prosperous from the poor in terms of food. In his account of the expedition, Byrd marveled that poor white North Carolinians "at the winding up of the year scarcely have bread to eat" despite the fertility of their environs.[6] Byrd accounted for poor white people's scanty provisions by diagnosing "a thorough aversion to labor" among them because, he insisted, staple foodstuffs practically supply themselves to residents: "Indian corn is of so great increase, that a little pains will subsist a very large family with bread, and then they may have meat without any pains at all."[7] Byrd's *History of the Dividing Line* kicks off a tradition of treating poor white deprivation as a personal pathology rather than as a political or economic problem. In Byrd's narrative, signs of lack betoken poor white southerners' laziness. In other affluent writers' accounts, indications of hunger denote poor white people's unwholesome appetites. According to these sources, poor white people experience unhealthy cravings that prompt them to gorge not on food but on clay, snuff, and racism. In such texts, elites rewrite a social ill – the economic inequality that can give rise to malnutrition and starvation – as a personal ill: a debased appetite given free rein by weak-willed individuals.

To wealthier observers, tactics for assuaging hunger can look like strategies for satisfying unnatural appetites. From colonial to contemporary times, poor southerners have consumed clay to ease hunger pains.[8] Yet a number of works by middle- and upper-class writers treat clay eating not as a temporary antidote to undernourishment but as an addiction. In one of Augustus Baldwin Longstreet's southwestern humor stories, the poor white protagonist's clay eating harms its practitioner but amuses its chronicler. Ransy Sniffle's diet of "red clay and blackberries" is played for laughs and cited as the cause of "a complexion that a corpse would have disdained to own." Signs of malnutrition including "fleshless and elevated" shoulders and a weight of ninety-five pounds give rise to chuckles rather than concerns. Other references to dietary insufficiency showcase the narrator's aptitude for droll understatement, as in his description of Sniffle's "abdominal rotundity that was quite unprepossessing."[9]

Nonfiction writers, less amused by clay eating than Longstreet, often depict it as a deplorable habit. Emily Burke, who worked as a teacher in Georgia during the 1840s, condemned the practice as a "senseless habit."[10] John Patterson Green, who spent a few years in the Carolinas in the early 1870s, identified clay eating as one of poor white people's "peculiar habits."[11] The author of an 1888 article in *Scientific American*, a popular science magazine, described poor white people in Byrd's old stomping ground – North Carolina – who were "addicted to the habit of clay eating." Despite declaring them "veritable living skeletons," the article takes pains to show that depravity, not deprivation, ails these poor whites by telling of a child who could not be coaxed to partake of "a big dish of bread and meat and potatoes" because he only had eyes for clay. By insisting that they "devour [clay] with as much avidity as a toper swallows a glass of whisky," the essay drives home the message that addiction, not inequality, bedevils poor white clay eaters.[12] Elite-authored accounts routinely chalk up physical markers of malnourishment to a diseased appetite rather than a diseased social system by treating clay eating as a risible or reprehensible habit.

Like clay eating, snuff dipping can afford temporary relief from hunger pains. Historian Jack Temple Kirby has identified tobacco as an important part of southern folk medicine, because it curbs hunger and dulls the tooth and gum aches that often plague the malnourished.[13] But middle- and upper-class writers almost always see dipping snuff, which involves placing tobacco between the cheek and gum, usually with the aid of a stick or brush, as little more than a disgusting habit. Writing during the Civil War, pastor John Hill Aughey excoriated the "filthy and disgusting habit" of snuff dipping that prevailed among poor white people.[14] Touring the South after the war, journalist Edward King found that "the poor white still clings to many of his eccentricities," including the "disgusting habit" of dipping snuff.[15]

In a social science–styled analysis published in 1860, Daniel Hundley used snuff dipping to recast the social problem of poverty as a personal disorder. Like Longstreet's story, Hundley's study describes poor white people as gaunt and cadaverous, suggesting that they are "lank, lean, angular, and bony" with a "sallow complexion."[16] Yet Hundley's account rebuts the idea that dietary deficiencies cause these bony bodies and wan faces, asserting that "it is yet a rare thing that any of them suffer from hunger."[17] Instead, his text diagnoses a "disgusting habit of snuff-dipping" as what ails them.[18] In an article about Georgia cotton mill workers published in 1891, Clare de Graffenried censured mill hands guilty of "excessive indulgence in this stimulant." Like the *Scientific American* article comparing clay eaters to whiskey drinkers, de Graffenried's *Century* essay relates dipping to drunkenness, arguing that "snuff-dippers might be mistaken for inebriates, having the ashy, rickety, depraved aspect that follows a long debauch."[19] Nearly a century after de Graffenried published her work, Virginia Foster Durr confirmed that well-off white people continued to use these strategies for reframing social inequalities as personal proclivities. In her 1985 autobiography, Durr recounted how her parents taught her to understand poor people's hunger: "If they had pellagra and worms and malaria and if they were thin and hungry and immoral, it was just because that was the way they were. It was in their blood. They were born to be poor white trash. They dipped snuff and drooled tobacco juice. If they smelt bad and were dirty, well, they liked being that way."[20] Using appetite-suppressing snuff. Suffering from pellagra, a disease caused by vitamin deficiency. Looking "thin and hungry." These markers of malnutrition morph into personal quirks – "that was the way they were" – personal preferences – "they liked being that way" – and even congenital conditions – "It was in their blood. They were born to be poor white trash" – in better-off people's accounts of poverty. By treating clay eating and snuff dipping as unwholesome consumption practices, middle- and upper-class observers' accounts rewrite social ills like food scarcity and economic inequality as personal ills stemming from debased appetites.

In the elite imaginary, the most common nonnutritive substance poor white southerners feast on is racism. In James Gilmore's 1862 travelogue, the author's pseudonymous alter ego, Edmund Kirke, describes a poor white woman whose appetite for racial distinctions trumps her hunger for food. Kirke and Scipio, his enslaved driver, take refuge in a poor white family's home during a storm. After his request for a cup of tea brings word that "haint a morsel to eat or drink in the house," Kirke shares his chicken, sweet potatoes, cornbread, and other traveling provisions.[21] But when Kirke invites Scipio to take a seat at the table and partake in the meal, the poor white matron vehemently objects. "Her eyes flashing with anger," she declares that she will not break bread with a man she calls "a good-for-nothin', no account nigger."[22] Despite describing her as "half-starved," Kirke's narrative suggests that the woman cannot be all *that* hungry if she chooses discrimination over satiation.[23] This wartime narrative downplays poor white hunger at the same time that it emphasizes poor white racism.

During the civil rights era, forward-looking white writers depicted poor white people as the southerners gobbling up racism as a means of distancing themselves from the injustices of the Jim Crow South, which were coming in for national (and even international) rebuke in this period. Lillian Smith's *Killers of the Dream* collapses nutritional lack and intellectual lack in the "starved minds and bodies" of poor white people, portraying racism as a palliative for their physical and psychological hungers (165). Poor white southerners, "fed little except scraps of 'skin color' and 'white supremacy,'" glut themselves on racism and segregation to sate their starved intellects (171). In this way, poor white people "eat Jim Crow" (178). Nourished by this hateful diet, the white proletariat purportedly becomes not simply unlike the white bourgeoisie but unknowable to its members. As Smith asked rhetorically, "How can we who were fed so bountifully feel what it means to live with a mind emptied of words, bereft of ideas and facts, unknowing of books and man-made beauty?" (163). Like Byrd's *History of the Dividing Line* centuries earlier, *Killers of the Dream* draws a clear line between prosperous whites and poor whites, contrasting the mental and physical nourishment enjoyed by people like Smith with the experiences of those whose minds are "emptied of words," "unknowing of books," and "bereft of ideas."

Recognizing how stories of poor white people's unwholesome diets rewrite hunger as a personal proclivity rather than a political problem helps us reconsider some of the weird food-focused scenes in southern literature. The ending of *To Kill a Mockingbird* puzzles me. Why is Scout dressed as a ham during her climactic encounter with Bob Ewell? In terms of the storyline, Scout hams it up as part of a pageant about Maycomb County, joining classmates dressed as butterbeans, peanuts, and other foodstuffs in representing the area's agricultural products. And the costume serves a crucial function in the narrative, because it saves Scout's life by absorbing slashes from Bob Ewell's knife. But, still, why a ham?

When it comes to poor white people, food separates the wheat from the chaff in *To Kill a Mockingbird*, distinguishing the redeemable Cunninghams from the irredeemable Ewells. The Cunninghams are repeatedly associated with food. Mr. Cunningham pays for Atticus's legal services with hickory nuts and turnip greens. When Scout invites her classmate Walter Cunningham to lunch at her house, he eagerly "pile[s] food on his plate" (32). Maycomb's finest citizens, too, are associated with food. The women who count themselves among what the novel terms "Fine Folks" may leave the lion's share of cooking responsibilities to domestic workers, but they do prepare desserts (173). For instance, Miss Maudie Atkinson is known for her Lane cake, and Aunt Alexandra makes charlotte for members of the missionary circle. Not content with just making cakes, such women also become cakes: the novel's opening pages tell us that "ladies," on summer evenings, "were like soft teacakes with frostings of sweat and sweet talcum" (6). By contrast, the absence of food marks the Ewells. Patriarch Bob Ewell subsists on "green whiskey," and because his relief checks furnish this liquid diet, his children suffer "hunger pains" (41). While Scout describes how the Ewells' neighbors' cabins released "delicious smells" of chicken, bacon, and other meats at Christmastime, she says that these "aromas ... vanished when we rode back past the Ewell residence" (229).

Within the Maycomb County agricultural economy celebrated by the school pageant, people like the Cunninghams produce food, and people like the Finches consume food, but people like the Ewells possess no food, and therefore no place in the community. This jibes with the new southern social order envisioned by Scout and endorsed by the novel, which departs from Aunt Alexandra's two-tiered model of white people – the best and the rest – by introducing a three-tiered system that distinguishes poor folks like the Cunninghams from trash like the Ewells. When Aunt Alexandra explains in no uncertain terms that Walter Cunningham is not a proper playmate for Scout "because – he – is – trash" (301), Scout vehemently disagrees, telling her brother, "that boy's not trash, Jem. He ain't like the Ewells" (302). The novel naturalizes this tripartite social order through food, using Scout's ham costume to demarcate the social strata of whiteness. For one thing, it makes a homophonic link between wealthy whites and hardworking poor whites, connecting cunning hams like Scout with Cunninghams like Walter. For another thing, it divides both the elite and the poor from the trash, marking out the latter as different not just socioeconomically but also metabolically. In the aftermath of Bob Ewell's attack on Scout, Maycomb residents insist that alcohol, not food, fueled him. Scout reports that he reeked of "stale whiskey" (352), and Sheriff Tate says Ewell had "enough liquor in him to make him brave enough to kill children" (360). Running on a heady mix of rotgut and class antagonism, Ewell lashes out against ham itself, stabbing the symbol of his exile from his community's agricultural producers and consumers.

Food and Class Consciousness

Allison's novel and Moss's memoir refute classist associations between material lack and intellectual lack by portraying the functions of literature in poor people's lives. *Bastard Out of Carolina* and *Change Me into Zeus's Daughter* brim with literary references. Characters recite lengthy passages of poetry, fill their spare moments with reading, enact dramatic scenes from plays, and compare themselves to fictional heroes and villains. This dense intertextual web gives rise to poor white class consciousness. In much twentieth-century literature, intertextual relationships create class consciousness for members of the middle and upper classes. Recognizing interrelationships among texts – by identifying literary allusions in modernist works or by being in on the game of postmodern parody – can connect (and cement the status of) the cognoscenti. In Allison's and Moss's texts, by contrast, intertextuality affords a two-pronged strategy for undermining representations of poor white ignorance and illiteracy, serving thematically to show how literature informs poor white characters' experiences and formally to illustrate how literary precursors shape poor white authors' writing.

Bastard Out of Carolina and *Change Me into Zeus's Daughter* bear witness to hunger while contesting the idea that it engenders "terrifying ignorance," as *Killers of the Dream* suggests (163). In Allison's and Moss's works, hungry people seek mental satiety, savoring mouthfuls of good words as temporary antidotes to empty stomachs. Allison's protagonist, Bone, observes that "hunger makes you restless," and to quell that restiveness, she would "read everything [she] hadn't read more than twice already."[24] Members of the Moss family read and recite lines from their favorite literary works to distract themselves from their hunger. Individuals' access to meals and to books varies, and their appetites for both seem insatiable. Bone is a ravenous reader, gobbling up library books, relatives' hand-me-down paperbacks, "secondhand books from racks at the thrift store," borrowed storybooks, and novels received as gifts (119). Although the Moss family loses a lot of books during evictions and other rushed relocations, parents and children have memorized so many poems that literature persists as a central part of their lives even after they lose track of their favorite tomes. Moss's chapter titles – drawn from works by Lewis Carroll, Stephen Crane, Emily Dickinson, Rainer Maria Rilke, and other writers – pay homage to the family's favorite and most frequently recited stories and poems.

Change Me into Zeus's Daughter challenges the linking of sustenance and sense seen in some middle- and upper-class writers' works by depicting physically hungry but intellectually sated poor white people. Moss's memoir opens with bare cupboards and growling stomachs. Moss, one of seven hungry children in her family, waits to see if her mother will be able to clean poison from corn and beans and thereby make the only available provisions safe to eat. To fill their minds while they wait to fill their bellies, the oldest child, Alice, "began reciting from her favorite book – *Alice's*

Adventures in Wonderland."[25] This act of literary recitation contests the yoking of "starved minds and bodies" that marks poor white people as doubly deprived in works by Smith, Byrd, and other well-off writers (165). Here, empty bellies catalyze active minds, because Alice uses a favorite story to distract herself and her siblings from their hunger. In addition, Alice's act troubles the notion that literature is a luxury – a pleasant distraction for the leisure class. Even other grit lit writers' works treat reading as a rarified pastime. In Harry Crews's memoir, *A Childhood: The Biography of a Place* (1978), for example, the only book in the house is a Sears catalog. By contrast, Moss's family has read Carroll and a host of other authors featured in Mrs. Moss's old schoolbooks. By engaging with Carroll's work, Moss's memoir rebuts the idea that poor white people suffer interrelated intellectual and nutritional deficiencies.

Introducing Carroll's lines initiates a pointed intertextual dialogue. Carroll's *Alice* books are all about eating and drinking. From cakes labeled "eat me" to the Queen of Hearts' stolen tarts, from sneeze-inducing pepper to the Hatter's tea, Carroll's stories overflow with foodstuffs. After opening with *Alice's Adventures in Wonderland*, Alice next "jumped to her favorite parts of 'The Walrus and the Carpenter,'" several lines of which appear in the memoir (19). This work – a narrative poem about using one's wits to secure one's dinner – appeared in *Through the Looking-Glass* (1871), Carroll's follow-up to *Alice's Adventures in Wonderland* (1865). The poem's titular walrus and carpenter invite oysters to join them for a walk along the beach. After the stroll, the two feast on their new friends. The poem speaks to the Moss family's current situation because, in each text, meeting nutritional needs requires cleverness and resourcefulness; just as the walrus and the carpenter turn their companions into comestibles, the Moss family turns poison into provision.

Bastard Out of Carolina engages with literary precursors to expose how narratives authored by middle- and upper-class writers can beget a form of false consciousness in poor white readers. Bone reads not only to understand but also to escape her daily life. At times, she is pained by the chasm between novelistic fantasy and her own reality, observing that "the worst thing in the world was the way I felt when I wanted us to be like the families in the books in the library" (209). The social standing of "the families in the books" determines whether they provoke pining or repugnance, as Bone's response to Margaret Mitchell's work makes clear:

> Aunt Alma had given me a big paperback edition of *Gone with the Wind*, with tinted pictures from the movie, and told me I'd love it. I had at first,

but one evening I looked up from Vivien Leigh's pink cheeks to see Mama coming in from work with her hair darkened with sweat and her uniform stained. A sharp flash went through me. Emma Slattery, I thought. That's who I'd be, that's who we were. Not Scarlett with her baking-powder cheeks. I was part of the trash down in the mud-stained cabins, fighting with the darkies and stealing ungratefully from our betters, stupid, coarse, born to shame and death. I shook with fear and indignation. (206)

Gone with the Wind reveals the perils of escaping into fiction for poor white readers. At first, lost in cross-class fantasy, Bone enjoys the story. Later, however, she realizes that she "was part of the trash" and would "be" Emmie Slattery, not Scarlett O'Hara (206). As Matthew Guinn observes, with this revelation, "Bone sees the narrative of her own life within the larger cultural narrative that has scripted her into an assigned role."[26] This role, largely unchanging across centuries, casts poor white southerners as "stupid," racist ("fighting with the darkies"), and dirty – although here the red clay soil of Georgia does not cake the mouth, as it did in late nineteenth-century travelogue writers' descriptions of poor white clay eaters, but the cabin. Bone's encounter with *Gone with the Wind* shows how class consciousness awakened by middle-class white writers' representations of poor white identity can engender "shame" and "fear" (206).

Change Me into Zeus's Daughter and *Bastard Out of Carolina* explore how literature feeds poor white people's intellectual hungers and shapes their understandings of their class identities. In *Change Me into Zeus's Daughter*, members of the Moss family draw sustenance from Lewis Carroll's work, which helps them palliate their hunger. *Bastard Out of Carolina* evokes Margaret Mitchell's work in order to purge it, creating space to show that knowledge, not ignorance, can stymie poor white people – knowledge, that is, of their circumscribed role in a literary tradition created by middle-class white people. In *Killers of the Dream*, Smith wrote that the poor white, kept mentally starved by a social order offering him little but white supremacist claptrap, had recourse to "few symbols out of which to create bridges between himself and the rest of the earth's people" (161). While perceptive about some of the privations suffered by poor white people, Smith failed to see that her own works construct fences rather than bridges, because they curtail options for poor white identity. By representing how poor white people define themselves in union with or in opposition to literary depictions of hunger and poverty, Allison's and Moss's texts examine literature's role in fostering poor white southerners' class consciousness.

From Feast to Famine

Born early in the Cold War period, Allison and Moss began their lives during what historian Susan Levine has described as "a remarkably complacent time when it came to questions of poor people in America."[27] Depression-era images of rail-thin, rickets-suffering southerners had given way to a postwar picture of unprecedented national prosperity and plenty. Convinced that an abundant domestic food supply had all but eradicated hunger, "midcentury nutritionists explored eating habits and food-related conditions like rickets and malnutrition only in foreign settings."[28] Yet Moss, born in 1954, experienced childhood malnutrition so severe that it impacted her physical development, producing what she called "a twisted, mummy face" that she transformed through surgery in adulthood (307).

In their collection on southern food writing, David Davis and Tara Powell observe that "the prevailing trend in American popular culture, extending from nineteenth-century accounts of plantation groaning tables overloaded with regional delicacies to Paula Deen's much-mocked obsession with butter, has been to associate southern food with abundance and extravagance, but the reality of southern food is that it is based more on ingenuity born of privation and necessity."[29] Allison's and Moss's works contest popular culture's picture of southern extravagance by repurposing key ingredients from nineteenth-century patricians' accounts of plenty to bear witness to mid-twentieth-century poor people's privation.

Foods spill from the pages of elites' accounts of plantation life. As literary critic Mary Titus observes, stories of sumptuous plantation feasts were meant to "testify to the aristocratic status of their host and hostess and suggest that nature blesses their social order."[30] As a result, rose-colored renderings of the antebellum era routinely feature catalogs of comestibles. In her postbellum memoir about antebellum life, Letitia Burwell illustrated the hospitality and prosperity of Virginia planters by detailing the meals served at their homes. At a plantation named Elkwood, dinner would be prepared for a half-dozen more people than were expected so that guests could be accommodated at a moment's notice. And these "were no commonplace dinners," because "every day was a feast-day at Elkwood."[31] Another plantation's foodstuffs were its foremost claims to fame: "Oaklands was famous for many things: its fine light-bread, its cinnamon cakes, its beat biscuit, its fricasseed chicken, its butter and cream, its wine-sauces, its plum-puddings."[32]

Other writers put accounts of plantation abundance into enslaved people's mouths to make it seem as though everyone who inhabited the plantation shared in its bounty. In a proslavery novel by Caroline Lee Hentz, an enslaved man named Albert finds himself "mortified" by a northern wedding banquet, which lacks the "many barbecued pigs ... stuffed hams and roasted turkeys, to say nothing of cakes, confectionaries and wines" of a southern celebration.[33] Appraising the northern bride's cakes with a "supercilious smile," Albert disparages her by joining internalized racism with intrepid regionalism: "Is that all the cake you're going to have? ... Why, we give more than that to the niggers."[34] In Susan Dabney Smedes's *Memorials of a Southern Planter* (1887), Mammy Harriet points to southern abundance in recalling her own "tearin'-down weddin'" complete with "a mutton – a round o' beef – tukkeys – cakes, one on t'other – trifle."[35] The black southerners depicted by upper-crust white writers describe decadent, plentiful meals. Unlike Frederick Douglass, Harriet Jacobs, and other authors of slave narratives who testified to enslaved people's experiences of hunger, Hentz and Smedes held that enslaved people had plenty to eat. Furthermore, in place of fatback, cornmeal, and molasses – the mainstays of enslaved people's diets in the US South – varied menus brimming with meats and cakes fill elite white writers' specious portrayals of enslavement.

Allison and Moss took up this practice of cataloging culinary delights but put it to different ends. The sixth chapter of *Bastard Out of Carolina* opens with a list of down-home delectables: "the one piece of meat, the exact taste of buttery corn, tomatoes so ripe they split and sweeten the air, beans so crisp they snap between the teeth, gravy like mother's milk singing to your bloodstream" (71). But far from a meal Bone expects to eat, this is the food "you dream about" when "hunger makes you restless" (71). Like Allison's novel, Moss's memoir imaginatively invokes enticing foods as an inventory of what is missing from the family's diet. The first chapter of *Change Me into Zeus's Daughter* depicts bountiful scarcity:

> Nothing to put up and stack on the pantry shelves for winter, no steam from boiling kettles fogging the kitchen windows, the aroma seeping into every corner of the house: tomato sauce, soup stocks, creamed corn, sweet bread-and-butter pickles, succotash, green beans, white navy beans, speckled pinto beans. Not one jar to open when the coldest days arrived, when it hurt to breathe the air. There had been no summer tomato sandwiches smeared thick with mayonnaise on white bread baked in the oven, no corn on the cob dripping with butter, no crispy cucumbers to eat, straight from the garden, still warm from the sun. (19–20)

Moss's memoir registers hunger through a laundry list of absent items, chronicling foods that do not fill the cupboards and staples that will not be savored at mealtime. Their fledgling garden having been "baked" by the sun before its seedlings could take root, family members harvest unmet expectations (19). By recounting the fresh foods she will not eat during the summer – "no summer tomato sandwiches," "no corn," and "no crispy cucumbers" – as well as the canned goods she will not make use of in the winter – "not one jar to open" – the narrator depicts seasons of starvation. Although redolent with sensory delights – kettles' aromas, cucumbers' warmth, dripping butter's taste – the passage's insistent negation makes clear that this meal is a mirage: the dream of a hungry child. To represent postwar poverty, Allison's and Moss's works turn the plantation celebrants' cornucopia of foodstuffs from a celebration of bounty to a litany of lack.

When middle- and upper-class writers shift their attention from the plantation to the family farm, they swap fricasseed chicken for fried chicken but persist in depicting copious amounts of food. In his contribution to *I'll Take My Stand*, Andrew Lytle celebrated the bucolic bounty of the yeoman farmer's board:

> Merriment rises up from the hot, steaming vegetables, all set about the table, small hills around the mountains of meat at the ends, a heaping plate of fried chicken, a turkey, a plate of guineas, or a one-year ham, spiced, and if company is there, baked in wine. A plate of bread is at each end of the table; a bowl of chitterlings has been set at the father's elbow; and pigs' feet for those that like them.[36]

Lytle's essay renders a topographic map of agrarian abundance, including "hills" of vegetables and "mountains of meat." Animal proteins abound on this farming family's table, because they enjoy chicken, turkey, guineas or ham, chitterlings, and pigs' feet. Produce, too, features in this midday meal in the form of "fat beans and juicy corn" and "potatoes flavored like pecans."[37] Lytle's picture of the well-fed southern agrarian is typical; as historian Ted Ownby asserts, until the 1930s, "the majority of writers adhered to the popular assumption that farming people were not truly poor."[38] While gentlemen farmers and one-horse farmers eat differently – the former relish international delights, stocking their cellars with items like "an abundance of the ... best old Madeira wine, all the way from Madeira,"[39] while the latter are locavores avant la lettre – both enjoy ample fare. Blessed with stock-filled barns and fertile fields, Lytle's farmer finds that "the abundance of nature ... fill[s] his dining-room with satisfaction and well-being."[40]

Allison's novel and Moss's memoir depict the same foods as Lytle's essay. However, these poor white writers' visions of agricultural abundance mark out class difference less by what one eats than by whether one eats. The "fat beans and juicy corn" that grace Lytle's farmer's table appear in Allison's and Moss's works as visions of wished-for victuals. Bone's hunger spawns dreams of "buttery corn" and "beans so crisp they snap between the teeth" (71), while Moss laments her family's lack of wintertime canned beans and creamed corn and summertime "corn on the cob dripping with butter" (20). Alimentary staples populate hungry children's thoughts in these books, driving home the point that poverty can produce not just differences but deficiencies in people's diets. Meals of meat with corn, tomatoes, and beans that Bone dreams about and hyperbolically describes as "perfect food, the best food, magical meals, famous and awe-inspiring" (71) seem mundane rather than magical given that, in Lytle's text, they are part of the farmer's workaday supper.

Characters' commonplace cravings shine a light on the deep divide between the nation's agricultural wealth and poverty-stricken people. Sociologist Janet Poppendieck has observed that when hunger was "rediscovered" in the late 1960s, "even people who had been involved in antipoverty action programs were shocked; they had imagined that somehow American agricultural abundance would protect the poor in America from severe food deprivation."[41] Allison and Moss, telling stories about an era perceived as prosperous (the postwar period) during a decade perceived as prosperous (the 1990s), refuted the idea of unvarying abundance in an effort to make their experiences of hunger legible. Bone indulges in food fantasies as a mental reprieve from her insufficient bread-based diet – one that, made up of biscuits with gravy and crackers with ketchup, yields "hunger wrapped around a starch belly" (72). Moss savors visions of garden-fresh foods in a chapter that opens with her head throbbing from hunger and ends with her mother calling her sister to beg her "to come and get her starving children" (33). Allison and Moss adapted middle- and upper-class writers' visions of southern agricultural abundance to their own ends, using them to demonstrate the region's affliction rather than its health.

While Allison and Moss were suffering the hunger that marks their stories, historian C. Vann Woodward was thinking about how such hardships characterize southern experience writ large. In his landmark 1958 essay "The Search for Southern Identity," Woodward argued that "generations of scarcity and want constitute one of the distinctive historical experiences of the Southern people."[42] Yet hunger is often an anomalous experience in elites' stories of southern life. When Scarlett O'Hara, gaunt and bedraggled, declares that she will never be hungry again, readers believe her. For Scarlett, hunger is an extraordinary occurrence born of exceptional circumstances. For Bone's mother, hunger is inescapable. When Anney insists, "I was never gonna have my kids know what it was like. Never was gonna have them hungry," she bewails her inability to shield her children from the hunger that she, too, experienced as a child (73). Using famineways, Allison's and Moss's texts depict the hunger often ignored or erased in narratives authored by wealthier people.

Hunger continues to be written out of stories of the South, which makes recognizing and bearing witness to deprivation as urgent for us today as it was for Allison and Moss in the 1990s. In Kathryn Stockett's bestseller *The Help* (2009), for example, though African American domestic workers in 1960s Mississippi prepare different meals for the white families they work for than they eat themselves, everyone has enough to eat. Aibileen, one of the novel's three first-person narrators who represent "the help" referred to in the novel's title, observes that her vegetable garden "looks like the Garden of Eden," and it yields "good turnip greens, eggplant, okra by the bushel, all kind a gourds."[43] But this does not square with domestic workers' own accounts from this era; whereas *The Help* depicts only dietary difference, many workers' narratives document deprivation. For instance, Anne Moody's memoir *Coming of Age in Mississippi* (1968) describes the lives of black domestic workers in Mississippi during the civil rights era. Moody and her mother both worked in white women's homes, but this employment did not earn them a living wage. As a result, Moody admitted, "we went hungry all the time."[44]

The Peckeresque

Not long after Jimmy Carter, the son of a Georgia peanut farmer, took office as the thirty-ninth president of the United States, Harry Crews, the son of a Georgia tenant farmer, took the publishing world by storm by releasing a first-of-its-kind volume: an insider's account of the lives of Georgians whose "first and primary consideration, always, was not to starve."[45] Published by Harper and Row in 1978, Crews's *A Childhood: The Biography of a Place* was the first major autobiography authored by a poor white southerner. A few years before *A Childhood* appeared, Crews took some shots across the bow at the kinds of narratives about poor white southern life his memoir would upend. In an *Esquire* article from 1976, for instance, he decried gauzy views of rural poverty. Commenting on a movie depicting "a farm family, poor but God knows honest, out there on the land building character through hunger and hard work," Crews denounced it as "immoral and dangerous." In a forceful rebuttal to the film's main takeaways – that "deprivation was ... rewarding" and "a little pain here and there ... would teach important lessons" – Crews's essay tells of watching a man in need of dental care who, lacking both transportation to the dentist and money to pay for treatment, was forced to extract his own diseased tooth with a pair of pliers.[46] By describing how he saw in the suffering man's eyes the same thing one saw "in the eyes of a trapped fox when it has not quite been able to chew through its own leg," Crews gave the lie to Hollywood's soft-pedaled poverty.[47]

Although he had published more than half a dozen novels by the time his memoir came out, early reviewers and Crews himself recognized that *A Childhood* represented a new direction in his work. Many of Crews's novels present, as Jean Stafford wrote in her review of *Naked in Garden Hills* (1969), "a Hieronymus Bosch landscape in Dixie."[48] *A Childhood* opens up a different vista. As James Atlas rightly noted in his review of Crews's memoir, the author's "penchant for the bizarre has been subdued" in *A Childhood*.[49] Departing from the fantastical and bizarre panorama of his fiction, Crews's memoir describes "a part of America that has rarely, except in books like this, been properly discovered."[50] In his own account of his writerly maturation, Crews suggested that he had to overcome feelings of "fear and loathing for what I was and who I was" before he could write about growing up in "the worst hookworm-and-rickets part of Georgia" during the Great Depression.[51]

A Childhood paved the way for Allison's semi-autobiographical novel and Moss's memoir by whetting publishers' and readers' appetites for poor white southerners' own stories about their experiences. Although I argue in the remainder of this section that Allison and Moss worked to get out of the looming shadow of Crews's fiction in their own writings, there is evidence that Crews's nonfiction shaped their texts. Where, for example, did the name Boatwright, the surname Allison gave to the family at the center of her novel, come from? I think it came from *A Childhood*. In Crews's memoir, the "Boatwright boys" are neighbors the writer's father, Ray Crews, worked for.[52] Less important than the content of the anecdote that introduces the Boatwrights – a rollicking tale about how Ray and a friend scared a moonshiner – is the effect the story had on Crews:

> It was in that moment and in that knowledge that I first had the notion that I would someday have to write about it all, but not in the convenient and comfortable metaphors of fiction, which I had been doing for years. It would have to be done naked, without the disguising distance of the third person pronoun. Only the use of *I*, lovely and terrifying word, would get me to the place where I needed to go.[53]

This idea of writing about one's own experiences as writing naked is one that Allison has taken up in discussing her semi-autobiographical novel. Asked what it felt like to know that lots of people were learning about her life by reading *Bastard Out of Carolina*, Allison explained that "emotionally to be that naked" turned out to be "a little bit higher pitch" than she had anticipated.[54] The trope of nakedness also figures in her advice to young authors. Urging would-be writers "to confront their own lives in their fiction," Allison advised, "show yourself naked."[55]

Allison and Moss also followed Crews in embracing, in Crews's evocative phrasing, "the use of *I*, lovely and terrifying word." This trio of writers coalesced not around the genre of the first-person memoir – Allison, after all, wrote a novel – but around the form of the first-person narrative. Like Addie Bundren, who repudiates townspeople's attempts to paint with a broad brush members of her family and people of her class by asserting "I would be I" (174), the poor white southern narrators who take center stage in these late twentieth-century texts harness the power of self-definition by speaking in the first person. In an essay in her book *Skin: Talking about Sex, Class, and Literature* (1994), Allison reflected on the power of pronouns in a way that speaks, I think, to her decision to structure her best-known novel as a first-person narrative. "Me and my family, we had always been *they*," Allison observed.[56] By claiming the first-person narrative stance in writing against others' declarations about what "*they*" are like, Allison and Moss took to task not only middle-class predecessors whose works erase poor white people's hungers but also contemporaries with class origins on a par with their own whose publications distort and discount poor white women's experiences.

Allison and Moss are among the handful of women who write grit lit, a genre that portrays "the 'grit' or grittiness of real life, stark violence, and economic despair" for poor white southerners.[57] Harry Crews may deserve credit for coining the genre's zingy appellation: Crews referred to himself as a "grit," and for a year (July 1976–August 1977) wrote a column called "Grits" in the monthly men's magazine *Esquire*.[58] Scholars routinely credit grit lit with contesting negative representations of poor white people. In an early essay defining the genre, Eric Bledsoe contends that grit lit aims at "forcing its readers to reexamine long-held stereotypes and beliefs while challenging the literary roles traditionally assigned poor whites."[59] More recently, Jean Cash has declared that grit lit works demonstrate "the value of working-class southerners and their culture."[60]

Given such capacious claims about form's ideological work, why do so few women write grit lit? However they define it, critics cannot help but acknowledge that male writers dominate the genre. In an anthology called *Grit Lit: A Rough South Reader* (2012), just three of the twenty-three featured authors are women. A collection titled *Rough South, Rural South: Region and Class in Recent Southern Literature* (2016) includes eighteen short essays about grit lit writers, only four of whom are women. In his introduction to *Grit Lit*, editor Brian Carpenter suggests that grit lit has remained "by and large a boys club" because of its "taste for violence and the hypermasculine."[61] Despite its history, Carpenter proposes that the form's future could be female, insisting that "the field is wide open for Rough South stories by and about women beyond the accustomed roles of vixen or victim."[62] But this claim seems optimistic at best, disingenuous at worst. For one thing, if a taste for the hypermasculine is endemic to grit lit, then is the field open to female authors only to the extent that they write about hypermasculine characters and events? For another thing, has the form been "wide open" to women writers since its inception? If not, what has changed that would encourage women to join the fold? If so, then why have women not been writing grit lit stories?

Overstated masculinity is a hallmark of some – but not all – grit lit. Class, not gender, is the common denominator across definitions of the genre; grit lit tells stories about poor southerners, and their grittiness can take different forms. While some grit lit writers portray the "grit in your workboots," as Tom Franklin observes, others depict the grit and grime on your flats: vestiges of another shift slinging hash or serving beers.[63] Because more poor and working-class white women in the United States work in customer service roles like waitressing than in manufacturing or construction jobs requiring work boots, restaurant work figures in several grit lit works by women, including *Bastard Out of Carolina*. In the same vein, while male grit lit writers zoom in on "the .38 in somebody's waistband outside the bar" – Franklin's colorful evocation of the violence and hypermasculinity that he considers twin pillars of the form[64] – female grit lit authors more often turn attention to that man's home in order to spotlight a woman whose parenting responsibilities, economic precarity, and interactions with the criminal justice system are influenced by the number of nights her male partner spends at that bar with that gun in his waistband.

Grit lit began as a male-authored form. But when women started writing their own gritty stories about poor white southerners, they consciously carved out a room of their own in the genre, using their narratives to fill in gaps left by their forerunners' oversights and chauvinisms. Rather than defining grit lit as a boys' club, then, I want to disentangle two distinct strands of it, making the case that the genre consists of a male tradition and a female countertradition. The male tradition, though long treated as a sui generis form, in fact owes a debt to the picaresque. Like the picaresque, men's grit lit takes shape as prose fiction starring a roguish but engaging lower-class hero whose adventures can unfold episodically.[65] I will distinguish this stripe of grit lit by dubbing it the peckeresque: a fitting name given the force protagonists' sexual urges exert as well as the attention paid to male genitalia in these stories. A novel by Tim McLaurin illustrates the genre's preoccupation with the pecker by focusing on a character whose "philosophy" is to "use your pecker as a compass."[66] In one of Larry Brown's short stories, after a woman tearfully told her husband that a "pervert" exposed himself to her, her spouse "asked her how long this particular pecker was."[67] Characters in Cormac McCarthy's novel *Suttree* take up the question of how a man engaged in perilous sexual activity might keep "the head of his pecker" free from injury.[68] As these examples suggest, peckers abound in peckeresque fiction.

Allison's and Moss's grit lit challenges the peckeresque. Contrasting their works with novels by influential male predecessors helps reveal how *Bastard Out of Carolina* and *Change Me into Zeus's Daughter* depart from some of the formal conventions of the peckeresque. The peckeresque's founding fathers, Harry Crews and Cormac McCarthy, published their first novels in 1968 and 1965, respectively, and were well-known and well-regarded authors by the 1990s, when Allison and Moss released their first books. In 1992, for example, when *Bastard Out of Carolina* came out, McCarthy won the National Book Award for Fiction for *All the Pretty Horses*.[69] (Thanks to her debut novel, Allison was also a finalist for the award that year.) In 1992, Larry Brown and Tim McLaurin were up-and-coming grit lit writers with seven books between them: two novels and two short story collections for Brown and two novels and a memoir for McLaurin. Today, both authors' works are grit lit mainstays. Bringing Allison's novel and Moss's memoir into dialogue with their forerunners' fictional works – specifically, with McCarthy's *Suttree* (1979), McLaurin's *The Acorn Plan* (1988), Brown's *Joe* (1991), and Crews's *Scar Lover* (1992) – lays bare grit lit's gendered fault lines.

In her analysis of misogyny, philosopher Kate Manne distinguishes between the human being and the human giver, whom she defines as "a woman who is held to owe many if not most of her distinctly human capacities to a suitable boy or man, ideally, and his children, as applicable."[70] The human giver turns up in works by McCarthy and McLaurin, performing a constellation of caregiving acts unreservedly – as though she owed such efforts to the men she performs them for – and using her caregiving labor to compensate for or distract from bodily attributes that make her less desirable to her male partners. McCarthy's novel tells the story of Cornelius Suttree, a man who abandons his life of privilege (and his wife and child) to spend his days fishing on the Tennessee River and philandering in Knoxville. For a while, Suttree takes up with Joyce, a lover who supports him in high style by working as a prostitute. When Suttree decides that Joyce's "heavy thighs" and "paunch" make her less appealing, she compensates for her supposedly compromised physical charms by buying him more – and more expensive – stuff (404). In his article on *Suttree*, Matthew Potts describes the compensatory economy that structures the pair's relationship, observing that "Suttree's occasional disgust at Joyce's body is counterpoised with his comfort among the material goods – the 'womby lassitude' – that her body makes available to him. When he complains about her weight, for example, Joyce buys Suttree a Jaguar."[71] Potts's commentary encapsulates how Joyce takes shape in the text as a human giver. Owing Suttree "love, pleasure, nurture, sustenance, and comfort,"[72] she amps up one when another dwindles, increasing the quantity and quality of creature comforts she provides to offset Suttree's decreasing satisfaction with her physique.

In *The Acorn Plan*, the coming-of-age story of Billy Riley, the central human giver is Billy's Aunt Ruby. Ruby feeds men in her professional life – she works as a waitress – and in her personal life, preparing countless meals for her male relatives and boyfriends. Ruby works tirelessly but never seems tired, performing a second shift of preparing and serving meals at home as soon as she finishes each day's round of serving truck stop patrons. She feeds Bubble, her brother, whenever his alcoholism leaves him ill or impecunious. She stuffs nephew Billy with food, serving him bacon and eggs when he drops by her house in the morning, dishing up coffee and pie during after-work visits, and preparing health-restoring foods while he is in the hospital and afterward, when he recuperates at her home. She lavishes meals on beau Harold until he asks for something even more substantial – her life savings – and then she gives him that, too.

Perhaps Ruby hopes food will distract the men she loves from two attributes that the text treats as flaws: her age and her weight. Ruby herself ascribes her low standards for her romantic partners to these traits, observing, "I'm getting older and fatter every day" when Billy asks why she has taken up with truck driver Harold Crumpler.[73] The narrator spends more than a page chronicling her progression from an "overweight" newborn to a "fat" little girl to an adolescent who grew "broader, her hips fanning out, her breasts much too large for a twelve-year-old."[74] As a middle-aged woman who weighs "twenty extra pounds," in the narrator's estimation, Ruby prepares for sex with Harold by first feeding him a meal that was "damn near a feast," then undressing in the dark so that he can catch glimpses of her body only when passing vehicles' headlights illuminate her bedroom.[75] Like Joyce in *Suttree*, Ruby embodies and even extends Manne's definition of the human giver, directing "emotional, social, reproductive, and caregiving labor" as well as money she earns from paid labor toward her romantic partner.[76]

In *Bastard Out of Carolina*, Bone's mother also works as a waitress in a diner. But whereas Ruby works for the social commerce, Anney works to support her family. Ruby treats her workplace first and foremost as a hunting ground for the truckers she dates in endless succession – a practice that prompts her brother to christen her with the unflattering moniker "trucker-fucker."[77] Having made her way through "dozens of regulars" looking for Mister Right, she then turns to new customers in search of "one special road cowboy."[78] Anney works for the money; Allison's novel introduces her job by observing, "the tips made all the difference" (8). *Bastard Out of Carolina* treats the family's financial situation exactingly, noting the cost of groceries – eighty dollars per month – and the careful "columns of figures" that Anney records to manage household finances (66).[79] Another important difference between the two characters emerges from how they respond to being sexualized in the workplace. Ruby welcomes sexual attention from customers. When Harold leaves a two-dollar tip after his first visit to the café, Ruby rejoices not because the money will help pay bills but because it signals his interest in her. By contrast, Anney must "tug her apron higher, refuse dates, pinches, suggestions" to make it through each shift (14). Though dependent on customers' tips, Anney "firmly passed back anything that looked like a down payment on something she didn't want to sell" (9).

Despite working "twenty-plus years in a truck-stop cafe," Ruby seems to suffer neither physical nor economic injuries from decades of low-wage work that keeps her on her feet.[80] For example, she has the energy and income necessary to host a yearly Thanksgiving banquet, inviting not only family members but also people "she thought worthy or needing."[81] Anney perpetually struggles to feed herself and her children by cobbling together grocery purchases, meals at the diner where she works, and vegetables from relatives' gardens. To assist in these efforts, family members use foods as gifts and as forms of payment. When Aunt Raylene wants Bone's help around her house, for instance, she "pay[s] in kind" with the yield from her garden: "fresh tomatoes, okra, two jars of chow-chow" (181). When Raylene babysits Bone and Reese as a favor to Anney, she brings along some of "her home-canned blackberries" (261). The novel describes how Raylene makes a skillet cobbler for the girls, listing like a recipe would the sugars, fruit, and biscuit dough that go into it as well as the time it takes to cook. In this way, Allison's text represents women's caretaking as a form of labor. By specifying that Raylene contributes home-canned blackberries to her nieces' meal, *Bastard Out of Carolina* points to the work that goes into growing and harvesting (if garden-grown) or foraging (if wild) and preserving the fruit – hours of effort that Raylene undertakes to help nourish her sister's children. This is a far cry from McLaurin's novel, in which Ruby almost magically produces foods whenever men appear. When Billy dropped by unannounced, for example, Ruby "hurried" into the kitchen and, after a single intervening sentence, returned with coffee and chocolate pie.[82]

In peckeresque novels, women hunger for men above all else. Early in *The Acorn Plan*, Ruby hugged her nephew Billy "as if there was a hunger inside her only he could feed."[83] Larry Brown's *Joe* centers on a friendship between the title character, Joe Ransom, and Gary Jones, a young man Joe employs. Gary's father, Wade, spends most of his money on alcohol, and so his wife and children often go hungry. Yet Gary's mother craves Wade more than food, throwing herself at him and "kissing him all over his face" one day when he returns home without provisions.[84] Joe's ex-wife laments "all them baloney sandwiches" that she and her children ate because Joe would wager – and lose – the grocery money.[85] Yet immediately after voicing this reproach, she initiates sex with her ex, explaining, "I need it."[86] By portraying women who are hungrier for men than for food, Brown's novel downplays the consequences of male characters prioritizing their own desires above their families' needs.

Is it to physically enact this hunger for men that so many female characters perform fellatio? Whatever the reason, oral sex abounds in peckeresque novels. To ingratiate himself with his fares, a taxi driver in *Suttree* offers to take the men to the Green Room, where women would "as soon suck a peter as look at ye" (338). In *Joe*, Joe pays a prostitute to perform oral sex on Gary in order to "break [him] in."[87] In Joe's mind, sponsoring Gary's first sexual experience is part and parcel of befriending and mentoring the younger man. In *The Acorn Plan*, one woman uses oral sex rather than speech to communicate. After Bubble and Wilma come up with a home-sharing plan, Wilma "slipped onto her knees ... unzipped Bubble's trousers and took him in her mouth, and committed herself to the agreement in the only way she knew."[88] In *Scar Lover*, giving head substitutes for getting emotional support. During her father's cremation, Sarah had approached her boyfriend, "put her head in his lap ... unzipped his fly, and damn nearly gotten him off" – an act she hoped would take "her mind off how ugly everything was."[89]

Food, not fellatio, salves women's emotional wounds in Moss's memoir. In the midst of a chaotic eviction in which Moss's emotions and her family's possessions are tossed about pell-mell, a neighbor Moss barely knows gives her a plate of melon and bacon. Savoring this snack as she sits among her family's sidewalk-flung clothes and furnishings, Moss describes the food as "sweet as honey in my mouth" (125). This phrase appears in Revelation 10:10 and Ezekiel 3:3; in each context, the speaker describes the taste of God's word. Quoting this line underscores the spiritual implications of the neighbor woman's act, drawing attention to how her gesture brings together loving one's neighbor, feeding the hungry, and comforting the afflicted. In addition, redeploying this Biblical simile illuminates a key way in which *Change Me into Zeus's Daughter* and *Bastard Out of Carolina* depart from the formal characteristics of the peckeresque. Whereas most peckeresque works (including the four I am concentrating on) use third-person point of view, Moss's memoir and Allison's novel are told in the first person. So, in contrast to Crews's novel, in which a third-person narrator describes Sarah's mouth in terms of Pete's desires and pleasures – "he wanted her mouth right where it was" the narrator observes of the mid-cremation fellatio[90] – Moss's memoir makes use of a first-person possessive pronoun to articulate how eating this meal provides pleasure and succor to Moss herself.

This fellation fixation is symptomatic of the peckeresque's broader disinterest in what women might think or wish to say. Offering dating advice, McLaurin's Bubble counsels his nephew to prioritize sleeping with a woman over understanding her: "Just screw her and don't worry about what's in her mind."[91] Characters in other peckeresque novels work to keep whatever thoughts might be in women's heads safely contained therein. To stop his girlfriend from talking, Crews's Pete "kissed her. It was the only way, that or hit her, so he stopped her mouth ... with a kiss."[92] After his girlfriend moves out, Brown's Joe decides that life "was easier without her. He didn't have to listen to anything."[93] In the midst of the fight that ends his relationship with Joyce, McCarthy's Suttree hears her "shouting at him," but he does not stop to listen because "he seemed to have heard it all before" (411). In truth, though, "all he could make out was his name," so his inattention springs not from knowledge of her concerns but from indifference to them (411).

Rather than listening to and meaningfully partnering with women, peckeresque protagonists feed on them. Peckeresque novels routinely link women's bodies with foodstuffs – most commonly, fruits and meats. At a brothel, Joe encounters a woman with a "bosom like mangoes."[94] To Pete, Sarah's genitalia feel like a "peeled plum."[95] Suttree's friend Gene Harrogate takes this trope a step further. This "moonlight melonmounter" (48) leaves a farmer with a field of "violated fruit" (32): watermelons that Harrogate penetrated with his penis. While Harrogate serves time for this act, his fellow prisoners taunt him with plans for a "combination fruitstand and whorehouse" featuring "melons in black negligees" (49). For other men in McCarthy's novel, women morph into meats. Men dining together turn from savoring veal cutlets to craving "lovely young cuntlets" (302). Women's breasts are "plump" both to Harrogate, who fantasizes about "plump young midnight tits" (144), and to Suttree, who gropes a "plump young tit" (246). The adjective "plump" can, of course, be applied to people, but it also frequently characterizes meat, gracing the name of a poultry company called Gold'n Plump, launched in 1978 (the year before McCarthy published *Suttree*), and figuring in Ball Park Franks' memorable advertising slogan, "they plump when you cook 'em," formulated in 1965. Elsewhere in *Suttree*, McCarthy employed "plump" to depict meats – "plump hares" await their fates in cages at a meat market (67) – and the melons Harrogate molests, which catch his fancy with their "plump forms supine and dormant" (31–2).

Bastard Out of Carolina and *Change Me into Zeus's Daughter* focus on decidedly inedible female figures. Although her birth certificate christens her Ruth Anne Boatwright, Allison's heroine is known to everyone as Bone. This nickname thwarts the peckeresque's sexualization of the female body by signifying Ruth Anne's hardness, bringing her more into line with the peckeresque's depictions of men (wielders of boners) than with its portrayals of women who, in several texts, incarnate permeability – Suttree, for example, has a lover whose "legs fell open bonelessly" (352). Ruth Anne's sobriquet also makes her less palatable than women in peckeresque fiction by associating her with an inedible part of an animal instead of with meat. Moss and her sisters do not look delectable because their bodies bear scars from nutritional deficiencies and psychological traumas. Alice, Moss's oldest sister, carries into adulthood "the nervous tic that developed when she was in her teens" (39). This sort of stress-induced physical response would likely repulse a peckeresque hero like Suttree, who leaves one paramour when her eyes, "tearful or speckled with rage," started to evince anxious feelings (405). In addition, malnutrition makes Moss "thin as a rail" (220). Peckeresque protagonists are drawn to voluptuous physiques, admiring not just "plump" breasts and thighs but also "full" ones. Suttree, for example, spends an evening cavorting with "a ripe young thing" with "full pale thighs" (76). Another time, he hits the dance floor with a "fullthighed" woman (246). And on the night he meets Joyce, the narrative twice draws attention to her "full breasts" (389, 393).

Allison's novel and Moss's memoir represent the experiences of young girls profoundly impacted by their fathers' failings – a thematic concern conveyed in both writers' book titles. The name of Allison's novel points to the fact that Bone is "certified a bastard by the state of South Carolina" (3). Bone has few ties to her biological father; he and Anney never married, he saw his daughter only once, and he does not contribute to her support. But his absence determines her legal identity, conferring the bastardy that state officials note on Bone's birth certificate. Although some scholars argue that Bone "struggles with the shame of being a 'bastard,'"[96] in fact only Anney experiences such feelings.[97] For Bone, what indelibly marks her is not the label of illegitimacy but that stigma's impact on her mother, who marries Glen because she mistakenly imagines he would "make a good daddy" (13). By shifting attention from neglectful fathers to neglected daughters, *Bastard Out of Carolina* reveals the consequences of the parental inattention and abandonment depicted in peckeresque writers' works.

Moss's title asks that she be transformed into Venus, the daughter of Greek mythology's supreme god. In a chapter called "Goddess of Beauty," the Moss family sits outside its dilapidated rental house while Stewart, Moss's father, points out bright Venus in the night sky. Moving from contemplating the planet to the deity, Moss rhapsodizes over a fantasy of becoming "Venus: goddess of beauty, much-loved daughter of Zeus, stonecutters' muse" (136). Moss feels undersupplied with beauty and love in part because the nutritional deficiencies she suffered during childhood had produced what she terms an "unsightly, tangled face" to which people often responded cruelly (100) – the epilogue tells of two occasions when men suggested that she put a bag over her head. Moss's narrative describes her father, who "forgot to feed" his children, not only spending his earnings on alcohol for himself rather than on food for his family but also feeding his friends rather than his kids (49). One night when he brought a brand-new buddy home from the bar, for example, he insisted that his wife make eggs and toast for the two of them even though he knew those ingredients were intended for his children's breakfasts. "When someone not entitled ate them, someone else went without" Moss explains, making clear the implications of such largesse in an economy of scarcity (151).[98]

By uncloaking the costs of her father's extrafamilial relationships, Moss's memoir critiques the rose-tinted bromances at the heart of the peckeresque tradition. Peckeresque protagonists neglect or abandon wives and children, meeting their sexual needs via womanizing and their emotional needs via homosocial hobnobbing. Brown's Joe distances himself from his family both while married – he was "too busy" to help care for his son and daughter – and afterward, when he identifies his ex-wife (using startlingly dissociating language) as a "thin girl with brown hair and skin like an Indian who'd born his children."[99] Over the course of the narrative, Joe has sex with this ex-wife, with a young woman named Connie, and with a woman he meets at a honky-tonk, but his central interpersonal connection is not with any of them; it is with Gary. In McLaurin's novel, Bubble and Billy have women as sexual partners, but their most meaningful relationship is with each other. Suttree's closest friend is Gene, and his social circle consists of male friends from prison and from Knoxville's fringes and underworlds. Literary critic David Cowart has praised *Suttree* for rousing the reader's sympathy for such figures, observing that "the most abject – Ab Jones, J-Bone, the ragpicker – prove remarkably selfless, even heroic."[100] But it is not a fluke that all of these figures are men. While Ab Jones, J-Bone, the ragpicker, and other male characters progress from abjection to heroism, women in the novel take the reverse trip, devolving from selfless figures into abject ones.[101]

The three women who selflessly love Suttree – his wife, Joyce, and Wanda – all suffer life-changing losses. His wife loses her son (and her husband, of course, since Suttree abandons his family). Joyce seems to lose her mind, degenerating across their brief relationship – it spans twenty-five pages of the 471-page novel – from a successful hustler to a woman in the throes of "a kind of fit" of kicking and screaming and sobbing and ripping up money and tossing it to the wind (409). Wanda loses her life. In Suttree's first outing with her, the young woman takes narrative shape as a riot of nubile female flesh: "young breasts" with "nipples so round and swollen" and "white thighs" (350). Twelve pages later, her body ravaged by a rockslide, Wanda is "sheared limbs and rags of meat" (362).

Suttree enacts female characters' abjection not only thematically but also formally. Wanda and Joyce transform from proper nouns into pronouns upon entering into Suttree's sexual consciousness. Suttree meets Wanda when he starts working with her family, and in this context Wanda's first name appears four times as characters discuss how she can contribute to the mussel-brailing enterprise that brings them all together.[102] But as soon as Wanda becomes sexually appealing to Suttree and then sexually involved with him (a development requiring just two pages of intervening interaction), her name permanently drops from the narrative. At a café, Joyce introduces herself to Suttree and he responds by greeting her by name. Her name never again appears in the novel. Joyce is the pair's breadwinner, providing food, lodging, and increasingly decadent superfluities, starting with grooming supplies including "a pigskin shavingbag ... with all manner of things that he hardly knew the use of, the powders and colognes and lotions" (395), moving to frippery like "alligator shoes ... a camelhair overcoat ... [and] beltless gabardine slacks" (400), and culminating in a Jaguar convertible, the ne plus ultra of Joyce's generosity. Yet McCarthy's syntax situates Joyce as Suttree's appendage by repeatedly identifying her as "his." Diction further sidelines Joyce by identifying her neither by her name nor by her role in Suttree's life (e.g., as lover or girlfriend) but by derogatory terms for sex workers. The combined effect is that Joyce, despite sponsoring every outing, takes textual shape as Suttree's sullied sidekick in phrases describing Suttree with "his trollop and his toddy" (399), "Suttree and his soiled dove" (401), and "Suttree and his whore" (410).

* * *

A week before Christmas in 1995, the *New York Times Magazine* ran a feature story on Dorothy Allison. Situated amid pages and pages of advertisements appealing to the petit bourgeois and the posh – watches by Swiss Army and Chopard; bags from the Gap and Louis Vuitton – the article weaves in several well-known authors' appraisals of Allison's work. Studs Terkel praised Allison for her knowledge of outsiders' experiences. Randall Kenan expressed concern that her characters cleave too close to stereotypes about poor southerners. And George Garrett offered this take on Allison's work: "It's as if the people in Dorothea Lange photographs, in the work of Margaret Bourke-White and Walker Evans, were able to speak."[103] Just let that statement sink in for a moment. Now, to be fair, I think I know what Garrett meant. Because the Americans depicted in these photographers' most famous works are known to the wider world only through the haunting portraits of them captured during the Great Depression, we know their faces rather than their stories.

Yet it is vitally important to recognize that the people in these photographs were able to speak, and did speak. And the things they said often upended middle-class artists' and audiences' narratives about them. Florence Thompson, the woman pictured in Dorothea Lange's famous

"Migrant Mother" photograph, found it galling to be treated as the face of poor whites' suffering during the Depression because she was in fact a Native American woman.[104] Describing their encounter decades later, Lange acknowledged that she was not interested in who Thompson really was, observing, "I did not ask her name or her history."[105] In the same vein, Erskine Caldwell and Margaret Bourke-White's *You Have Seen Their Faces* (1937) pairs photographs captured with Bourke-White's gotcha technique – she would, by her own account, trigger the shutter suddenly when people's "faces or gestures gave us what we were trying to express" so that her subjects were "imprisoned on a sheet of film before they knew what had happened" – with captions written in the first person (as though spoken by the individuals pictured) that were in truth composed by Caldwell and Bourke-White.[106] In an introductory note to *You Have Seen Their Faces*, the pair explained that "the legends under the pictures are intended to express the authors' own conceptions of the sentiments of the individuals portrayed; they do not pretend to reproduce the actual sentiments of these persons."[107] That last claim is an important one. Although they are placed in quotation marks under the photographs and use folksy vocabulary and nonstandard syntax, the "legends," as Caldwell and Bourke-White termed them (the myths, the widespread but unverified beliefs), do not aim to express "the actual sentiments of these persons."[108] *You Have Seen Their Faces* is, in Alan Trachtenberg's estimation, "an inventive work, more documentary fiction than strict documentation or sociological analysis."[109] "Imprisoned" on the page, in Bourke-White's startlingly forthright wording, real poor white people become imaginary poor white characters in Caldwell and Bourke-White's text, their bodies made to convey what their middle-class chroniclers "were trying to express" and their (falsified) words voicing these middle-class artists' "own conceptions" of what poor white southerners should think and feel.

Poor white southerners "were able to speak," to return to George Garrett's phrasing, and did speak, long before Dorothy Allison and Barbara Robinette Moss became writers. But in the late twentieth century, knowing that some middle-class people were listening to what poor white people had to say (and knowing, too, that many poor white readers were hungry for new kinds of stories about economically disadvantaged Americans), Allison and Moss used famineways to tell about poor white southerners' experiences of hunger. Discussing *Bastard Out of Carolina* not long after it was published, Allison explained the central role that hunger plays in her characters' lives by observing that "being poor in this country is about being constantly hungry, because the thing that you get, the emotional sustenance you get is never enough, so that hunger becomes a way of life."[110] To be sure, middle-class writers' works are not necessarily deficient in emotional sustenance, as I work to show in my analyses of novels and short stories by Chesnutt, Faulkner, and O'Connor. By the same token, poor white authors' texts may not assuage readers' cravings. This chapter argues that *Suttree*, *The Acorn Plan*, *Joe*, and *Scar Lover* might fail to satisfy those with an appetite for well-rounded representations of poor white women's experiences. The coda continues on this path, exploring why a more recent book by a white writer who grew up poor – *Hillbilly Elegy* – might leave readers who hanker for fresh ideas about poor white people feeling unsated.

Coda

This book has worked to show how, across generations and across movements and genres, American authors have represented poor white southerners as out of step with what is going on in middle-class Americans' lives. In the late nineteenth century, a period awash in social and personal improvement schemes of all stripes, poor white southerners were routinely depicted as unimprovable – as "less plastic to civilization than any other race in America," as Clare de Graffenried wrote in the *Century* in 1891.[1] During the interwar period, a time profoundly shaped by the modernist credo "make it new," poor white southerners were frequently pictured as unmodern. At midcentury, as civil rights activists scored victories against racially unjust social, political, and commercial systems, poor white southerners were often presented as unprogressive. At the end of the twentieth century, amid a health and wellness craze – step aerobics, the Thighmaster, Jazzercise, and the Abdominizer were all popular in this era – poor white southerners were routinely portrayed as unhealthy. And today?

If two recent and celebrated books are any indication, early twenty-first-century writers often picture poor white southerners as unalive. In 2016, Arlie Hochschild, a titan in the field of sociology, published a study of the Tea Party Movement titled *Strangers in Their Own Land: Anger and Mourning on the American Right*. That same year, venture-capitalist-turned-writer J. D. Vance published *Hillbilly Elegy: A Memoir of a Family and Culture in Crisis*, which tells of Vance's experiences growing up in a poor white family whose members, although living in Ohio by the time he was born, had migrated from Kentucky. Both books depict the people they focus on as doubly unalive. For one thing, poor white people are portrayed as unalive to the core issues that plague them. Vance insists that his hometown contains "not a single person aware of his own laziness" – a charge that unites unoriginal allegations of shiftlessness with timeworn accusations of ignorance.[2] Hochschild contends that the Louisianans she studied suffer "structural amnesia," which renders them unaware that "pollution, health, schooling,

[and] poverty" are among their most pressing problems.³ For another thing, both writers' book titles intimate that the populations they look at are, in some sense, not alive. Vance's text is an "elegy," or a lament for the dead. Hochschild's subtitle identifies her field site as a place of "mourning." Presenting poor white people as unattuned to life-threatening hazards in their communities and in their own lives makes them seem out of sync with today's wellness culture. Taking shape through corporate programs aiming to improve employees' health (and reduce employers' health-related expenses) and through pricey spa treatments, exercise regimens, and self-improvement programs, wellness culture is a behemoth force in twenty-first-century life.⁴

Rather than informing poor white Americans about mental and physical health risks and empowering them to surmount such hazards, though, *Hillbilly Elegy* and *Strangers in Their Own Land* aim to enlighten middle-class readers about what it feels like for poor white people to be so unalive. In his book's introduction, Vance explains that he wrote *Hillbilly Elegy* to help his audience understand "what it *feels like* to nearly give up on yourself."⁵ Feelings are also the focus of Hochschild's study, which strives to reveal the "'deep story,' a story that *feels as if* it were true," that her ethnographic subjects embrace.⁶ But Hochschild and Vance also, and perhaps unknowingly, lay bare another deep story: the story of how well-off white Americans are thinking about poor white people in the opening decades of the twenty-first century. Although they make use of familiar stereotypes about poor white people, including that they are lazy and eat unhealthily, Vance and Hochschild employ these ideas differently than their similarly stereotype-steeped predecessors by portraying poor whites as unalive. In keeping with my contention that representations of poor white people are barometers of the anxieties gripping middle-class white Americans in the periods in which they are produced, I want to suggest that this two-pronged unaliveness – a one-two punch of unawareness and unhealthiness – is a major bugbear haunting better-off people today.

To paint a picture of the Louisiana communities in which she conducted interviews for *Strangers in Their Own Land,* Hochschild inventories the differences between Berkeley, California, where she lives, and Lake Charles, Louisiana, where she completed much of the fieldwork for the book:

> Certain absences also reminded me I was not at home: no *New York Times* at the newsstand, almost no organic produce in grocery stores or farmers' markets, no foreign films in movie houses, few small cars, fewer petite sizes in clothing stores.... In some cafés, virtually everything on the menu was fried. There were no questions before meals about gluten-free entrees.⁷

Hochschild's description characterizes Louisiana by its deficiencies, dilating on "absences." Sociologist Steph Lawler, drawing on Pierre Bourdieu, has noted that middle-class observers portray lower-status communities in terms of lack: not "a lack of material resources, but a lack of 'taste,' knowledge, and the 'right ways of being and doing.'"[8] *Class, Whiteness, and Southern Literature* traces out how this rhetoric of lack shapes four eras of literary history, making the case that successive waves of unimprovable, unmodern, unprogressive, and unhealthy poor white characters in southern literature act as foils for the identities middle-class Americans wish to claim for themselves. *Strangers in Their Own Land* illustrates how this rhetoric of lack persists in our own era, because what Lawler has identified as the "right ways of being and doing" that some middle-class observers claim are absent in lower-status communities are what Hochschild found in short supply in Louisiana. Her account makes clear that Lake Charles has newsstands, farmers' markets, theaters, clothing boutiques, and restaurants. But these venues sell the wrong goods. Even when it turns from listing what is missing to describing what is present, Hochschild's description renders abundance as absence. Finding herself in a place full of large vehicles and garments in larger sizes, Hochschild perceived the locale as deficient in small cars and small clothes.[9]

Elizabeth Currid-Halkett's study of twenty-first-century elites helps account for the specific unavailable items Hochschild namechecks. The upper echelon of today's society, which Currid-Halkett terms the aspirational class, is tied together less by income level than by "*a shared set of cultural practices and social norms*":

> The unifying characteristic shared by members of this new elite cultural formation is their acquisition and valuing of knowledge.... Reading cultural commentary, being up-to-date on the news (preferably via the *New York Times, Wall Street Journal,* or *Financial Times*), and eating organic food are but a number of ways by which they connect with one another irrespective of their economic means.[10]

Reading Hochschild's work by the light of Currid-Halkett's analysis reveals that *Strangers in Their Own Land* corroborates one of my book's core arguments, exemplifying how writers define middle- and upper-class Americans in terms of what distinguishes them from poor white southerners. In her first chapter, Hochschild asserts that her own social milieu is made up of people who "read the *New York Times* daily" and "eat organic food."[11] By noting, just a few pages later, that the retailers she visited in Lake Charles did not sell the *New York Times* or stock a wide variety of organic foods, Hochschild suggests that these Louisianans do not partake in the social norms and cultural practices that tie together members of the aspirational class. The weirdness of Hochschild's description of her field site – Why not characterize a locale by the newspapers its populace *does* read? Why consider print media at all given that, when Hochschild was conducting her fieldwork in the early 2010s, more *New York Times* subscribers accessed the paper digitally than in print?[12] – is accounted for by how this information helps establish her readers' (rather than her interviewees') identities. Today's elites "strive to feel informed and legitimate in their belief that they have made the right and reasonable decision based on facts (whether regarding the merit of organic food ... or electric cars)."[13] Believing that poor whites' poor decisions lead to poor health (the two prongs of unaliveness) acts as ballast for privileged people's desired self-conceptions as informed consumers whose good decisions will lead to good health.

Hochschild's treatment of her field site's foodways jumps into a conversation interlacing eating and ethics. Members of the professional middle class "demonstrate their moral superiority through their consumption choices."[14] In Progressive Era Appalachia, middle- and upper-class people made and ate biscuits, which they considered healthy and hygienic, and turned up their noses at cornbread, which "symbolized ignorance, disease, and poverty."[15] Today, many members of the middle and upper classes work to avoid the foodstuffs Hochschild mentions in describing her experiences dining out in Louisiana: fried foods and foods containing gluten. Fried foods are anathema to raw foods diets, among others, and people following ketogenic diets, Paleolithic diets, and other diet plans recently in vogue sidestep gluten. Organic food is an especially powerful status signifier. According to Currid-Halkett, "While in Veblen's time status was a function of the product itself, in the twenty-first century status emerges from how the product is made and its point of origin."[16] This shift from the Gilded Age's conspicuous consumption to today's conspicuous production means that eating organic foods, which are perceived as "superior, more environmentally friendly, and more humane," is one way that more prosperous people can endeavor to brandish their moral ascendancy.[17]

Whereas *Strangers in Their Own Land* obliquely suggests that pesticide-laden produce and trans-fats-heavy fried foods are sapping poor white southerners' vitality, *Hillbilly Elegy* explicitly, and misleadingly, links poor white people's diets to their deaths. "Our eating and exercise habits seem designed to send us to an early grave," Vance writes, finding sepulchral motives behind dietary practices that scholars link to economic constraints.[18] He continues by elaborating on this erroneous connection: "A recent study found that ... the life expectancy of working-class white folks is going down. We eat Pillsbury cinnamon rolls for breakfast, Taco Bell for lunch, and McDonald's for dinner."[19] The study mentioned here is surely Anne Case and Angus Deaton's work; these economists have documented how "deaths of despair" are claiming the lives of white Americans without college degrees at such a rate that overall life expectancy in the United States has declined.[20] Half of these deaths occurred in Appalachia.[21] Case and Deaton found three main culprits behind this increase in mortality, although they are not, as Vance suggests, Pillsbury rolls, Taco Bell, and McDonald's. Instead, drug overdoses, suicides, and alcohol-related liver diseases caused these deaths.[22] The opioid epidemic's heavy toll is well known to Vance, who in 2017 announced that he was going to return to his home state and turn his attention to battling opiate addiction.[23] But food is at the heart of an enduring deep story about what ails poor white Americans. From Ransy Sniffle's diet of "red clay and blackberries" to Honey Boo Boo's roadkill and sketti dinners, poor white southerners have long been associated with foods that better-off people deem unappetizing or unhealthy.[24] Although fast food consumption actually decreases as income decreases, so that lower-income Americans eat fast food less often than either middle- or upper-income people, the feels-as-if story suggests that, unalive to the health risks of such foods, poor white Americans are killing themselves one quick meal at a time.[25]

Hillbilly Elegy and *Strangers in Their Own Land* may reveal an emerging set of generic conventions for addressing poor white life in the opening decades of the twenty-first century. Both books, I want to suggest, make use of the motif of katabasis. A Greek word meaning "descent," katabasis can involve traveling from a country's interior down to its coast, but in literary works katabasis often refers to journeying into the underworld. This book shines a light on how well-off white people represent themselves as refined, modern, racially progressive, and tasteful across the long twentieth century by depicting poor white people as trashy, behind the times, racist, and gross. Perhaps in taking recourse to a motif that intertwines traveling down the social ladder with traveling to the land of the dead, twenty-first-century writers lay bare middle- and upper-class Americans' anxieties about their own mortality. Identifying poor white communities as hotspots for deadly social problems (violence and drug addiction: foci of Vance's memoir) and for public health crises (environmental pollution and poor nutrition: issues Hochschild's study emphasizes) may appeal in our wellness-obsessed era as a way to quarantine malignancies far from the communities in which richer people shop, eat, and live. For readers of *Strangers in Their Own Land* or *Hillbilly Elegy*, closing the book on such experiences of despondence and disease means just that: While offering middle-class readers glimpses of an unfamiliar netherworld, each book ultimately keeps that world safely confined within its covers.

Vance's and Hochschild's works accentuate the space between the bourgeoisie and the poor by highlighting a series of supposed points of contrast between the two classes. For example, *Hillbilly Elegy* unleashes harsh words of righteous indignation against poor people who were "living off of government largesse" because they "gamed the welfare system."[26] Vance is not the first American to make claims about the prevalence of welfare fraud, of course.[27] But it is worth noting how anxieties about people gaming government benefit systems cluster around a subset of social welfare programs: those disbursed through financial allotments rather than tax exemptions. Tax breaks with social welfare objectives including supporting charitable organizations, accessing higher education, saving for retirement, and owning a home – which constitute what political scientist Christopher Howard refers to as America's "hidden welfare state" – arouse much less tongue wagging than financial allotment programs that tackle social welfare tasks like feeding the hungry and providing healthcare for the poor.[28] Consider, for example, attitudes toward two of the largest federal housing assistance programs: the housing choice voucher program (Section 8) and the mortgage interest deduction. Although Americans often fail to think of the latter program as governmental housing assistance, the mortgage interest deduction functions, in the words of sociologist Matthew Desmond, as "a generous public-housing program for the rich."[29] More than half of high-income households claim the mortgage interest deduction, whereas only eleven percent of low-income households avail themselves of either Section 8 assistance or the mortgage interest deduction. As a result, the government spends four times more on the domicile of the average high-income household in any given year than on the average low-income one.[30] But *Hillbilly Elegy* lets this form of "living off of government largesse" fly under the radar – perhaps because this program is one likely to benefit Vance and his readership.[31]

Vance's memoir delivers an old message via a new messenger. The blurb on the inside flap of *Hillbilly Elegy*'s dust jacket describes the text as "a passionate and personal analysis of a culture in crisis – that of poor, white Americans" that recounts "the disintegration of this group ... searingly from the inside." Bringing grit lit's insider account of poor white life together with Appalachian outmigration literature's stories of families' lives after leaving the South, Vance's narrative arises "searingly from the inside" of the community it describes.[32] But what his grit lit forebears depict as – no surprise here – gritty, Vance portrays as grim. A "hub of misery," his hometown is on the precipice between life and death because it is "hemorrhaging jobs."[33] Members of his community face a "grim future" because they are part of "a culture that increasingly encourages social decay" by conditioning its members to feel helpless: "There is a lack of agency here – a feeling that you have little control over your life and a willingness to blame everyone but yourself."[34] Purporting to offer a cultural account of poverty experienced by white midwesterners with Appalachian roots – a gesture signaled most clearly by his book's subtitle, which promises to detail a "culture in crisis" – *Hillbilly Elegy* leans heavily on the culture of poverty thesis, an idea introduced by anthropologist Oscar Lewis more than a half-century ago. In a 1968 essay called "The Culture of Poverty," Lewis asserted, "The people in the culture of poverty have a strong feeling of marginality, of helplessness, of dependency, of not belonging. They are like aliens in their own country, convinced that the existing institutions do not serve their interests and needs."[35] Given that this short excerpt from Lewis's article sets forth both Vance's and Hochschild's central claims, it seems likely that Lewis's work influenced these writers. Vance replaces Lewis's specific terms with synonyms – the marginalized are the "socially isolated," those who feel helpless manifest a "lack of agency," dependent people are specifically "food stamp recipients who show little interest in honest work" – and traces this culture back to Appalachia, identifying these "values" (as he acerbically terms them) as "hillbilly values [that] spread widely along with hillbilly people."[36] Hochschild, too, seems just to reword Lewis: "aliens in their own country" sounds an awful lot like "strangers in their own land."

Unfazed by the staleness of Vance's stereotypes, readers and reviewers proclaimed *Hillbilly Elegy* "essential reading for this moment in history" (*New York Times* op-ed columnist David Brooks's words, from a glowing account of Vance's memoir) and treated its author as the foremost diagnostician of what ails poor white Americans.[37] Yet the book's central claims range from the half-century-old culture of poverty thesis to the three-century-old notion that poor whites' laziness causes their poverty. Depicting them as patients whose bodies resist the treatment capable of curing their malady, *Hillbilly Elegy* describes poor white people as "immune to hard work."[38] Further tainting this purported indolence with hints of impropriety, the text suggests that poor white people have "little interest in honest work."[39] How does this hoary concept maintain its foothold generation after generation?

Clichéd ideas about poor white people's laziness endure because they shore up a vision of the United States as a land of opportunity where, with hard work, anyone can make it. This American dream depends on equality of opportunity – which is where it goes awry. In the realm of higher education, for example, everyone – faculty members and administrators, parents and students – wants to believe that hard work is what earned our students (and ourselves) a place at the seminar table. Yet we know that the college admissions process advantages economically privileged people. Grades are an important consideration in the admissions process, and high schools attended by affluent students – private institutions as well as public schools in which few students qualify for free or reduced price lunch – have the highest rates of grade inflation.[40] Middle-class students are also more likely to seek help on assignments, flexibility with deadlines, and other academic advantages that can positively impact their grades.[41] In addition, social class influences applicants' scores on standardized tests, which have long been another key component of college applications. Lani Guinier calls the SAT a "wealth test," explaining that it "is normed to white, upper-middle-class performance" and citing the College Board's own figures showing that SAT scores move in lockstep with family income, inching steadily upward from average scores of 1326 for students whose families earn less than $20,000 to 1714 for those with family incomes above $200,000.[42] Extracurricular activities matter, too. Participating in clubs, teams, and volunteer activities – which can be difficult for students with after-school jobs, unreliable access to transportation, or limited funds for things like sporting equipment, musical instruments, and travel costs – can give more well-to-do students a leg up when it comes to college admissions. Wealthier students are also more likely to pick the *right* extracurricular endeavors. After-school activities that middle- and upper-class urbanites generally shun – including participating in organizations like Future Farmers of America and 4-H – actually hurt applicants' chances for admission.[43] But Vance pooh-poohs such concerns, treating them as symptomatic of the fatalism that beleaguers poor white people.[44] *Hillbilly Elegy* tells of bootstrapping oneself to a bachelor's degree.[45]

Claims about poor whites' laziness counterbalance a feels-as-if story about how elites earn their success by working hard. This dichotomizing belief system takes root early in Americans' lives. In her ethnographic analysis of affluent white middle-school-aged children, Margaret A. Hagerman asked her interviewees about "how rich people become rich." In their answers, the kids "all make some mention of 'hard work' and meritocracy, proposing that poor people are poor because they are 'lazy' or 'make bad choices' or 'don't save their money.'"[46] Slightly older elites offered slightly more politic takes on poverty – prep school students interviewed by sociologist Shamus Khan suggested that less advantaged people "were unlucky, had different values, or were from a past generation where opportunities weren't as available" – but continued to maintain that hard work was the linchpin of prosperous people's success.[47] Yet after analyzing material collected during his prep-school fieldwork, Khan and his fellow ethnographer Colin Jerolmack concluded that privileged students value the rhetoric, rather than the reality, of hard work and meritocracy:

> In interviews, most students construct a narrative of having achieved by dint of their hard work; meanwhile, observations reveal that most students seldom work hard and actually marginalize the few that do. The reason for this discrepancy between their words and actions, we contend, is that in a world marked by greater openness, students recognize the importance of rhetorically embracing meritocracy – even as they work in practice to protect the advantages they have most often inherited.[48]

In *Strangers in Their Own Land*, Hochschild explains that "a deep story is a *feels-as-if* story – it's the story feelings tell, in the language of symbols."[49] Poor white southerners are pivotal figures in the American imaginary because of the starring role they play in a feels-as-if story about how the nation works. Although Americans' visions of their nation as a classless society hold sway from sea to shining sea, they are nowhere more pervasive than in the South. Southerners feel more optimistic about their chances of achieving social mobility than people in other parts of the country even though they experience upward mobility less frequently than other Americans.[50] And well-off people have invoked the specter of the southern poor white layabout to naturalize the social order since at least the early eighteenth century, when William Byrd compared North Carolina to Lubberland. In each chapter of this book, I explore works by writers who devised formal techniques capable of challenging stereotypes about poor white lassitude. Chesnutt's conjure stories make clear that what planter John critiques as laziness when practiced by the poor is what he celebrates as leisure when people of his ilk do it. Faulkner's *As I Lay Dying* calls into question Anse's reputation for laziness both by pointing to his work-related injuries and by hinting at his neighbors' motivations for calling him lazy. O'Connor's short stories underscore how farm owners like Mrs. Turpin use claims about poor white people's laziness to throw into relief their own industriousness. Allison's novel and Moss's memoir depict poor white women's endless paid and unpaid labors. Only time will tell what works by established, emerging, or yet-to-appear writers will contest the classist representations of unalive poor white southerners promulgated by Vance and Hochschild. Perhaps the ghosts haunting characters in Karen Russell's *Swamplandia!* (2011), Jesmyn Ward's *Sing, Unburied, Sing* (2017), and other recently published southern novels portend possibilities for using the undead to critique problematic depictions of poor white people as unalive.

Hochschild's work fortifies social class divides by underscoring the chasm between the people she wrote about and the people she wrote for. Speaking about *Strangers in Their Own Land* at Stanford University in February 2017, Hochschild shared with audience members one of the takeaways from her time in Louisiana: "They know what we think of them," she said.[51] This startled me when I heard it.[52] For one thing, it seemed too obvious to need to be said. How could people inhabiting a culture inundated with images of poor white southerners as dirty, tacky, lazy, angry, ignorant, backwards, racist, jobless, toothless reprobates possibly not know what "we" think of them? For another thing, I wondered what made Hochschild so sure that a bright line separated the people she spoke to from the people she spoke about. But, in fact, she was on solid ground on both fronts. Like Dante returning from the Inferno, Hochschild returned from Louisiana to share her katabatic narrative with people distant – geographically as well as economically – from the southerners she had met.

They know what we think of them. Yet "we" keep losing track of what we think about them – and why it is that we spend so much time thinking about them. Katabasis is, ultimately, "a journey of self-discovery."[53] Accordingly, the ideas about poor white people with which Hochschild returned from Louisiana are ideas that help Hochschild and people like her understand themselves. And such notions, although treated as revelations by some twenty-first-century readers of *Strangers in Their Own Land* and *Hillbilly Elegy*, are long-in-the-tooth stereotypes.[54] Successive generations, and successive movements and genres, use poor whites as points of contrast for better-off whites' desired self-conceptions as people who are refined, modern, racially progressive, tasteful, and now, it seems, thriving. By surveying these efforts' effects on literary forms, *Class, Whiteness, and Southern Literature* traces out the history of this practice from the Gilded Age to the present.

Recognizing the poor white southerner as "a race problem" – the phrase captioning E. W. Kemble's drawing of a poor white man that was reproduced and discussed in the introduction – enriches our understanding of American literary history. Poor white people appear throughout American literary works as distorted forms personifying whatever middle- and upper-class white people want to dissociate from. This accounts for why so many different texts – modernist novels and midcentury short stories, local color sketches and grit lit tales, antebellum memoirs and early twenty-first-century memoirs – depict poor white southerners in ways that engage or even inflame intraracial antagonisms. Was Huck Finn black? No. Are local color tales' "Appalachian hillbillies [stand-ins] for Russian Jews and Chinese"?[55] No. Social class structures not only American society but also the American imaginary, and these characters from late nineteenth-century fiction bear witness to anxieties about rural white poverty that found outlet in the reports and essays of the eugenics movement as well as in the sketches and short stories of the local color movement. Such antagonisms and anxieties continued to shape American literature and culture throughout the twentieth century and, as recent books by Hochschild and Vance indicate, still dog us in the twenty-first century. Accounting for the ideological work done by fictional representations of poor white people means acknowledging and amending the ways that previous critical approaches have obscured classism's formative role in southern literature. To do otherwise would be poor scholarship. Not to mention poor form.

Notes

Introduction

1. E. W. Kemble, "Illustrating Huckleberry Finn," *Colophon: A Book Collectors' Quarterly* 1 (February 1930): n.p.
2. W. E. B. Du Bois, *The Souls of Black Folk: Essays and Sketches* (Chicago: A. C. McClurg, 1903), vii.
3. Kemble's drawings first appeared in the *Century* alongside selections from Mark Twain's *Adventures of Huckleberry Finn* that were published in successive issues of the magazine (December 1884–February 1885). In the next (March 1885) issue, Kemble illustrated "Hodson's Hide-Out," a local color story by Maurice Thompson about poor white Alabamians.
4. Joel Chandler Harris, "Azalia," *Century Illustrated Monthly Magazine* 34, August 1887, 549.
5. Harry Stillwell Edwards, "An Idyl of 'Sinkin' Mount'in,'" *Century Illustrated Monthly Magazine* 36, October 1888, 896.
6. Charles Egbert Craddock [Mary Noailles Murfree], "The 'Harnt' That Walks Chilhowee," *Atlantic Monthly* 51, May 1883, 660–3.
7. Harry Stillwell Edwards, "A Battle in Crackerdom," *Century Illustrated Monthly Magazine* 43, January 1892, 458, 459.
8. For an important early article on this subject, see Charles H. Nilon, "The Ending of *Huckleberry Finn*: 'Freeing the Free Negro,'" *Mark Twain Journal* 22, no. 2 (Fall 1984): 21–7.
9. Scholars interested in Twain's engagement with eugenics most often discuss *Pudd'nhead Wilson* (1894), a novel that responds to studies of twins and fingerprints published by Francis Galton, the father of eugenics.
10. Donald A. MacKenzie, *Statistics in Britain, 1865–1930: The Social Construction of Scientific Knowledge* (Edinburgh: Edinburgh University Press, 1981), 18.
11. Nicole Hahn Rafter, "White Trash: Eugenics as Social Ideology," *Society* 26, no. 1 (November–December 1988): 44.
12. Mark Twain, *Adventures of Huckleberry Finn* (New York: W. W. Norton, 1999), 75.

13 Frederick Douglass, "The Race Problem" (Bethel Library and Historical Association, Metropolitan A.M.E. Church, Washington, DC, October 21, 1890), 10, Daniel Murray Pamphlet Collection, Library of Congress, https://lccn.loc.gov/74171961.
14 Marietta Holley, *Samantha on the Race Problem* (New York: Dodd, Mead, 1892), 248.
15 Among the most influential historical studies of poor white southerners are Charles C. Bolton, *Poor Whites of the Antebellum South: Tenants and Laborers in Central North Carolina and Northeast Mississippi* (Durham, NC: Duke University Press, 1994); Wayne Flynt, *Dixie's Forgotten People: The South's Poor Whites* (Bloomington: Indiana University Press, 1979); Jeff Forret, *Race Relations at the Margins: Slaves and Poor Whites in the Antebellum Southern Countryside* (Baton Rouge: Louisiana State University Press, 2006); and Keri Leigh Merritt, *Masterless Men: Poor Whites and Slavery in the Antebellum South* (New York: Cambridge University Press, 2017).
16 The first decade of the twenty-first century saw the publication of perceptive anthropological and sociological examinations of poor white people; see, for example, John Hartigan Jr., *Odd Tribes: Toward a Cultural Analysis of White People* (Durham, NC: Duke University Press, 2005); Kirby Moss, *The Color of Class: Poor Whites and the Paradox of Privilege* (Philadelphia: University of Pennsylvania Press, 2003); and Matt Wray, *Not Quite White: White Trash and the Boundaries of Whiteness* (Durham, NC: Duke University Press, 2006).
17 Arlie Russell Hochschild's *Strangers in Their Own Land: Anger and Mourning on the American Right* (New York: New Press, 2016) and J. D. Vance's *Hillbilly Elegy: A Memoir of a Family and Culture in Crisis* (New York: HarperCollins, 2016) generated a lot of buzz – in part because they were credited with helping to explain how Donald Trump won the 2016 presidential election.
18 Richard H. Brodhead, *Cultures of Letters: Scenes of Reading and Writing in Nineteenth-Century America* (Chicago: University of Chicago Press, 1993), 137.
19 Shelley Fisher Fishkin contends that "the model for Huck Finn's voice was a black child instead of a white one and that this child's speech sparked in Twain a sense of the possibilities of a vernacular narrator" in *Was Huck Black? Mark Twain and African-American Voices* (New York: Oxford University Press, 1993), 4. The voices of black southerners – in literature and in life – undoubtedly shaped Twain's art. So too did the poor white vernacular speakers Twain read about in southwestern humor stories and local color sketches and encountered throughout his life.
20 *Autobiography of Mark Twain*, ed. Harriet Elinor Smith, vol. 1 (Berkeley: University of California Press, 2010), 397.
21 The fact that most American epithets for poor whites – including cracker, hillbilly, redneck, and white trash – originated in the South suggests the outsized role that poor white southerners play in rousing class-based anxieties in the United States.

22 C. Vann Woodward, *The Burden of Southern History* (Baton Rouge: Louisiana State University Press, 2008), 17.
23 Jennifer Rae Greeson, *Our South: Geographic Fantasy and the Rise of National Literature* (Cambridge, MA: Harvard University Press, 2010), 1.
24 Evert Jansen Wendell, "Boys' Clubs in New York," in *The Poor in Great Cities* (New York: Charles Scribner's Sons, 1895), 159.
25 Willard Parsons, "The Story of the Fresh-Air Fund," *Scribner's Magazine* 9, April 1891, 518.
26 Clare de Graffenried, "The Georgia Cracker in the Cotton Mills," *Century Illustrated Monthly Magazine* 41, February 1891, 484.
27 Alexandra Minna Stern, "'We Cannot Make a Silk Purse Out of a Sow's Ear': Eugenics in the Hoosier Heartland," *Indiana Magazine of History* 103, no. 1 (March 2007): 20.
28 Charles W. Chesnutt, *The Colonel's Dream* (New York: Random House, 2005), 302.
29 Kenneth S. Lynn, *Mark Twain and Southwestern Humor* (Boston: Little, Brown, 1959), 68, 69.
30 Skitt [Hardin E. Taliaferro], "Ham Rachel, of Alabama," in *Fisher's River (North Carolina) Scenes and Characters* (New York: Harper and Brothers, 1859), 267.
31 Margaret Mitchell, *Gone with the Wind* (New York: Macmillan, 1963), 537.
32 Ibid., 509.
33 Ibid., 537.
34 Scarlett O'Hara twice notes that poor white Confederate soldiers have sallow faces; this coloration is perhaps one of the clues Scarlett and her sisters use to decipher the socioeconomic status of the troops they encounter. In giving her nineteenth-century poor whites yellowish hues, Mitchell followed in the footsteps of earlier accounts of poor white Georgians including (to offer just a couple of examples from titles mentioned already) Clare de Graffenried's essay "The Georgia Cracker in the Cotton Mill" and Harry Stillwell Edwards's story "A Battle in Crackerdom."
35 Mitchell, *Gone with the Wind*, 537, 3.
36 E. P. Thompson, *The Making of the English Working Class* (New York: Random House, 1963), 9.
37 Lillian Smith, *Killers of the Dream* (New York: W. W. Norton, 1994), 163. All subsequent references are to this edition and appear parenthetically in the text.
38 Pierre Bourdieu, *Practical Reason: On the Theory of Action* (Stanford, CA: Stanford University Press, 1998), 9.
39 Joel Williamson, *The Crucible of Race: Black/White Relations in the American South since Emancipation* (New York: Oxford University Press, 1984), 292.
40 Gavin Jones's *American Hungers: The Problem of Poverty in U.S. Literature, 1840–1945* (Princeton, NJ: Princeton University Press, 2007) discusses more than a century's worth of sharecroppers, beggars, and factory hands who appear in American literature. Keith Gandal examines 1890s representations of the urban poor in *The Virtues of the Vicious: Jacob Riis, Stephen Crane, and*

the Spectacle of the Slum (New York: Oxford University Press, 1997). Amy Schrager Lang's *The Syntax of Class: Writing Inequality in Nineteenth-Century America* (Princeton, NJ: Princeton University Press, 2003) delves into how mid-nineteenth-century novels engage with class differences and handle class conflicts.

41 Studies focusing specifically on poor whites in southern literature include Sarah Robertson, *Poverty Politics: Poor Whites in Contemporary Southern Writing* (Jackson: University Press of Mississippi, 2019); Susan J. Tracy, *In the Master's Eye: Representations of Women, Blacks, and Poor Whites in Antebellum Southern Literature* (Amherst: University of Massachusetts Press, 1995); Sylvia Jenkins Cook, *From Tobacco Road to Route 66: The Southern Poor White in Fiction* (Chapel Hill: University of North Carolina Press, 1976) and *Erskine Caldwell and the Fiction of Poverty: The Flesh and the Spirit* (Baton Rouge: Louisiana State University Press, 1991); and Shields McIlwaine, *The Southern Poor-White from Lubberland to Tobacco Road* (Norman: University of Oklahoma Press, 1939).

42 Laura Hapke, *Labor's Text: The Worker in American Fiction* (New Brunswick, NJ: Rutgers University Press, 2001); Janet Zandy, *Hands: Physical Labor, Class, and Cultural Work* (New Brunswick, NJ: Rutgers University Press, 2004).

43 Eric Schocket, *Vanishing Moments: Class and American Literature* (Ann Arbor: University of Michigan Press, 2006); Joe Shapiro, *The Illiberal Imagination: Class and the Rise of the U.S. Novel* (Charlottesville: University of Virginia Press, 2017).

44 Barbara Foley, *Radical Representations: Politics and Form in U.S. Proletarian Fiction, 1929–1941* (Durham, NC: Duke University Press, 1993); Paula Rabinowitz, *Labor and Desire: Women's Revolutionary Fiction in Depression America* (Chapel Hill: University of North Carolina Press, 1991).

45 Michael Denning, *Mechanic Accents: Dime Novels and Working-Class Culture in America* (London: Verso, 1987); Lori Merish, *Archives of Labor: Working-Class Women and Literary Culture in the Antebellum United States* (Durham, NC: Duke University Press, 2017).

46 Rick Bragg, *The Most They Ever Had* (San Francisco: MacAdam/Cage, 2009), 14.

47 Ibid., 17.

48 Daniel R. Hundley, *Social Relations in Our Southern States* (New York: Arno, 1973), 262.

49 Zandy, *Hands*, 90–2.

50 Ibid., 90.

51 Andrew Hoberek, *The Twilight of the Middle Class: Post–World War II American Fiction and White-Collar Work* (Princeton, NJ: Princeton University Press, 2005); Stephen Schryer, *Fantasies of the New Class: Ideologies of Professionalism in Post–World War II American Fiction* (New York: Columbia University Press, 2011); Robert Seguin, *Around Quitting Time: Work and Middle-Class Fantasy in American Fiction* (Durham, NC:

Duke University Press, 2001); and Christopher P. Wilson, *White Collar Fictions: Class and Social Representation in American Literature, 1885–1925* (Athens: University of Georgia Press, 1992).

52 Shannon Sullivan, *Good White People: The Problem with Middle-Class White Anti-Racism* (Albany: State University of New York Press, 2014), 8.
53 James Agee and Walker Evans, *Let Us Now Praise Famous Men: Three Tenant Families* (Boston: Houghton Mifflin, 2001), 5.
54 This image was not used in the 1941 edition of *Let Us Now Praise Famous Men* (which included thirty-one photographs) or the second edition, published in 1960, which reproduced sixty-two photographs by Evans.
55 Lincoln Kirstein, "Photographs of America: Walker Evans," in *American Photographs*, by Walker Evans (New York: Museum of Modern Art, 1988), 197.
56 In *The Real Thing: Imitation and Authenticity in American Culture, 1880–1940* (Chapel Hill: University of North Carolina Press, 1989), 239, Miles Orvell observes that Evans "found in the camera ... an instrument with a capacity for objective treatment of the visible world." In *In Visible Light: Photography and the American Writer, 1840–1940* (New York: Oxford University Press, 1987), 190, Carol Shloss contends that Evans "wanted people to rely on his photographs as unassailable and authoritative revelations of human life."
57 Dale Maharidge and Michael Williamson, *And Their Children after Them* (New York: Pantheon Books, 1989), 140.
58 In *Distinction: A Social Critique of the Judgement of Taste*, trans. Richard Nice (Cambridge, MA: Harvard University Press, 1984), 77, Pierre Bourdieu wrote that "tastes and distastes, sympathies and aversions ... forge the unconscious unity of a class." Evans's photographs of poor white southerners in Hale County lay bare these unconscious processes. The middle and upper classes can respond sympathetically to the *object* – the work of art – and thereby come together as the cognoscenti of the arts. At the same time, the photographs do little to trouble longstanding stereotypes about poor white people, and thus can inflame adverse feelings that reinforce class divides.
59 May Lou Zoll, "Susanna," *Peterson Magazine* 6, January 1896, 85, 86.
60 De Graffenried, "Georgia Cracker," 490.
61 William Faulkner, *Absalom, Absalom!* (New York: Vintage International, 1990), 149.
62 Peter Sekaer captured photographs of Evans at work in 1935 in Bethlehem, Pennsylvania, that make clear how Evans and his tripod-mounted large-format camera cast the shadows visible in half of the pictures Evans took of Flora Tingle in front of a barn. Sekaer's prints, although not on view at the Metropolitan Museum of Art, can be seen on the museum's website.
63 Evans misidentified this woman as Dora Mae Tengle, and so this is the name associated with her photographs in the Farm Security Administration's Office of War Information Photograph Collection held at the Library of Congress. Agee assigned pseudonyms to the Alabamians he wrote about in *Let Us Now Praise Famous Men*; this woman appears in that text as Paralee Ricketts. The

real name of the nineteen-year-old woman captured on film that summer in Hale County was Flora Tingle.
64 W. J. T. Mitchell, *Picture Theory: Essays on Verbal and Visual Representation* (Chicago: University of Chicago Press, 1994), 294.
65 Agee and Evans, *Let Us Now Praise Famous Men*, 322.
66 Nancy Glazener identifies the *Atlantic Monthly*, *Century Illustrated Monthly Magazine*, *Scribner's Magazine*, and other prominent magazines published during the Gilded Age as the "*Atlantic* group" in *Reading for Realism: The History of a U.S. Literary Institution, 1850–1910* (Durham, NC: Duke University Press, 1997).

Chapter 1

1 Amy Kaplan, "Nation, Region, and Empire," in *Columbia History of the American Novel*, ed. Emory Elliott (New York: Columbia University Press, 1991), 251.
2 Ibid.
3 Brodhead, *Cultures of Letters*, 137.
4 Stephanie Foote, *Regional Fictions: Culture and Identity in Nineteenth-Century American Literature* (Madison: University of Wisconsin Press, 2001), 6.
5 Eric J. Sundquist, "Realism and Regionalism," in *Columbia Literary History of the United States*, ed. Emory Elliott (New York: Columbia University Press, 1988), 509.
6 Brodhead, *Cultures of Letters*, 119.
7 Ibid., 120.
8 Frank Luther Mott, *A History of American Magazines*, vol. 2 (Cambridge, MA: Harvard University Press, 1938), 494.
9 Glazener, *Reading for Realism*, 24.
10 The *Atlantic Monthly* published "The Goophered Grapevine" in 1887, "Po' Sandy" in 1888, and "Dave's Neckliss" in 1889. Houghton Mifflin, the *Atlantic Monthly*'s parent company, brought out *The Conjure Woman* in 1899.
11 Natalie J. Ring, *The Problem South: Region, Empire, and the New Liberal State, 1880–1930* (Athens: University of Georgia Press, 2012), 136.
12 Rayford Whittingham Logan, *The Negro in American Life and Thought: The Nadir, 1877–1901* (New York: Dial, 1954), 52.
13 Brodhead, *Cultures of Letters*, 117.
14 "Then and Now in the Old Dominion," *Atlantic Monthly* 9, April 1862, 500.
15 E. H. Derby, "Resources of the South," *Atlantic Monthly* 10, October 1862, 506.
16 E. Atkinson, "Taxation No Burden," *Atlantic Monthly* 10, July 1862, 118.
17 "American Civilization," *Atlantic Monthly* 9, April 1862, 510.
18 See, for example, "The Reign of King Cotton," *Atlantic Monthly* 7, April 1861, 456–7; and Edmund Kirke [James R. Gilmore], "John Jordan," *Atlantic Monthly* 16, October 1865, 434–45.

19 Hundley, *Social Relations*, 254.
20 Ibid., 258.
21 In the early days of Reconstruction, correspondents for the *Atlantic Monthly* and other periodicals traveled throughout the South, tasked with reporting on conditions there. While my quotations come from book-length accounts of these tours, two of the three writers I cite – Andrews and Trowbridge – published in the *Atlantic Monthly* during this same period.
22 Whitelaw Reid, *After the War: A Tour of the Southern States, 1865–1866* (New York: Harper and Row, 1965), 325.
23 Sidney Andrews, *The South since the War: As Shown by Fourteen Weeks of Travel and Observation in Georgia and the Carolinas* (Boston: Ticknor and Fields, 1866), 177.
24 Ibid., 336.
25 See, for example, J. T. Trowbridge, *The South: A Tour of Its Battle-Fields and Ruined Cities* (New York: Arno, 1969), 185; and Reid, *After the War*, 221.
26 Hundley, *Social Relations*, 251.
27 J. W. De Forest, "Drawing Bureau Rations," *Harper's New Monthly Magazine* 36, May 1868, 794.
28 De Forest may have come by his notion of natural selection from reading Darwin's seminal text or from perusing a work influenced by Darwin's analysis – perhaps Francis Galton's 1865 essay "Hereditary Talent and Character," in which Galton used his cousin Darwin's idea of natural selection to posit connections between heredity and morality.
29 De Forest, "Drawing Bureau Rations," 798.
30 Richard L. Dugdale, *"The Jukes": A Study in Crime, Pauperism, Disease and Heredity; Also, Further Studies of Criminals*, 3rd ed. (New York: G. P. Putnam's Sons, 1877), 8.
31 Nicole Hahn Rafter, *Creating Born Criminals* (Urbana: University of Illinois Press, 1997), 38.
32 D. O. Kellogg, "The Pauper Question," *Atlantic Monthly* 51, May 1883, 639.
33 Henry W. Holland, "Heredity," *Atlantic Monthly* 52, October 1883, 450.
34 Octave Thanet [Alice French], "The Indoor Pauper: A Study," *Atlantic Monthly* 47, June 1881, 756.
35 Edwards, "A Battle in Crackerdom," 464.
36 For an overview of this debate, see the first chapter of Emily Satterwhite's *Dear Appalachia: Readers, Identity, and Popular Fiction since 1878* (Lexington: University Press of Kentucky, 2011).
37 Emma E. Brown, "Children's Labor: A Problem," *Atlantic Monthly* 46, December 1880, 791.
38 Daniel Pick, *Faces of Degeneration: A European Disorder, c. 1848–c. 1918* (Cambridge: Cambridge University Press, 1989), 195.
39 Charles Egbert Craddock [Mary Noailles Murfree], "The Romance of Sunrise Rock," *Atlantic Monthly* 46, December 1880, 776.
40 Ibid., 776, 778.
41 Ibid., 778.

42 Ibid., 780, 777, 783, 778.
43 Edward King, "The Great South," *Scribner's Monthly* 8, August 1874, 386–7.
44 De Graffenried, "Georgia Cracker," 484.
45 Ibid.
46 Thanet [French], "Indoor Pauper," 756.
47 Charles Egbert Craddock [Mary Noailles Murfree], "Over on the T'other Mounting," *Atlantic Monthly* 47, June 1881, 747.
48 Ibid., 742.
49 D. O. Kellogg, "The Principle and Advantage of Association in Charities," *Journal of Social Science* 12 (December 1880): 88.
50 Kellogg, "Pauper Question," 639.
51 Craddock [Murfree], "The 'Harnt,'" 660–3.
52 Ibid., 674, 663, 674, 667.
53 Holland, "Heredity," 450.
54 Charles Egbert Craddock [Mary Noailles Murfree], "A Playin' of Old Sledge at the Settlemint," *Atlantic Monthly* 52, October 1883, 544–5.
55 Ibid., 548–9, 551.
56 Ibid., 545, 550.
57 Ibid., 545, 547, 545.
58 William Byrd, *The Westover Manuscripts: Containing the History of the Dividing Line Betwixt Virginia and North Carolina; A Journey to the Land of Eden, A.D. 1733; and A Progress to the Mines. Written from 1728 to 1736, and Now First Published* (Petersburg, VA: Edmund and Julian C. Ruffin, 1841), 27–8.
59 Frederick Law Olmsted, *A Journey in the Seaboard Slave States: With Remarks on Their Economy* (New York: Dix and Edwards, 1856), 506–7.
60 Andrews, *South since the War*, 177.
61 W. G. Ramsay, "The Physiological Differences between the European (or White Man) and the Negro," *Southern Agriculturist and Register of Rural Affairs: Adapted to the Southern Section of the United States* 12, no. 6 (June 1839): 293.
62 Edmund Ruffin, *The Political Economy of Slavery; or, The Institution Considered in Regard to its Influence on Public Wealth and the General Welfare* (Washington, DC: Lemuel Towers, 1857), 15.
63 Thomas Nelson Page, *In Ole Virginia; or, Marse Chan and Other Stories* (Nashville: J. S. Sanders, 1991), 10. All subsequent references are to this edition and are given in the text.
64 Thomas Nelson Page, *The Negro: The Southerner's Problem* (New York: Charles Scribner's Sons, 1904), 80.
65 Charles W. Chesnutt, *The Conjure Woman and Other Conjure Tales*, ed. Richard H. Brodhead (Durham, NC: Duke University Press, 1993), 32. All subsequent references are to this edition and are cited in the text. I am following Brodhead in referring to the conjure tales as the seven stories published as *The Conjure Woman* in 1899 as well as seven additional stories that employ the conjure formula.

66 Thorstein Veblen, *The Theory of the Leisure Class: An Economic Study of Institutions* (New York: Macmillan, 1912), 43.
67 Ibid., 40.
68 In a 1903 essay, for instance, Chesnutt praised Washington as an educator imparting "manual training, *thrift* and character-building" (emphasis mine) but also decried his political positions, which "have not always been so wise nor so happy." Charles W. Chesnutt, "The Disenfranchisement of the Negro," in *The Negro Problem: A Series of Articles by Representative American Negroes of To-day*, ed. Booker T. Washington et al. (New York: James Pott, 1903), 110.
69 Booker T. Washington, *Up from Slavery: An Autobiography* (New York: Doubleday, 1901), 73.
70 Booker T. Washington, "The Awakening of the Negro," *Atlantic Monthly* 78, September 1896, 323.
71 Ibid., 328.
72 Craddock [Murfree], "A Playin' of Old Sledge," 545.
73 Sherwood Bonner, *Suwanee River Tales* (Boston: Roberts Brothers, 1884), 3, 9.
74 Michael Flusche, "On the Color Line: Charles Waddell Chesnutt," *North Carolina Historical Review* 53, no. 1 (January 1976): 23. Richard Brodhead offers a similar but even more forceful take on the plantation formula as enemy territory, arguing that Chesnutt viewed "the Joel Chandler Harris – Thomas Nelson Page formula as a deeply distortionary representation enforced by organs of dominant-cultural expression." See Brodhead, *Cultures of Letters*, 206.
75 Brodhead, *Cultures of Letters*, 196.
76 Kenneth M. Price, "Charles Chesnutt, the *Atlantic Monthly*, and the Intersection of African-American Fiction and Elite Culture," in *Periodical Literature in Nineteenth-Century America*, ed. Kenneth M. Price and Susan Belasco Smith (Charlottesville: University Press of Virginia, 1995), 265.
77 Mark Twain, *Life on the Mississippi* (Boston: James R. Osgood, 1883), 442.
78 Chesnutt was familiar with Cable's local color collection *Old Creole Days* (1879) and novel *The Grandissimes* (1880). Tourgée's novel *A Fool's Errand* (1879), a story of race and class relations in the Reconstruction South (set on a former plantation), inspired a March 1880 journal entry in which Chesnutt moved from contemplating the handsome royalties garnered by Tourgée's bestseller to imagining himself "writ[ing] a far better book about the South than Judge Tourgee or Mrs. Stowe has written." Charles W. Chesnutt, *The Journals of Charles W. Chesnutt*, ed. Richard H. Brodhead (Durham, NC: Duke University Press, 1993), 125.
79 Kenneth W. Warren observes that plantation fiction's "romanticized views of blacks" could serve those "who wished to discredit or roll back civil rights gains" while also offering a pre-industrial fantasy "allowing whites to indulge their nostalgia for a lifestyle that was no longer available to them." Warren,

Black and White Strangers: Race and American Literary Realism (Chicago: University of Chicago Press, 1993), 119.

80 I disagree with Brodhead's contention that Chesnutt's letters reveal that he felt "ambivalent" about plantation fiction or saw it as "deeply distortionary." To be sure, in his letters Chesnutt critiqued Harris's and Page's works, lamenting their black characters' "dog-like fidelity and devotion" toward enslavers and decrying the writers' representations of "the sentimental and devoted negro who prefers kicks to half-pence." But Chesnutt also observed that "the writings of Harris and Page ... have furnished my chief incentive to write something upon the other side of this very vital question," which suggests that Chesnutt took issue with not the plantation formula but rather the sociopolitical orientation of its major practitioners and embraced the opportunity to flesh out "the other side" for readers. Brodhead, *Cultures of Letters*, 206; Chesnutt, *To Be an Author: Letters of Charles W. Chesnutt, 1889–1905*, ed. Joseph R. McElrath Jr. and Robert C. Leitz III (Princeton, NJ: Princeton University Press, 1997), 65, 66, 167.

81 See Lacy K. Ford, *Deliver Us from Evil: The Slavery Question in the Old South* (New York: Oxford University Press, 2009), 352 for Virginians' responses to the insurrection.

82 John M. Grammer, "Plantation Fiction," in *A Companion to the Literature and Culture of the American South*, ed. Richard Gray and Owen Robinson (Malden, MA: Blackwell, 2004), 64.

83 Quoted in Jean Fagan Yellin, *The Intricate Knot: Black Figures in American Literature, 1776–1863* (New York: New York University Press, 1972), 59.

84 Drew Gilpin Faust, introduction to *The Ideology of Slavery: Proslavery Thought in the Antebellum South, 1830–1860*, ed. Drew Gilpin Faust (Baton Rouge: Louisiana State University Press, 1981), 4.

85 Tracy, *In the Master's Eye*, 179.

86 Ibid., 180, 185.

87 Ibid., 179.

88 Caroline Lee Hentz, *The Planter's Northern Bride* (Philadelphia, PA: T. B. Peterson, 1854), 32.

89 Ibid., 31–2.

90 William R. Taylor, *Cavalier and Yankee: The Old South and American National Character* (New York: Harper and Row, 1961), 96.

91 Grammer, "Plantation Fiction," 69.

92 Anthony Wilson, "Narrative and Counternarrative in *The Leopard's Spots* and *The Marrow of Tradition*," in *The Oxford Handbook of the Literature of the U.S. South*, ed. Fred Hobson and Barbara Ladd (New York: Oxford University Press, 2016), 215; Trent A. Watts, *One Homogeneous People: Narratives of White Southern Identity, 1890–1920* (Knoxville: University of Tennessee Press, 2010), 56.

93 Robert Hemenway, introduction to *Uncle Remus: His Songs and His Sayings*, by Joel Chandler Harris (New York: Penguin, 1982), 20.

94 Ibid.

95 Social continuity characterizes "Legends of the Old Plantation," a section of *Uncle Remus* filled with framed animal tales, not "His Sayings," a group of short, explicitly political stories about life in the South during Reconstruction. But both sets of stories expose Harris's apprehensions about social change. For example, tales in "His Sayings" criticize post-Emancipation educational opportunities and paint a dire picture of free black labor in the South, suggesting that chain gangs and migration are among African Americans' best options.
96 Joel Chandler Harris, *Uncle Remus: His Songs and His Sayings* (New York: Penguin, 1982), 76.
97 Ibid., 121.
98 Ibid., 129.
99 Ibid., 130.
100 Hemenway, introduction to Harris, *Uncle Remus*, 19.
101 Harris, *Uncle Remus*, 130.
102 Ibid.
103 Eric J. Sundquist, *To Wake the Nations: Race in the Making of American Literature* (Cambridge, MA: Belknap Press of Harvard University Press, 1993), 287.
104 Lucinda H. MacKethan argues that "the grave deficiencies of the masters [Page] created for 'No Haid Pawn' and 'Ole 'Stracted' have the inevitable effect of calling to judgment the system as a whole." I disagree. In each story, the antagonist is an outsider – a French Creole from the West Indies and a socially aspirant white, respectively – and each text spotlights how out of sync the interloper is with the Virginia cavalier tradition: the West Indian's "personal characteristics and habits were unique in that country" (168), while Ephraim's landlord, unlike a ruling-class white person, "don' know nuttin 'bout black folks [because he] ain' nuver been fotch up wid 'em" (147). Page's tales affirm the southern social system by demonstrating the disastrous consequences of diverging from its hierarchical organization of whites. See MacKethan, "Plantation Fiction, 1865–1900," in *The History of Southern Literature*, ed. Louis D. Rubin Jr. (Baton Rouge: Louisiana State University Press, 1985), 214.
105 Henry W. Grady, "The South and Her Problem," in *Life of Henry W. Grady Including His Writings and Speeches: A Memorial Volume*, ed. Joel Chandler Harris (New York: Cassell, 1890), 100.
106 Robert C. Nowatzki, "'Passing' in a White Genre: Charles W. Chesnutt's Negotiations of the Plantation Tradition in *The Conjure Woman*," *American Literary Realism, 1870–1910* 27, no. 2 (Winter 1995): 24.
107 Harris, *Uncle Remus*, 130.
108 Sundquist, *To Wake the Nations*, 286.
109 Faulkner, *Absalom, Absalom!*, 187. Formerly enslaved people's accounts confirm that some planters did refuse to receive poor white callers at the front door. Robert Williams, for one, explained that when poor white people

"would come 'roun to de big house, dey had to come to de back do', an' de white folks would ask dem, 'What in de hell do you want?'" Charles L. Perdue Jr., Thomas E. Barden, and Robert K. Phillips, eds., *Weevils in the Wheat: Interviews with Virginia Ex-Slaves* (Charlottesville: University of Virginia Press, 1976), 326.
110 Harris, *Uncle Remus*, 130.
111 Here and elsewhere, plantation fiction showcases family-like affective ties between enslaved people and enslavers while assiduously avoiding the fact that centuries of state-sanctioned rape had produced real familial ties between the two groups.
112 See, for example, the conclusion of "The Conjurer's Revenge."
113 Robert Hemenway, "The Functions of Folklore in Charles Chesnutt's *The Conjure Woman*," *Journal of the Folklore Institute* 13, no. 3 (1976): 301.
114 Judith Fetterley and Marjorie Pryse, *Writing Out of Place: Regionalism, Women, and American Literary Culture* (Urbana: University of Illinois Press, 2003), 18.
115 Heather Tirado Gilligan, "Reading, Race, and Charles Chesnutt's 'Uncle Julius' Tales," *ELH* 74, no. 1 (Spring 2007): 204.
116 Price, "Intersection," 264.
117 Brodhead, *Cultures of Letters*, 206.
118 William Alexander Percy, *Lanterns on the Levee: Recollections of a Planter's Son* (Baton Rouge: Louisiana State University Press, 2006), 283.
119 Ibid.
120 Ibid., 18.
121 Watts, *One Homogeneous People*, 43.

Chapter 2

1 William Faulkner, *As I Lay Dying* (New York: Vintage, 1990), 229. All subsequent references are to this edition and page numbers are included in the text.
2 See André Bleikasten, *Faulkner's "As I Lay Dying,"* trans. Roger Little, rev. and enl. ed. (Bloomington: Indiana University Press, 1973), 13; and Michael Millgate, *The Achievement of William Faulkner* (New York: Random House, 1966), 108.
3 See Cleanth Brooks, *William Faulkner: The Yoknapatawpha Country* (New Haven, CT: Yale University Press, 1963), 143–4. At least two scholars – John T. Matthews and Warwick Wadlington – have noted that Jewel addresses the "wrong" man in this scene, although both interpret this scene differently than I do. See Matthews, "*As I Lay Dying* in the Machine Age," in *National Identities and Post-Americanist Narratives,* ed. Donald E. Pease (Durham, NC: Duke University Press, 1994), 91–2; and Wadlington, "*As I Lay Dying*": *Stories Out of Stories* (New York: Maxwell Macmillan International, 1992), 94–6.

4 William Faulkner, *As I Lay Dying: Holograph Manuscript and Carbon Typescript*, ed. Thomas L. McHaney (New York: Garland, 1986), 190.
5 Grace Elizabeth Hale describes how white-on-black violence has been used to forge a sense of white unity in *Making Whiteness: The Culture of Segregation in the South, 1890–1940* (New York: Pantheon Books, 1998), esp. 227–39.
6 Fredric Jameson, *Postmodernism, or, The Cultural Logic of Late Capitalism* (Durham, NC: Duke University Press, 1991), 309.
7 Ibid., 311.
8 Julie Beth Napolin, "'Ravel Out into the No-Wind, No-Sound': The Audiophonic Form of *As I Lay Dying*," in *Fifty Years after Faulkner*, ed. Jay Watson (Jackson: University Press of Mississippi, 2016), 122–37; Libby Catchings, "Elegy, Effigy: Alchemy and the Displacement of Lament in *As I Lay Dying*," *Faulkner Journal* 28, no. 2 (Fall 2014): 25–38; Heather E. Holcombe, "Faulkner on Feminine Hygiene, or, How Margaret Sanger Sold Dewey Dell a Bad Abortion," *MFS: Modern Fiction Studies* 57, no. 2 (Summer 2011): 203–29; Susan Scott Parrish, *The Flood Year 1927: A Cultural History* (Princeton, NJ: Princeton University Press, 2017).
9 William Faulkner, "An Introduction to *The Sound and the Fury*," *Mississippi Quarterly* 26, no. 3 (Summer 1973): 412.
10 Richard C. Moreland, *Faulkner and Modernism: Rereading and Rewriting* (Madison: University of Wisconsin Press, 1990), 25.
11 Granville Hicks, *The Great Tradition: An Interpretation of American Literature since the Civil War*, rev. ed. (New York: Macmillan, 1935), 266–7.
12 Mike Gold, "Notes of the Month," *New Masses*, September 1930, 5.
13 John T. Matthews, "Faulkner and Proletarian Literature," in *Faulkner in Cultural Context: Faulkner and Yoknapatawpha, 1995*, ed. Donald M. Kartiganer and Ann J. Abadie (Jackson: University Press of Mississippi, 1997), 189.
14 See Erskine Caldwell, *Tobacco Road* (Athens: University of Georgia Press, 1995), 63; and Erskine Caldwell and Margaret Bourke-White, *You Have Seen Their Faces* (New York: Viking, 1937), 165.
15 Twelve Southerners, *I'll Take My Stand: The South and the Agrarian Tradition* (Baton Rouge: Louisiana State University Press, 1977), 12.
16 Ibid., 234.
17 Ibid., 12, 14.
18 Ibid., 71.
19 Daniel J. Singal, *The War Within: From Victorian to Modernist Thought in the South, 1919–1945* (Chapel Hill: University of North Carolina Press, 1982), 212.
20 My formulation of the sweat economy draws on Marx's discussion of estranged labor in the *Economic and Philosophic Manuscripts of 1844*; see Robert C. Tucker, ed., *The Marx-Engels Reader*, 2nd ed. (New York: W. W. Norton, 1978), 70–81.
21 Faulkner, *Absalom, Absalom!*, 78.

22 Ibid., 183, 191. With this critique of brutish toil that far outstrips its reward, which describes Sutpen's sister's domestic labors, Faulkner might have been specifically challenging Andrew Lytle. In his contribution to *I'll Take My Stand*, Lytle waxed poetic over the value that farm women's labors accrue by being tedious and time consuming. For instance, contrasting the effort of making butter – milking, straining, cooling, churning, salting, molding, and again cooling – with the ease of purchasing it, Lytle insisted that women do well to embrace the more labor-intensive option, writing that "the process has been long, to some extent tedious, but profitable, because insomuch as it has taken time and care and intelligence, by that much does it have a meaning." Twelve Southerners, *I'll Take My Stand*, 223.
23 William Faulkner, *Collected Stories of William Faulkner* (New York: Vintage, 1977), 12.
24 Twelve Southerners, *I'll Take My Stand*, xlvii.
25 Calvin Bedient, "Pride and Nakedness: *As I Lay Dying*," *Modern Language Quarterly* 29, no. 1 (March 1968): 73.
26 Dorothy J. Hale, "*As I Lay Dying*'s Heterogeneous Discourse," *NOVEL: A Forum on Fiction* 23, no. 1 (Autumn 1989): 20.
27 See Tucker, *Marx-Engels Reader*, 79, 74–5.
28 Matthews, "Machine Age," 75.
29 See Tucker, *Marx-Engels Reader*, 302–29, esp. 307–8.
30 Scholars tackling Faulkner's treatment of time often draw on French philosopher Henri Bergson's theories of time and consciousness. These analyses, steeped in the intricacies of Bergson's ideas about duration, stress the aesthetic logic of temporal fluidity at the expense of its social significance. Given that Cleanth Brooks and André Bleikasten argue, respectively, that Faulkner found in Bergson "confirmation ... of something that he already knew," making the relationship between the two men one of "confluence rather than influence," I will not engage with Bergson's work in my analysis. See Brooks, *William Faulkner: Toward Yoknapatawpha and Beyond* (New Haven, CT: Yale University Press, 1978), 255; and Bleikasten, *The Ink of Melancholy: Faulkner's Novels from "The Sound and the Fury" to "Light in August"* (Bloomington: Indiana University Press, 1990), 374.
31 Jay Watson, "The Rhetoric of Exhaustion and the Exhaustion of Rhetoric: Erskine Caldwell in the Thirties," *Mississippi Quarterly* 46, no. 2 (Spring 1993): 219.
32 Leigh Anne Duck, *The Nation's Region: Southern Modernism, Segregation, and U.S. Nationalism* (Athens: University of Georgia Press, 2006), 99.
33 Bleikasten, *Faulkner's "As I Lay Dying,"* 132; Cook, *From Tobacco Road*, 39.
34 Susan Willis, "Learning from the Banana," *American Quarterly* 39, no. 4 (Winter 1987): 587.
35 Matthews, "Machine Age," 83.
36 As Charles A. Peek rightly remarks, the Bundrens are "unable to achieve the American dream whether through frontiersmanship (Jewel), a work ethic (Cash), patriotic service (Darl), or education (Addie)," and this failure to find

success along the roads that purportedly lead to it fuels "the insistent force of [their] desires" for consumer goods. Peek, "'A-laying There, Right Up to My Door': As American *As I Lay Dying*," in *Faulkner in America: Faulkner and Yoknapatawpha 1998*, ed. Joseph R. Urgo and Ann J. Abadie (Jackson: University Press of Mississippi, 2001), 131.

37 Georg Simmel described a "metropolitan blasé attitude." See Simmel, *Simmel on Culture: Selected Writings*, ed. David Frisby and Mike Featherstone (London: Sage Publications, 1997), 178.
38 Cook, *From Tobacco Road*, 41.
39 William Goodell Frost, "Our Contemporary Ancestors in the Southern Mountains," *Atlantic Monthly* 83, March 1899, 311.
40 Ibid., 319.
41 Ibid., 313.
42 Lothrop Stoddard, *The Revolt against Civilization: The Menace of the Under Man* (New York: Charles Scribner's Sons, 1922), 22.
43 A. N. J. den Hollander, "The Tradition of 'Poor Whites,'" in *Culture in the South*, ed. William T. Couch (Chapel Hill: University of North Carolina Press, 1934), 425.
44 Evan Watkins, *Throwaways: Work Culture and Consumer Education* (Stanford, CA: Stanford University Press, 1993), 39.
45 As these snippets make clear, Faulkner peppered MacGowan's language with some of the same nonstandard grammatical features that mark rural characters' speech. These linguistic similarities underscore the educational and cultural correspondences between people like MacGowan and people like the Bundrens – connections that MacGowan tries to downplay by repeatedly distinguishing Dewey Dell's country ways from his citified ways. But his idiolect undermines these efforts. Across the chapter he narrates, MacGowan offers up half a dozen instances of "aint," more than a dozen double negatives, and many incorrect verb tenses, including "I says." Anse, Armstid, Darl, Samson, and Tull also use "I says," but sparingly, whereas MacGowan deploys this formulation forty-six times in his chapter.
46 Matthews, "Machine Age," 72–3.
47 This passage has traditionally been addressed in terms of the relationship between character and language in the novel, with critics accounting for the ostensible disparity between young Vardaman and his sophisticated narration; see, for example, Stephen M. Ross, "'Voice' in Narrative Texts: The Example of *As I Lay Dying*," *PMLA* 94, no. 2 (March 1979): 302; and Eric J. Sundquist, *Faulkner: The House Divided* (Baltimore: Johns Hopkins University Press, 1983), 29–30.
48 Brooks, *William Faulkner: Yoknapatawpha Country*, 154–5.
49 Ted Atkinson, *Faulkner and the Great Depression: Aesthetics, Ideology, and Cultural Politics* (Athens: University of Georgia Press, 2006), 180.
50 Julia Leyda, "Reading White Trash: Class, Race, and Mobility in Faulkner and Le Sueur," *Arizona Quarterly* 56, no. 2 (Summer 2000): 44.

51 This jibes with sociologist Jennifer Sherman's observation that "morality is often the most potent and visible in situations where few other types of social distinctions exist," and her discovery, from ethnographic fieldwork and interviews, that work ethic is a major determinant of moral capital among poor white people living in rural areas. Sherman, *Those Who Work, Those Who Don't: Poverty, Morality and Family in Rural America* (Minneapolis: University of Minnesota Press, 2009), 4.
52 Daniel J. Singal, *William Faulkner: The Making of a Modernist* (Chapel Hill: University of North Carolina Press, 1997), 147.
53 Kenneth M. Ludmerer, *Genetics and American Society: A Historical Appraisal* (Baltimore: Johns Hopkins University Press, 1972), 78.
54 Paul A. Lombardo, *Three Generations, No Imbeciles: Eugenics, the Supreme Court, and* Buck v. Bell (Baltimore: Johns Hopkins University Press, 2008), 137.
55 Harry Hamilton Laughlin, *The Legal Status of Eugenical Sterilization: History and Analysis of Litigation under the Virginia Sterilization Statute, which Led to a Decision of the Supreme Court of the United States Upholding the Statute* (Chicago: Fred J. Ringley, 1930), 17.
56 Ian Robert Dowbiggin, *Keeping America Sane: Psychiatry and Eugenics in the United States and Canada, 1880–1940* (Ithaca, NY: Cornell University Press, 1997), 129.
57 Edward J. Larson, *Sex, Race, and Science: Eugenics in the Deep South* (Baltimore: Johns Hopkins University Press, 1995), 121.
58 Elizabeth Yukins, "'Feeble-Minded' White Women and the Spectre of Proliferating Perversity in American Eugenics Narratives," in *Evolution and Eugenics in American Literature and Culture, 1880–1940: Essays on Ideological Conflict and Complicity*, ed. Lois A. Cuddy and Claire M. Roche (Lewisburg, PA: Bucknell University Press, 2003), 167.
59 Jay Watson, "Genealogies of White Deviance: The Eugenic Family Studies, *Buck v. Bell*, and William Faulkner, 1926–1931," in *Faulkner and Whiteness*, ed. Jay Watson (Jackson: University Press of Mississippi, 2011), 42.
60 Daylanne K. English, *Unnatural Selections: Eugenics in American Modernism and the Harlem Renaissance* (Chapel Hill: University of North Carolina Press, 2004), 173.
61 Buck v. Bell, 274 US 200 (1927).
62 Nicole Hahn Rafter, *White Trash: The Eugenic Family Studies, 1877–1919* (Boston: Northeastern University Press, 1988), 2.
63 Brooks, *William Faulkner: Yoknapatawpha Country*, 148.
64 Paul S. Nielsen, "What Does Addie Bundren Mean, and How Does She Mean It?" *Southern Literary Journal* 25, no. 1 (Fall 1992): 34.
65 Singal, *William Faulkner*, 150.
66 Donald M. Kartiganer, "Modernism as Gesture: Faulkner's Missing Facts," *Renaissance and Modern Studies* 41 (1998): 23.

67 Wendy Kline, *Building a Better Race: Gender, Sexuality, and Eugenics from the Turn of the Century to the Baby Boom* (Berkeley: University of California Press, 2001), 18.
68 Michael A. Rembis, "'Explaining Sexual Life to Your Daughter': Gender and Eugenic Education in the United States during the 1930s," in *Popular Eugenics: National Efficiency and American Mass Culture in the 1930s*, ed. Susan Currell and Christina Cogdell (Athens: Ohio University Press, 2006), 101.
69 Diana York Blaine, "The Abjection of Addie and Other Myths of the Maternal in *As I Lay Dying*," *Mississippi Quarterly* 47, no. 3 (Summer 1994): 432–3.
70 English, *Unnatural Selections*, 2.
71 Anne A. Fernihough, *Freewomen and Supermen: Edwardian Radicals and Literary Modernism* (New York: Oxford University Press, 2013), 45.
72 W. Grant Hague, *The Eugenic Mother and Baby: A Complete Home Guide* (New York: Hague, 1913), 110.
73 Rafter, *White Trash*, 25.
74 Mary Douglas, *Purity and Danger: An Analysis of Concepts of Pollution and Taboo* (New York: Routledge, 2003), 36.
75 Hartigan, *Odd Tribes*, 114.
76 Simmel, *Simmel on Culture*, 118–19.
77 W. Somerset Maugham, *On a Chinese Screen* (New York: George H. Doran, 1922), 142–3.
78 George Orwell, *The Road to Wigan Pier* (London: Secker and Warburg, 1986), 119.
79 Ibid., 122.
80 According to Peabody, when he asked Cash why he pressed on in the journey to Jefferson after breaking his leg, Cash observed (of the smell of putrefaction), "hit was gittin right noticeable" (138). But this admission, coming at second hand and after the fact, differs from Vardaman's disclosure.
81 Susan B. Miller, *Disgust: The Gatekeeper Emotion* (Hillsdale, NJ: Analytic, 2004), 20.
82 William Ian Miller, *The Anatomy of Disgust* (Cambridge, MA: Harvard University Press, 1997), 8.
83 Ibid., 248.
84 In a now-classic first-person essay describing how she became aware of her own race-based privilege, Peggy McIntosh defines white privilege as "an invisible package of unearned assets which I can count on cashing in each day, but about which I was 'meant' to remain oblivious." See McIntosh, "White Privilege and Male Privilege: A Personal Account of Coming to See Correspondences through Work in Women's Studies," in *Critical White Studies: Looking behind the Mirror*, ed. Richard Delgado and Jean Stefancic (Philadelphia, PA: Temple University Press, 1997), 291.
85 United States Bureau of the Census, *Population 1920*, vol. 1 of *Fourteenth Census of the United States Taken in the Year 1920* (Washington, DC: Government Printing Office, 1921), 47.

Chapter 3

1. Katherine Henninger takes this response as the title of her article, "'My Childhood Is Ruined!': Harper Lee and Racial Innocence," *American Literature* 88, no. 3 (2016): 597–626.
2. Tierney McAfee, "Parents Change 14-Month-Old Son Atticus' Name After *Go Set a Watchman* Controversy," *People*, July 24, 2015, http://people.com/books/parents-change-son-atticus-name-after-go-set-a-watchman-controversy/.
3. Eudora Welty, "Where Is the Voice Coming From?," in *The Collected Stories of Eudora Welty* (New York: Harcourt Brace Jovanovich, 1980), 604.
4. This move aligns Lee, Smith, and Welty with broader national trends in the decades after World War II. As Leah Gordon shows in *From Power to Prejudice: The Rise of Racial Individualism in Midcentury America* (Chicago: University of Chicago Press, 2015), in this era white liberals came to understand racism as a product of individual psychology rather than structural inequality.
5. Lora Romero, *Home Fronts: Domesticity and Its Critics in the Antebellum United States* (Durham, NC: Duke University Press, 1997), 4.
6. Margaret Earley Whitt, "The Pivotal Year, 1963: Flannery O'Connor and the Civil Rights Movement," in *A Political Companion to Flannery O'Connor*, ed. Henry T. Edmondson III (Lexington: University Press of Kentucky, 2017), 80; Katherine Hemple Prown, *Revising Flannery O'Connor: Southern Literary Culture and the Problem of Female Authorship* (Charlottesville: University Press of Virginia, 2001), 13–14.
7. Eudora Welty, *One Writer's Beginnings* (Cambridge, MA: Harvard University Press, 1983), 39.
8. Welty, "Where Is the Voice," 603.
9. See Twain, *Huckleberry Finn*, 39–40.
10. Byrd, *Westover Manuscripts*, 16.
11. Hundley, *Social Relations*, 262.
12. W. J. Cash, *The Mind of the South* (New York: Vintage Books, 1991), 24.
13. Vance, *Hillbilly Elegy*, 7.
14. Welty, "Where Is the Voice," 606.
15. Ibid., 604.
16. Eudora Welty, "The Art of Fiction XLVII," *Paris Review* 55 (Fall 1972): 86.
17. Ibid., 87.
18. Ibid.; Reed Massengill, *Portrait of a Racist: The Man Who Killed Medgar Evers?* (New York: St. Martin's, 1994), 52, 37.
19. Welty, "Art of Fiction," 87, 86.
20. Nadine Hubbs, *Rednecks, Queers, and Country Music* (Berkeley: University of California Press, 2014), 19.
21. John Hartigan Jr., *Racial Situations: Class Predicaments of Whiteness in Detroit* (Princeton, NJ: Princeton University Press, 1999), 8.
22. Welty, *One Writer's Beginnings*, 39.

23 Steph Lawler, *Identity: Sociological Perspectives* (Cambridge: Polity, 2008), 133.
24 Welty, "Art of Fiction," 86.
25 Welty, "Where Is the Voice," 607, 603.
26 Twain, *Huckleberry Finn*, 125; Massengill, *Portrait of a Racist*, 17.
27 Welty, "Where Is the Voice," 605; Massengill, *Portrait of a Racist*, 91.
28 Pete Daniel, *Lost Revolutions: The South in the 1950s* (Chapel Hill: University of North Carolina Press, 2000), 196.
29 Charles M. Payne, *I've Got the Light of Freedom: The Organizing Tradition and the Mississippi Freedom Struggle* (Berkeley: University of California Press, 1995), 34–5.
30 Welty, "Where Is the Voice," 606; Massengill, *Portrait of a Racist*, 108.
31 Welty, preface to *Collected Stories*, xi.
32 Adam Nossiter, *Of Long Memory: Mississippi and the Murder of Medgar Evers* (Reading, MA: Addison-Wesley, 1994), 108.
33 Casey N. Cep, "A Murder in Deep Summer," *New Yorker*, July 18, 2013, www.newyorker.com/books/page-turner/a-murder-in-deep-summer.
34 Julie Buckner Armstrong, "Civil Rights Movement Fiction," in *The Cambridge Companion to American Civil Rights Literature*, ed. Julie Buckner Armstrong (New York: Cambridge University Press, 2015), 95.
35 John Hartigan Jr., "Who Are These White People? 'Rednecks,' 'Hillbillies,' and 'White Trash' as Marked Racial Subjects," in *White Out: The Continuing Significance of Racism*, ed. Ashley W. Doane and Eduardo Bonilla-Silva (New York: Routledge, 2003), 111.
36 Flannery O'Connor, *The Habit of Being* (New York: Farrar, Straus and Giroux, 1979), 537.
37 Dorothy J. Hale, "Part I: Form and Function," in *The Novel: An Anthology of Criticism and Theory, 1900–2000*, ed. Dorothy J. Hale (Oxford: Blackwell, 2006), 25.
38 Flannery O'Connor, *Everything That Rises Must Converge* (New York: Farrar, Straus and Giroux, 1965), 191. All subsequent references to "Greenleaf" and "Revelation" come from this edition; page numbers are indicated parenthetically in the text.
39 Cash, *The Mind of the South*, 24, describes a slumped posture – "a striking lankness of frame and slackness of muscle" – as "the very hallmark of the [poor white] type." Historian Jeff Forret traces out the antebellum roots of the stereotype of poor white southerners as "idle, lazy, and indolent" and "dirty and disease-ridden" in *Race Relations at the Margins*, 2.
40 Welty, "Art of Fiction," 86.
41 The poor white woman's racial opinions are strident and hateful. In response to Turpin's insistence that "you got to love [black employees] if you want em to work for you," for instance, the poor white woman emits "a bark of contempt" (199). As her treatment of this character makes clear, O'Connor did not respond to her fellow white women writers' classist calumny by creating idealized anti-racist poor white characters.

42 Gregory R. Johnson offers a different take on the women's comments, contending that Turpin's "rather elaborate set of prejudices against white trash" are "show[n] ... to be well-founded," in part because the poor white woman "turned out to be a typical lower-class racist..., whereas Mrs. Turpin and the upper-class lady were careful to distinguish between good and bad black people, and professed themselves unable to do without good black friends." Johnson, "Pagan Virtue and Christian Charity: Flannery O'Connor on the Moral Contradictions of Western Culture," in *The Moral of the Story: Literature and Public Ethics*, ed. Henry T. Edmondson III (Lanham, MD: Lexington Books, 2000), 243.

43 For more about the expectation that African Americans would call at the back door when visiting white people's houses, as well as some of the strategies black southerners deployed to avoid this indignity, see Charles J. Johnson, *Patterns of Negro Segregation* (New York: Harper and Brothers, 1943), 128–31.

44 Rebecca Sharpless, *Cooking in Other Women's Kitchens: Domestic Workers in the South, 1865–1960* (Chapel Hill: University of North Carolina Press, 2010), 144. Sharpless's study offers several accounts of domestic workers whose employers required them to use segregated dishware; in one especially appalling case, the cook was told to use the dog's dish for her meals.

45 In *To Kill a Mockingbird*, cook and caretaker Calpurnia sleeps on a cot in the kitchen when she stays overnight in the Finches' home.

46 Memoirist and activist Anne Moody remembered that one white woman in Mississippi who employed her mother "didn't pay Mama much money at all, but she would give her the dinner leftovers to bring home for us at night." Moody, *Coming of Age in Mississippi* (New York: Dial, 1968), 13.

47 In the antebellum South, some planters required poor white people to call at the back door of the plantation house. See Eugene D. Genovese, "'Rather Be a Nigger Than a Poor White Man': Slave Perceptions of Southern Yeomen and Poor Whites," in *Toward a New View of America: Essays in Honor of Arthur C. Cole*, ed. Hans L. Trefousse (New York: Burt Franklin, 1977), 82.

48 Ralph C. Wood, *The Comedy of Redemption: Christian Faith and Comic Vision in Four American Novelists* (Notre Dame, IN: University of Notre Dame Press, 1988), 131.

49 Lillian Smith, *How Am I to Be Heard? Letters of Lillian Smith*, ed. Margaret Rose Gladney (Chapel Hill: University of North Carolina Press, 1993), 318.

50 Welty, preface to *Collected Stories*, xi.

51 For influential interpretations of *Killers of the Dream* that praise Smith's analysis of southern society and her treatment of poor white people, see Margaret Rose Gladney, introduction to *Killers of the Dream*, by Lillian Smith (New York: W. W. Norton, 1994); and Robert H. Brinkmeyer, "Marginalization and Mobility: Segregation and the Representation of Southern Poor Whites," in *Reading Southern Poverty between the Wars, 1918–1939*, ed. Richard Godden and Martin Crawford (Athens: University of Georgia Press, 2006), 223–38.

52 W. E. B. Du Bois, *Black Reconstruction in America: An Essay Toward a History of the Part Which Black Folk Played in the Attempt to Reconstruct Democracy in America, 1860–1880* (New York: Russell and Russell, 1962), 700. Influential works of whiteness studies including David R. Roediger's *The Wages of Whiteness: Race and the Making of the American Working Class* (London: Verso, 1991) and George Lipsitz's *The Possessive Investment in Whiteness: How White People Profit from Identity Politics* (Philadelphia, PA: Temple University Press, 1998) follow in the footsteps of Du Bois (and Smith) in exploring how the social, psychological, and material benefits of whiteness structure American society and fuel anti-black racism.

53 Manning Marable, *How Capitalism Underdeveloped Black America* (Boston: South End, 1983), 106.

54 Eduardo Bonilla-Silva, *Racism without Racists: Color-Blind Racism and the Persistence of Racial Inequality in America*, 4th ed. (Lanham, MD: Rowman and Littlefield, 2014), 305.

55 William Fitzhugh Brundage, *Lynching in the New South: Georgia and Virginia, 1880–1930* (Urbana: University of Illinois Press, 1993), 38.

56 Hale, *Making Whiteness*, esp. 206–7.

57 C. Ralph Stephens, ed., *The Correspondence of Flannery O'Connor and the Brainard Cheneys* (Jackson: University Press of Mississippi, 2008), 29. Virginia Wray reads O'Connor's decision to decline Smith's invitation differently than I do, seeing it as evidence of "her own unreadiness in 1955 for the kind of regional knowledge and self-knowledge" Smith was trying to inculcate. See Wray, "Flannery O'Connor and Lillian Smith: A Missed Opportunity?," *Flannery O'Connor Review* 5 (2007): 36.

58 Smith, *How Am I to Be Heard?*, 183.

59 Flannery O'Connor, *A Good Man Is Hard to Find and Other Stories* (San Diego: Harcourt Brace Jovanovich, 1983), 208, 209. All subsequent references to "A Circle in the Fire," "The Displaced Person," and "Good Country People" are from this edition; page numbers are indicated in the body of the text.

60 Claudia Durst Johnson, *"To Kill a Mockingbird": Threatening Boundaries* (New York: Twayne Publishers, 1994), 13–14.

61 "AFI's 100 Years ... 100 Heroes & Villains," American Film Institute, accessed November 3, 2021, www.afi.com/afis-100-years-100-heroes-villians/.

62 "Baby Names," Social Security Administration, accessed June 20, 2021, www.ssa.gov/oact/babynames/. The publication of *Go Set a Watchman* in 2015 perhaps temporarily tempered the popularity of the name Atticus, since the newer novel presents Atticus as a racist and segregationist. Between 2015 and 2016, the name lost ground, falling from spot 347 to 361.

63 Woodward, *Burden of Southern History*, 7.

64 Ibid., 6.

65 Harper Lee, *To Kill a Mockingbird* (Philadelphia, PA: J. B. Lippincott, 1960), 147. All subsequent references are from this edition. Page numbers are indicated between parentheses in the text.
66 Hartigan, *Odd Tribes*, 114.
67 Frederick Douglass Opie, "Molasses-Colored Glasses: WPA and Sundry Sources on Molasses and Southern Foodways," *Southern Cultures* 14, no. 1 (Spring 2008): 82.
68 Labor organizer Hosea Hudson remembered that in Alabama during the 1930s, poor and working-class white people were questioning racial inequality and embracing interracial organizing in record numbers, spurred by the deprivations of the Great Depression and the Communist Party's educational efforts. See Nell Irvin Painter, *The Narrative of Hosea Hudson: The Life and Times of a Black Radical* (New York: W. W. Norton, 1994), esp. 47–9.
69 Richard H. McAdams, "Empathy and Masculinity in Harper Lee's *To Kill a Mockingbird*," in *American Guy: Masculinity in American Law and Literature*, ed. Saul Levmore and Martha C. Nussbaum (New York: Oxford University Press, 2014), 252 and Katie Rose Guest Pryal, "Walking in Another's Skin: Failure of Empathy in *To Kill a Mockingbird*," in *Harper Lee's "To Kill a Mockingbird": New Essays*, ed. Michael J. Meyer (Lanham, MD: Scarecrow, 2010), 182 call attention to the limits of empathy in this scene by emphasizing that Cunningham's empathetic identification is with Atticus rather than with Tom Robinson.
70 In a number of letters sent to Eleanor Roosevelt during the Depression, for example, correspondents described the sorry state of their shoes and asked the First Lady to help them acquire some in better repair – perhaps, as some writers suggested, by sending them a pair that she no longer needed. See Robert Cohen, ed., *Dear Mrs. Roosevelt: Letters from Children of the Great Depression* (Chapel Hill: University of North Carolina Press, 2002).
71 Matt Wray contends that "hookworm disease and southern poor whites were intimately and biologically linked" in the national imagination during the early twentieth century – the result, in no small measure, of how the popular press reported on the efforts of the Rockefeller Sanitary Commission for the Eradication of Hookworm Disease (RSC), a five-year (1909–1914) philanthropic public health initiative that sought to eliminate hookworm disease in the South. Wray, *Not Quite White*, 114.
72 O'Connor, *Habit of Being*, 411.
73 Ibid.
74 Perhaps Lee would have appreciated this comparison. According to journalist Marja Mills, whose memoir recounts her friendship with Harper and her sister Alice during the eighteen months she lived next door to them, Harper Lee fondly reminisced about the Miss Minerva series over dinner one night in 2005. Mills, *The Mockingbird Next Door: Life with Harper Lee* (New York: Penguin, 2014), 220.
75 Frances Boyd Calhoun, *Miss Minerva and William Green Hill* (Chicago: Reilly and Britton, 1910), 20.

76 Ibid., 22–3.
77 Lee echoed – by design, I suspect – Justice Oliver Wendell Holmes Jr.'s infamous declaration in the *Buck v. Bell* decision that "three generations of imbeciles are enough." *Buck v. Bell*, 274 US 200 (1927).
78 "I'm just a country boy" is the motto of another 1950s character who, like Pointer, adopts a hayseed persona that finds a ready audience among middle-class whites. For Lonesome Rhodes in the 1957 film *A Face in the Crowd*, this slogan evolves from the ostensibly unselfconscious utterance of an ingénue to the self-satisfied sneer of a masterful manipulator whose bumpkin persona paves the way to wealth and prestige.
79 O'Connor, *Habit of Being*, 537.
80 Edward Kessler, *Flannery O'Connor and the Language of Apocalypse* (Princeton, NJ: Princeton University Press, 1986), 44.
81 For wrestling fans' disparaging view of Monroe as white trash, see Daniel, *Lost Revolutions*, 126. For how Monroe integrated Ellis Auditorium, see Robert Gordon, *It Came from Memphis* (New York: Pocket Books, 1995), 34–5.
82 Victoria Valentine, "When Love Was a Crime," *Emerge*, June 1997, 60.
83 Robert Coles, *Flannery O'Connor's South* (Baton Rouge: Louisiana State University Press, 1980), xxvi.

Chapter 4

1 Jean Anthelme Brillat-Savarin, *The Physiology of Taste: Or Meditations on Transcendental Gastronomy*, trans. M. F. K. Fisher (New York: Everyman's Library, 2009), 15.
2 Amos G. Warner, "Notes on the Statistical Determination of the Causes of Poverty," *Publications of the American Statistical Association* 1, no. 5 (March 1889): 184.
3 Ernest Matthew Mickler, *White Trash Cooking* (Berkeley: Ten Speed, 1986), 4.
4 As literary scholar Dina Smith has noted, *White Trash Cooking* enjoyed "fabulous success with its predominantly white middle-class readers, garnering favorable reviews from such publications as the *Village Voice*, the *New York Review of Books*, and *Vogue*." Smith, "Cultural Studies' Misfit: White Trash Studies," *Mississippi Quarterly* 57, no. 3 (Summer 2004): 376.
5 Dorothy Allison, *Skin: Talking about Sex, Class, and Literature* (Ithaca, NY: Firebrand, 1994), 15.
6 Byrd, *Westover Manuscripts*, 28.
7 Ibid., 27–8.
8 Robert W. Twyman, "The Clay Eater: A New Look at an Old Southern Enigma," *Journal of Southern History* 37, no. 3 (August 1971): 446.
9 Augustus Baldwin Longstreet, "The Fight," in *Georgia Scenes* (Nashville: J. S. Sanders, 1992), 54.

10 Emily P. Burke, *Reminiscences of Georgia* (Oberlin, OH: J. M. Fitch, 1850), 205.
11 John Patterson Green, *Recollections of the Inhabitants, Localities, Superstitions, and KuKlux Outrages of the Carolinas: By a "Carpet-Bagger" Who Was Born and Lived There* (Cleveland: n.p., 1880), 159.
12 "Carolina Clay Eaters," *Scientific American* 58, May 19, 1888, 311.
13 Jack Temple Kirby, *Rural Worlds Lost: The American South, 1920–1960* (Baton Rouge: Louisiana State University Press, 1987), 192.
14 John Hill Aughey, *The Iron Furnace; or, Slavery and Secession* (Philadelphia, PA: William S. and Alfred Martien, 1863), 213.
15 Edward King, *The Great South: A Record of Journeys in Louisiana, Texas, the Indian Territory, Missouri, Arkansas, Mississippi, Alabama, Georgia, Florida, South Carolina, North Carolina, Kentucky, Tennessee, Virginia, West Virginia, and Maryland* (Hartford, CT: American, 1875), 774.
16 Hundley, *Social Relations*, 264.
17 Ibid., 261.
18 Ibid., 264.
19 De Graffenried, "Georgia Cracker," 491.
20 Virginia Foster Durr, *Outside the Magic Circle* (Tuscaloosa: University of Alabama Press, 1985), 31.
21 Edmund Kirke [James R. Gilmore], *Among the Pines; or, South in Secession-Time* (New York: J. R. Gilmore, 1862), 71.
22 Ibid., 73.
23 Ibid., 72.
24 Dorothy Allison, *Bastard Out of Carolina* (New York: Plume, 1992), 71. All subsequent references are to this edition and appear in parentheses in the text.
25 Barbara Robinette Moss, *Change Me into Zeus's Daughter* (New York: Scribner, 2001), 19. All later references are to this edition and are incorporated into the text.
26 Matthew Guinn, *After Southern Modernism: Fiction of the Contemporary South* (Jackson: University Press of Mississippi, 2000), 27.
27 Susan Levine, *School Lunch Politics: The Surprising History of America's Favorite Welfare Program* (Princeton, NJ: Princeton University Press, 2008), 105.
28 Ibid., 107.
29 David A. Davis and Tara Powell, "Reading Southern Food," in *Writing in the Kitchen: Essays on Southern Literature and Foodways*, ed. David A. Davis and Tara Powell (Jackson: University Press of Mississippi, 2014), 3–4.
30 Mary Titus, "The Dining Room Door Swings Both Ways: Food, Race, and Domestic Space in the Nineteenth-Century South," in *Haunted Bodies: Gender and Southern Texts*, ed. Anne Goodwyn Jones and Susan V. Donaldson (Charlottesville: University of Virginia Press, 1997), 245.
31 Letitia M. Burwell, *A Girl's Life in Virginia before the War* (New York: Frederick A. Stokes, 1895), 149, 150.
32 Ibid., 171–2.

33 Hentz, *Planter's Northern Bride*, 173.
34 Ibid.
35 Susan Dabney Smedes, *Memorials of a Southern Planter* (Baltimore: Cushings and Bailey, 1887), 55.
36 Twelve Southerners, *I'll Take My Stand*, 226.
37 Ibid., 227.
38 Ted Ownby, "Three Agrarianisms and the Idea of a South without Poverty," in *Reading Southern Poverty between the Wars, 1918–1939*, ed. Richard Godden and Martin Crawford (Athens: University of Georgia Press, 2006), 2.
39 Burwell, *A Girl's Life*, 149.
40 Twelve Southerners, *I'll Take My Stand*, 227.
41 Janet Poppendieck, *Free for All: Fixing School Food in America* (Berkeley: University of California Press, 2010), 58.
42 Woodward, *Burden of Southern History*, 17.
43 Kathryn Stockett, *The Help* (New York: Berkley Books, 2009), 19.
44 Moody, *Coming of Age in Mississippi*, 339.
45 Steve Oney, "The Making of the Writer," *New York Times*, December 24, 1978, Sunday Book Review, 17.
46 Harry Crews, "Pages from the Life of a Georgia Innocent," *Esquire*, July 1976, 30.
47 Ibid., 36.
48 Jean Stafford, review of *Naked in Garden Hills*, by Harry Crews, *New York Times*, April 13, 1969, Sunday Book Review, 5.
49 James Atlas, "Like It Was," review of *A Childhood: The Biography of a Place*, by Harry Crews, *Time*, October 23, 1978, 108.
50 Robert Sherrill, "A Son of the Hungry South," review of *A Childhood: The Biography of a Place*, by Harry Crews, *New York Times*, December 24, 1978, Sunday Book Review, 3.
51 Harry Crews, "Television's Junkyard Dog," *Esquire*, October 1976, 128.
52 Harry Crews, *A Childhood: The Biography of a Place* (Athens: University of Georgia Press, 1995), 22.
53 Ibid., 25.
54 Susanne Dietzel, "An Interview with Dorothy Allison," in *Conversations with Dorothy Allison,* ed. Mae Miller Claxton (Jackson: University Press of Mississippi, 2012), 51.
55 Allison, *Skin*, 219, 220.
56 Ibid., 13.
57 M. Thomas Inge, "Literature," in *Literature*, vol. 9 of *The New Encyclopedia of Southern Culture,* ed. M. Thomas Inge (Chapel Hill: University of North Carolina Press, 2008), 14. Robert Gingher offers a similar definition, describing grit lit works as "stories grounded in the grime or 'grit' of reality [that] typically deploy stark, sometimes violent narratives of poor white southerners"; see "Grit Lit," in *The Companion to Southern Literature: Themes,*

Genres, Places, People, Movements, and Motifs, ed. Joseph M. Flora and Lucinda H. MacKethan (Baton Rouge: Louisiana State University Press, 2002), 319.

58 In the October 1976 installment of his *Esquire* column, Crews proposed that his birthplace had made him a "grit," writing, "that swamp, all those goddamn mules, all those screwworms that I'd dug out of pigs ... had made me the grit I am and will always be." Crews, "Television's Junkyard Dog," 128.

59 Erik Bledsoe, "The Rise of Southern Redneck and White Trash Writers," *Southern Cultures* 6, no. 1 (Spring 2000): 68.

60 Jean W. Cash, introduction to *Rough South, Rural South: Region and Class in Recent Southern Literature*, ed. Jean W. Cash and Keith Perry (Jackson: University Press of Mississippi, 2016), xiii.

61 Brian Carpenter, introduction to *Grit Lit: A Rough South Reader*, ed. Brian Carpenter and Tom Franklin (Columbia: University of South Carolina Press, 2012), xxix.

62 Ibid., xxx.

63 Tom Franklin, preface to *Grit Lit: A Rough South Reader*, ed. Brian Carpenter and Tom Franklin (Columbia: University of South Carolina Press, 2012), viii.

64 Ibid.

65 Grit lit tales are rarely wholly episodic. However, in men's grit lit novels, protagonists' sexual escapades can take shape as episodes, or "discrete units of narrative that do not accumulate toward a definite, necessary end," which is how Matthew Garrett defines the episode in *Episodic Poetics: Politics and Literary Form after the Constitution* (New York: Oxford University Press, 2014), 11. In *Suttree* and *Joe*, for instance, the eponymous protagonists' sexual relationships with women do not influence the plot's trajectory and, in fact, function interchangeably – so much so that sexual partners can drop from the text in an instant. One of Suttree's lovers is killed by falling rocks: a sort of geologic deus ex machina. Women can also substitute for one another. In the antepenultimate chapter of *Joe*, the protagonist calls at the home of a rich woman who likes to spend money on him. Finding her gone, Joe visits a honky-tonk where he meets a different woman with money who eagerly spends it on him, treating him to porterhouse steaks and beers (and sex). Immediately after this bacchanalia – in the next paragraph – Joe grows tired of her and sneaks away while she sleeps, bringing this episode (and the chapter) to a close. This self-contained sexual interlude typifies the peckeresque's erotic episodes.

66 Tim McLaurin, *The Acorn Plan* (New York: W. W. Norton, 1988), 71.

67 Larry Brown, "Waiting for the Ladies," in *Big Bad Love: Stories* (Chapel Hill, NC: Algonquin Books, 1990), 79.

68 Cormac McCarthy, *Suttree* (New York: Random House, 1979), 33. All subsequent references are to this edition and appear in parentheses in the text.

69 Harry Crews published a dozen novels between 1968, when his first novel came out, and 1992, when Allison published her debut novel. Cormac

McCarthy published a half-dozen novels between 1965, when *The Orchard Keeper* appeared, and 1992. I focus on *Suttree* and *Scar Lover* because Robert Gingher cites them as works that define grit lit in *The Companion to Southern Literature*, 319.
70 Kate Manne, *Down Girl: The Logic of Misogyny* (New York: Oxford University Press, 2018), 301.
71 Matthew Potts, "'Their Ragged Biblical Forms': Materiality, Misogyny, and the Corporal Works of Mercy in *Suttree*," *Religion and Literature* 47, no. 2 (Summer 2015): 67.
72 Manne, *Down Girl*, 22.
73 McLaurin, *Acorn Plan*, 55.
74 Ibid., 44–5.
75 Ibid., 44, 78.
76 Manne, *Down Girl*, 301.
77 McLaurin, *Acorn Plan*, 77.
78 Ibid., 43, 35.
79 Doris, Moss's mother, puts her whole salary toward feeding her family. Moss writes that "every Friday Mother would cash her paycheck at the front courtesy counter" of Winn-Dixie and then shop for the week's provisions (193).
80 McLaurin, *Acorn Plan*, 35.
81 Ibid., 144.
82 Ibid., 120.
83 Ibid., 34.
84 Larry Brown, *Joe: A Novel* (Chapel Hill, NC: Algonquin Books, 1991), 192.
85 Ibid., 310.
86 Ibid.
87 Ibid., 268.
88 McLaurin, *Acorn Plan*, 90.
89 Harry Crews, *Scar Lover* (New York: Touchstone, 1992), 210.
90 Ibid.
91 McLaurin, *Acorn Plan*, 71.
92 Crews, *Scar Lover*, 40.
93 Brown, *Joe*, 293.
94 Ibid., 213.
95 Crews, *Scar Lover*, 41, 104.
96 Rachel Walerstein, "Recomposing the Self: Joyful Shame in Dorothy Allison's *Bastard Out of Carolina*," *Mosaic* 49, no. 4 (December 2016): 169. J. Brooks Bouson makes a similar claim in "'You Nothing but Trash': White Trash Shame in Dorothy Allison's *Bastard Out of Carolina*," *Southern Literary Journal* 34, no. 1 (Fall 2001): 106.
97 Anney's preoccupation with Bone's birth certificate is a through line in *Bastard Out of Carolina*. The first chapter describes Anney's attempts to get

an unstamped version of the document during Bone's early years – efforts motivated by the fact that "the stamp on that birth certificate burned her" (3). The novel ends with Anney giving Bone a "blank, unmarked, unstamped" copy of the record (309).

98 Other fathers in Moss's memoir also prioritize their own desires above their families' dietary needs. For instance, a man named Ralph trades his family's monthly food stamp allotment for a convertible.

99 Brown, *Joe*, 121, 27.

100 David Cowart, "Death and the Wastrel: McCarthy's *Suttree*," *Modern Philology* 115, no. 3 (February 2018): 406.

101 Other analyses of abjection in *Suttree* concentrate on men's experiences. For one of the more in-depth treatments of this subject, see J. Douglas Canfield, "The Dawning of the Age of Aquarius: Abjection, Identity, and the Carnivalesque in Cormac McCarthy's *Suttree*," *Contemporary Literature* 44, no. 4 (Winter 2003): 664–96.

102 Reese, Wanda's father, introduces her name to the text on page 332. On page 349, Wanda's name appears three times in a conversation about who will make the downstream run after Reese's son falls ill.

103 Alexis Jetter, "The Roseanne of Literature," *New York Times Magazine*, December 17, 1995, 56. As Jetter's title suggests, the article points to connections between Allison's writings and Roseanne Barr's then-popular sitcom.

104 Sally Stein discusses why Florence Thompson's Cherokee heritage matters for understanding Lange's famous 1936 photograph in "Passing Likeness: Dorothea Lange's 'Migrant Mother' and the Paradox of Iconicity," in *Only Skin: Changing Visions of the American Self*, ed. Coco Fusco and Brian Wallis (New York: International Center of Photography / Harry N. Abrams, 2003), 345–55.

105 Dorothea Lange, "The Assignment I'll Never Forget: Migrant Mother," *Popular Photography*, February 1960, 126.

106 Margaret Bourke-White, "Notes on Photographs," in Caldwell and Bourke-White, *You Have Seen Their Faces*, 187.

107 Caldwell and Bourke-White, *You Have Seen Their Faces*, n.p.

108 That these are middle-class makers' own ideas about poor white people's sentiments is perhaps a merit rather than a shortcoming of the book in the minds of some of its readers. In his review of *You Have Seen Their Faces*, for example, Malcolm Cowley gushed, "the quotations printed beneath the photographs are exactly right." See Cowley, "Fall Catalogue," *New Republic*, November 24, 1937, 78.

109 Alan Trachtenberg, foreword to *You Have Seen Their Faces*, by Erskine Caldwell and Margaret Bourke-White (Athens: University of Georgia Press, 1995), v.

110 Carolyn E. Megan, "Moving toward Truth: An Interview with Dorothy Allison," *Kenyon Review* 16, no. 4 (Autumn 1994): 77.

Coda

1. De Graffenried, "Georgia Cracker," 484.
2. Vance, *Hillbilly Elegy*, 57.
3. Hochschild, *Strangers in Their Own Land*, 131.
4. One indicator of wellness culture's influence is the wellness industry's profitability. Management consulting firm McKinsey and Company values the global wellness market at $1.5 trillion. See Shaun Callaghan, Martin Lösch, Anna Pione, and Warren Teichner, "Feeling Good: The Future of the $1.5 Trillion Wellness Market," McKinsey and Company, April 8, 2021, www.mckinsey.com/industries/consumer-packaged-goods/our-insights/feeling-good-the-future-of-the-1-5-trillion-wellness-market.
5. Vance, *Hillbilly Elegy*, 2; emphasis mine.
6. Hochschild, *Strangers in Their Own Land*, 16; emphasis in original.
7. Ibid., 19.
8. Lawler, *Identity*, 135.
9. This reference to petite-sized clothing seems like a polite misnomer. Petite clothes are designed to fit women of shorter stature (five foot four and under) and state-to-state height differences are negligible. But in 2015, the year before *Strangers in Their Own Land* was published, Louisiana had the nation's highest adult obesity rate: 36.3 percent. California, Hochschild's home state, had one of the lowest rates in the country (24.2 percent). See "Adult Obesity in the United States," State of Childhood Obesity, Robert Wood Johnson Foundation, accessed August 20, 2019, www.stateofobesity.org/adult-obesity/.
10. Elizabeth Currid-Halkett, *The Sum of Small Things: A Theory of the Aspirational Class* (Princeton, NJ: Princeton University Press, 2017), 18.
11. Hochschild, *Strangers in Their Own Land*, 10.
12. In 2012, fifty-five percent of *New York Times* subscribers most often read that paper on a computer or mobile device, whereas forty-one percent most commonly perused the print version of the *Times*. See "In Changing News Landscape, Even Television Is Vulnerable," Pew Research Center, September 27, 2012, www.pewresearch.org/politics/2012/09/27/in-changing-news-landscape-even-television-is-vulnerable/.
13. Currid-Halkett, *Sum of Small Things*, 18.
14. S. Margot Finn, *Discriminating Taste: How Class Anxiety Created the American Food Revolution* (New Brunswick, NJ: Rutgers University Press, 2017), 213.
15. Elizabeth S. D. Engelhardt, *A Mess of Greens: Southern Gender and Southern Food* (Athens: University of Georgia Press, 2011), 52.
16. Currid-Halkett, *Sum of Small Things*, 111.
17. Ibid., 56.
18. Vance, *Hillbilly Elegy*, 148. For scholarship explaining why Americans who have less money to spend on food might be constrained to less nutritious diets, see, for example, Caitlin Daniel, "Economic Constraints on Taste Formation and the True Cost of Healthy Eating," *Social Science and Medicine* 148 (January 2016): 34–41.

19 Vance, *Hillbilly Elegy*, 148.
20 Anne Case and Angus Deaton, "Mortality and Morbidity in the 21st Century," *Brookings Papers on Economic Activity* (Spring 2017): 397–476. Case and Deaton's research on white Americans' rising mortality rates first appeared as a 2015 working paper.
21 Steven H. Woolf, Heidi Schoomaker, Latoya Hill, and Christine M. Orndahl, "The Social Determinants of Health and the Decline in U.S. Life Expectancy: Implications for Appalachia," *Journal of Appalachian Health* 1, no. 1 (Spring 2019): 10.
22 Anne Case and Angus Deaton, *Deaths of Despair and the Future of Capitalism* (Princeton, NJ: Princeton University Press, 2020), 38.
23 Owen Daugherty, "J. D. Vance Talks Ohio's Opioid Epidemic," *Lantern*, April 17, 2017, www.thelantern.com/2017/04/j-d-vance-talks-ohios-opioid-epidemic/.
24 Longstreet, "The Fight," 54.
25 Cheryl D. Fryar, Jeffery P. Hughes, Kirsten A. Herrick, and Namanjeet Ahluwalia, "Fast Food Consumption among Adults in the United States, 2013–2016," NCHS Data Brief no. 322, National Center for Health Statistics, October 2018, www.cdc.gov/nchs/products/databriefs/db322.htm.
26 Vance, *Hillbilly Elegy*, 139.
27 Citizens and bureaucrats blur the line between economic misfortune and economic malfeasance. Legal scholar Kaaryn S. Gustafson has observed that in the wake of the 1996 welfare reform law – the Personal Responsibility and Work Opportunity Reconciliation Act – "the federal government and the states instituted a host of policies and practices that equated welfare receipt with criminality." Gustafson, *Cheating Welfare: Public Assistance and the Criminalization of Poverty* (New York: New York University Press, 2011), 51.
28 Christopher Howard, *The Hidden Welfare State: Tax Expenditures and Social Policy in the United States* (Princeton, NJ: Princeton University Press, 1997).
29 Matthew Desmond, "How Homeownership Became the Engine of American Inequality," *New York Times Magazine*, May 9, 2017, www.nytimes.com/2017/05/09/magazine/how-homeownership-became-the-engine-of-american-inequality.html.
30 Andrew Woo and Chris Salviati, "Imbalance in Housing Aid: Mortgage Interest Deduction vs. Section 8," Apartment List, October 17, 2017, www.apartmentlist.com/rentonomics/imbalance-housing-aid-mortgage-interest-deduction-vs-section-8/.
31 Historian Molly C. Michelmore observes that "most of the recipients of federal aid are not the suspect 'welfare queens' of the popular imagination, but rather middle-class homeowners, salaried professionals, and retirees" in *Tax and Spend: The Welfare State, Tax Politics, and the Limits of American Liberalism* (Philadelphia: University of Pennsylvania Press, 2012), 1. Yet it is precisely this bugbear of the popular imagination that *Hillbilly Elegy* conjures. After disavowing constructions of the welfare queen that make use of "unfair images of the lazy black mom," Vance promptly applies the stereotype to poor

white women: "I have known many welfare queens ... and all were white" (Vance, *Hillbilly Elegy*, 8). Like Harper Lee, Lillian Smith, and Eudora Welty a half-century before him, Vance deploys classism to bolster his anti-racist bona fides.
32 It is worthwhile to distinguish between Appalachian outmigration and the broader southern diaspora in discussing poverty because white Appalachian migrants to the Midwest experienced significantly higher rates of poverty than whites who moved to the Midwest from other parts of the South. See J. Trent Alexander, "Defining the Diaspora: Appalachians in the Great Migration," *Journal of Interdisciplinary History* 37, no. 2 (Autumn 2006): 219–47, esp. 232–5.
33 Vance, *Hillbilly Elegy*, 4, 1.
34 Ibid., 2, 7, 7.
35 Oscar Lewis, "The Culture of Poverty," *Trans-action* 1, November 1963, 17.
36 Vance, *Hillbilly Elegy*, 4, 7, 21, 21.
37 David Brooks, "Revolt of the Masses," *New York Times*, June 28, 2016, www.nytimes.com/2016/06/28/opinion/revolt-of-the-masses.html.
38 Vance, *Hillbilly Elegy*, 7.
39 Ibid., 21.
40 Michael Hurwitz and Jason Lee, "Grade Inflation and the Role of Standardized Testing," in *Measuring Success: Testing, Grades, and the Future of College Admissions*, ed. Jack Buckley, Lynn Letukas, and Ben Wildavsky (Baltimore: Johns Hopkins University Press, 2018), 64–93.
41 Jessica McCrory Calarco, *Negotiating Opportunities: How the Middle Class Secures Advantages in School* (New York: Oxford University Press, 2018).
42 Lani Guinier, *The Tyranny of the Meritocracy: Democratizing Higher Education in America* (Boston: Beacon, 2015), 20–1. The College Board released these figures correlating scores with incomes in 2013.
43 Thomas J. Espenshade and Alexandria Walton Radford, *No Longer Separate, Not Yet Equal: Race and Class in Elite College Admission and Campus Life* (Princeton, NJ: Princeton University Press, 2009), 126.
44 Vance, *Hillbilly Elegy*, 193.
45 *Hillbilly Elegy* discusses higher education and higher education discusses *Hillbilly Elegy*: a dozen colleges and universities selected Vance's memoir for their Common Reading programs during the 2017–2018 academic year. See Tim Cheng, "What Students Will Be Reading: Campus Common Reading Roundup, 2017–18," Penguin Random House Common Reads, June 20, 2017, http://commonreads.com/2017/06/20/campus-common-reading-roundup-2017–18/.
46 Margaret A. Hagerman, *White Kids: Growing Up with Privilege in a Racially Divided America* (New York: New York University Press, 2018), 184.
47 Shamus Rhaman Khan, *Privilege: The Making of an Adolescent Elite at St. Paul's School* (Princeton, NJ: Princeton University Press, 2011), 60.
48 Shamus Khan and Colin Jerolmack, "Saying Meritocracy and Doing Privilege," *Sociological Quarterly* 54, no. 1 (2013): 12.

49 Hochschild, *Strangers in Their Own Land*, 135.
50 Alberto Alesina, Stefanie Stantcheva, and Edoardo Teso, "Intergenerational Mobility and Preferences for Redistribution," *American Economic Review* 108, no. 2 (February 2018): 521–54; Raj Chetty, Nathaniel Hendren, Patrick Kline, and Emmanuel Saez, "Where Is the Land of Opportunity? The Geography of Intergenerational Mobility in the United States," *Quarterly Journal of Economics* 129, no. 4 (November 2014): 1553–623.
51 Arlie Russell Hochschild, "Strangers in Their Own Land: What Led to the Rise of Trump and What Now?" (Sociology Department Colloquium, Stanford University, Palo Alto, CA, February 23, 2017).
52 Thanks to Stanford's Center for Comparative Studies in Race and Ethnicity, which hosted me as a visiting scholar during the 2016–2017 academic year, I was in residence at Stanford and thus able to attend Hochschild's talk.
53 Erling B. Holtsmark, "The *Katabasis* Theme in Modern Cinema," in *Classical Myth and Culture in the Cinema*, ed. Martin M. Winkler (New York: Oxford University Press, 2001), 26.
54 A number of reviewers described these books as revealing hitherto unknown communities and concepts. For example, Barbara Ehrenreich called Hochschild's analysis "revelatory" in her blurb on the back cover of *Strangers in Their Own Land*. Amy Chua, in her back cover blurb for *Hillbilly Elegy*, wrote that the book "opens a window on a part of America usually hidden from view."
55 Brodhead, *Cultures of Letters*, 137.

Bibliography

Agee, James, and Walker Evans. *Let Us Now Praise Famous Men: Three Tenant Families.* Boston: Houghton Mifflin, 2001.
Alesina, Alberto, Stefanie Stantcheva, and Edoardo Teso. "Intergenerational Mobility and Preferences for Redistribution." *American Economic Review* 108, no. 2 (February 2018): 521–54.
Alexander, J. Trent. "Defining the Diaspora: Appalachians in the Great Migration." *Journal of Interdisciplinary History* 37, no. 2 (Autumn 2006): 219–47.
Allison, Dorothy. *Bastard Out of Carolina.* New York: Plume, 1992.
——. *Skin: Talking about Sex, Class, and Literature.* Ithaca, NY: Firebrand, 1994.
"American Civilization." *Atlantic Monthly* 9, April 1862, 502–11.
American Film Institute. "AFI's 100 Years … 100 Heroes & Villains." Accessed November 3, 2021. www.afi.com/afis-100-years-100-heroes-villians/.
Andrews, Sidney. *The South since the War: As Shown by Fourteen Weeks of Travel and Observation in Georgia and the Carolinas.* Boston: Ticknor and Fields, 1866.
Armstrong, Julie Buckner. "Civil Rights Movement Fiction." In *The Cambridge Companion to American Civil Rights Literature*, edited by Julie Buckner Armstrong, 85–103. New York: Cambridge University Press, 2015.
Atkinson, E. "Taxation No Burden." *Atlantic Monthly* 10, July 1862, 115–18.
Atkinson, Ted. *Faulkner and the Great Depression: Aesthetics, Ideology, and Cultural Politics.* Athens: University of Georgia Press, 2006.
Atlas, James. "Like It Was." Review of *A Childhood: The Biography of a Place*, by Harry Crews. *Time*, October 23, 1978, 108+.
Aughey, John Hill. *The Iron Furnace; or, Slavery and Secession.* Philadelphia, PA: William S. and Alfred Martien, 1863.
Bedient, Calvin. "Pride and Nakedness: *As I Lay Dying*." *Modern Language Quarterly* 29, no. 1 (March 1968): 61–76.
Blaine, Diana York. "The Abjection of Addie and Other Myths of the Maternal in *As I Lay Dying*." *Mississippi Quarterly* 47, no. 3 (Summer 1994): 419–39.
Bledsoe, Erik. "The Rise of Southern Redneck and White Trash Writers." *Southern Cultures* 6, no. 1 (Spring 2000): 68–90.
Bleikasten, André. *Faulkner's "As I Lay Dying."* Translated by Roger Little. Rev. and enl. ed. Bloomington: Indiana University Press, 1973.

The Ink of Melancholy: Faulkner's Novels from "The Sound and the Fury" to "Light in August." Bloomington: Indiana University Press, 1990.
Bolton, Charles C. *Poor Whites of the Antebellum South: Tenants and Laborers in Central North Carolina and Northeast Mississippi.* Durham, NC: Duke University Press, 1994.
Bonilla-Silva, Eduardo. *Racism without Racists: Color-Blind Racism and the Persistence of Racial Inequality in America.* 4th ed. Lanham, MD: Rowman and Littlefield, 2014.
Bonner, Sherwood. *Suwanee River Tales.* Boston: Roberts Brothers, 1884.
Bourdieu, Pierre. *Distinction: A Social Critique of the Judgement of Taste.* Translated by Richard Nice. Cambridge, MA: Harvard University Press, 1984.
Practical Reason: On the Theory of Action. Stanford, CA: Stanford University Press, 1998.
Bouson, J. Brooks. "'You Nothing but Trash': White Trash Shame in Dorothy Allison's *Bastard Out of Carolina*." *Southern Literary Journal* 34, no. 1 (Fall 2001): 101–23.
Bragg, Rick. *The Most They Ever Had.* San Francisco: MacAdam/Cage, 2009.
Brillat-Savarin, Jean Anthelme. *The Physiology of Taste: Or Meditations on Transcendental Gastronomy.* Translated by M. F. K. Fisher. New York: Everyman's Library, 2009.
Brinkmeyer, Robert H. "Marginalization and Mobility: Segregation and the Representation of Southern Poor Whites." In *Reading Southern Poverty between the Wars, 1918–1939,* edited by Richard Godden and Martin Crawford, 223–38. Athens: University of Georgia Press, 2006.
Brodhead, Richard H. *Cultures of Letters: Scenes of Reading and Writing in Nineteenth-Century America.* Chicago: University of Chicago Press, 1993.
Brooks, Cleanth. *William Faulkner: Toward Yoknapatawpha and Beyond.* New Haven, CT: Yale University Press, 1978.
William Faulkner: The Yoknapatawpha Country. New Haven, CT: Yale University Press, 1963.
Brooks, David. "Revolt of the Masses." *New York Times,* June 28, 2016. www.nytimes.com/2016/06/28/opinion/revolt-of-the-masses.html.
Brown, Emma E. "Children's Labor: A Problem." *Atlantic Monthly* 46, December 1880, 787–92.
Brown, Larry. *Joe: A Novel.* Chapel Hill, NC: Algonquin Books, 1991.
"Waiting for the Ladies." In *Big Bad Love: Stories,* 47–61. Chapel Hill, NC: Algonquin Books, 1990.
Brundage, William Fitzhugh. *Lynching in the New South: Georgia and Virginia, 1880–1930.* Urbana: University of Illinois Press, 1993.
Buck v. Bell, 274 US 200 (1927).
Burke, Emily P. *Reminiscences of Georgia.* Oberlin, OH: J. M. Fitch, 1850.
Burwell, Letitia M. *A Girl's Life in Virginia before the War.* New York: Frederick A. Stokes, 1895.
Byrd, William. *The Westover Manuscripts: Containing the History of the Dividing Line Betwixt Virginia and North Carolina; A Journey to the Land of Eden,*

A.D. 1733; and *A Progress to the Mines. Written from 1728 to 1736, and Now First Published.* Petersburg, VA: Edmund and Julian C. Ruffin, 1841.

Calarco, Jessica McCrory. *Negotiating Opportunities: How the Middle Class Secures Advantages in School.* New York: Oxford University Press, 2018.

Caldwell, Erskine. *Tobacco Road.* Athens: University of Georgia Press, 1995.

Caldwell, Erskine, and Margaret Bourke-White. *You Have Seen Their Faces.* New York: Viking, 1937.

Calhoun, Frances Boyd. *Miss Minerva and William Green Hill.* Chicago: Reilly and Britton, 1910.

Callaghan, Shaun, Martin Lösch, Anna Pione, and Warren Teichner. "Feeling Good: The Future of the $1.5 Trillion Wellness Market." McKinsey and Company, April 8, 2021. www.mckinsey.com/industries/consumer-pack aged-goods/our-insights/feeling-good-the-future-of-the-1-5-trillion-well ness-market.

Canfield, J. Douglas. "The Dawning of the Age of Aquarius: Abjection, Identity, and the Carnivalesque in Cormac McCarthy's *Suttree.*" *Contemporary Literature* 44, no. 4 (Winter 2003): 664–96.

"Carolina Clay Eaters." *Scientific American* 58, May 19, 1888, 311.

Carpenter, Brian. Introduction to *Grit Lit: A Rough South Reader,* xiii–xxxii. Edited by Brian Carpenter and Tom Franklin. Columbia: University of South Carolina Press, 2012.

Case, Anne, and Angus Deaton. *Deaths of Despair and the Future of Capitalism.* Princeton, NJ: Princeton University Press, 2020.

———. "Mortality and Morbidity in the 21st Century." *Brookings Papers on Economic Activity* (Spring 2017): 397–476.

Cash, Jean W. Introduction to *Rough South, Rural South: Region and Class in Recent Southern Literature,* xi–xiv. Edited by Jean W. Cash and Keith Perry. Jackson: University Press of Mississippi, 2016.

Cash, W. J. *The Mind of the South.* New York: Vintage Books, 1991.

Catchings, Libby. "Elegy, Effigy: Alchemy and the Displacement of Lament in *As I Lay Dying.*" *Faulkner Journal* 28, no. 2 (Fall 2014): 25–38.

Cep, Casey N. "A Murder in Deep Summer." *New Yorker,* July 18, 2013. www.newyorker.com/books/page-turner/a-murder-in-deep-summer.

Cheng, Tim. "What Students Will Be Reading: Campus Common Reading Roundup, 2017–18." Penguin Random House Common Reads, June 20, 2017. http://commonreads.com/2017/06/20/campus-common-reading-roundup-2017-18/.

Chesnutt, Charles W. *The Colonel's Dream.* New York: Random House, 2005.

———. *The Conjure Woman and Other Conjure Tales.* Edited by Richard H. Brodhead. Durham, NC: Duke University Press, 1993.

———. "The Disenfranchisement of the Negro." In *The Negro Problem: A Series of Articles by Representative American Negroes of To-day,* edited by Booker T. Washington et al., 79–124. New York: James Pott, 1903.

———. *The Journals of Charles W. Chesnutt.* Edited by Richard H. Brodhead. Durham, NC: Duke University Press, 1993.

To Be an Author: Letters of Charles W. Chesnutt, 1889–1905. Edited by Joseph R. McElrath Jr. and Robert C. Leitz III. Princeton, NJ: Princeton University Press, 1997.

Chetty, Raj, Nathaniel Hendren, Patrick Kline, and Emmanuel Saez. "Where Is the Land of Opportunity? The Geography of Intergenerational Mobility in the United States." *Quarterly Journal of Economics* 129, no. 4 (November 2014): 1553–623.

Cohen, Robert, ed. *Dear Mrs. Roosevelt: Letters from Children of the Great Depression.* Chapel Hill: University of North Carolina Press, 2002.

Coles, Robert. *Flannery O'Connor's South.* Baton Rouge: Louisiana State University Press, 1980.

Cook, Sylvia Jenkins. *Erskine Caldwell and the Fiction of Poverty: The Flesh and the Spirit.* Baton Rouge: Louisiana State University Press, 1991.

  From Tobacco Road to Route 66: The Southern Poor White in Fiction. Chapel Hill: University of North Carolina Press, 1976.

Cowart, David. "Death and the Wastrel: McCarthy's *Suttree.*" *Modern Philology* 115, no. 3 (February 2018): 391–411.

Cowley, Malcolm. "Fall Catalogue." *New Republic,* November 24, 1937, 78–9.

Craddock, Charles Egbert [Mary Noailles Murfree]. "The 'Harnt' That Walks Chilhowee." *Atlantic Monthly* 51, May 1883, 660–74.

  "Over on the T'other Mounting." *Atlantic Monthly* 47, June 1881, 737–49.

  "A Playin' of Old Sledge at the Settlemint." *Atlantic Monthly* 52, October 1883, 544–57.

  "The Romance of Sunrise Rock." *Atlantic Monthly* 46, December 1880, 775–86.

Crews, Harry. *A Childhood: The Biography of a Place.* Athens: University of Georgia Press, 1995.

  "Pages from the Life of a Georgia Innocent." *Esquire,* July 1976, 30+.

  Scar Lover. New York: Touchstone, 1992.

  "Television's Junkyard Dog." *Esquire,* October 1976, 95+.

Currid-Halkett, Elizabeth. *The Sum of Small Things: A Theory of the Aspirational Class.* Princeton, NJ: Princeton University Press, 2017.

Daniel, Caitlin. "Economic Constraints on Taste Formation and the True Cost of Healthy Eating." *Social Science and Medicine* 148 (January 2016): 34–41.

Daniel, Pete. *Lost Revolutions: The South in the 1950s.* Chapel Hill: University of North Carolina Press, 2000.

Daugherty, Owen. "J. D. Vance Talks Ohio's Opioid Epidemic." *Lantern,* April 17, 2017. www.thelantern.com/2017/04/j-d-vance-talks-ohios-opioid-epidemic/.

Davis, David A., and Tara Powell. "Reading Southern Food." In *Writing in the Kitchen: Essays on Southern Literature and Foodways,* edited by David A. Davis and Tara Powell, 3–12. Jackson: University Press of Mississippi, 2014.

De Forest, J. W. "Drawing Bureau Rations." *Harper's New Monthly Magazine* 36, May 1868, 792–9.

De Graffenried, Clare. "The Georgia Cracker in the Cotton Mills." *Century Illustrated Monthly Magazine* 41, February 1891, 483–98.

Denning, Michael. *Mechanic Accents: Dime Novels and Working-Class Culture in America*. London: Verso, 1987.

Derby, E. H. "Resources of the South." *Atlantic Monthly* 10, October 1862, 502–10.

Desmond, Matthew. "How Homeownership Became the Engine of American Inequality." *New York Times Magazine*, May 9, 2017. www.nytimes.com/2017/05/09/magazine/how-homeownership-became-the-engine-of-american-inequality.html.

Dietzel, Susanne. "An Interview with Dorothy Allison." In *Conversations with Dorothy Allison*, edited by Mae Miller Claxton, 40–52. Jackson: University Press of Mississippi, 2012.

Douglas, Mary. *Purity and Danger: An Analysis of Concepts of Pollution and Taboo*. New York: Routledge, 2003.

Douglass, Frederick. "The Race Problem." Bethel Library and Historical Association, Metropolitan A.M.E. Church, Washington, DC, October 21, 1890. Daniel Murray Pamphlet Collection, Library of Congress. https://lccn.loc.gov/74171961.

Dowbiggin, Ian Robert. *Keeping America Sane: Psychiatry and Eugenics in the United States and Canada, 1880–1940*. Ithaca, NY: Cornell University Press, 1997.

Du Bois, W. E. B. *Black Reconstruction in America: An Essay Toward a History of the Part Which Black Folk Played in the Attempt to Reconstruct Democracy in America, 1860–1880*. New York: Russell and Russell, 1962.

―――. *The Souls of Black Folk: Essays and Sketches*. Chicago: A. C. McClurg, 1903.

Duck, Leigh Anne. *The Nation's Region: Southern Modernism, Segregation, and U.S. Nationalism*. Athens: University of Georgia Press, 2006.

Dugdale, Richard L. *"The Jukes": A Study in Crime, Pauperism, Disease and Heredity; Also, Further Studies of Criminals*. 3rd ed. New York: G. P. Putnam's Sons, 1877.

Durr, Virginia Foster. *Outside the Magic Circle*. Tuscaloosa: University of Alabama Press, 1985.

Edwards, Harry Stillwell. "A Battle in Crackerdom." *Century Illustrated Monthly Magazine* 43, January 1892, 457–67.

―――. "An Idyl of 'Sinkin' Mount'in.'" *Century Illustrated Monthly Magazine* 36, October 1888, 895–907.

Engelhardt, Elizabeth S. D. *A Mess of Greens: Southern Gender and Southern Food*. Athens: University of Georgia Press, 2011.

English, Daylanne K. *Unnatural Selections: Eugenics in American Modernism and the Harlem Renaissance*. Chapel Hill: University of North Carolina Press, 2004.

Espenshade, Thomas J., and Alexandria Walton Radford. *No Longer Separate, Not Yet Equal: Race and Class in Elite College Admission and Campus Life*. Princeton, NJ: Princeton University Press, 2009.

Faulkner, William. *Absalom, Absalom!* New York: Vintage International, 1990.
———. *As I Lay Dying*. New York: Vintage, 1990.
———. *As I Lay Dying: Holograph Manuscript and Carbon Typescript*. Edited by Thomas L. McHaney. New York: Garland, 1986.
———. *Collected Stories of William Faulkner*. New York: Vintage, 1977.
———. "An Introduction to *The Sound and the Fury*." *Mississippi Quarterly* 26, no. 3 (Summer 1973): 410–15.
Faust, Drew Gilpin. Introduction to *The Ideology of Slavery: Proslavery Thought in the Antebellum South, 1830–1860*, 1–20. Edited by Drew Gilpin Faust. Baton Rouge: Louisiana State University Press, 1981.
Fernihough, Anne A. *Freewomen and Supermen: Edwardian Radicals and Literary Modernism*. New York: Oxford University Press, 2013.
Fetterley, Judith, and Marjorie Pryse. *Writing out of Place: Regionalism, Women, and American Literary Culture*. Urbana: University of Illinois Press, 2003.
Finn, S. Margot. *Discriminating Taste: How Class Anxiety Created the American Food Revolution*. New Brunswick, NJ: Rutgers University Press, 2017.
Fishkin, Shelley Fisher. *Was Huck Black? Mark Twain and African-American Voices*. New York: Oxford University Press, 1993.
Flusche, Michael. "On the Color Line: Charles Waddell Chesnutt." *North Carolina Historical Review* 53, no. 1 (January 1976): 1–24.
Flynt, Wayne. *Dixie's Forgotten People: The South's Poor Whites*. Bloomington: Indiana University Press, 1979.
Foley, Barbara. *Radical Representations: Politics and Form in U.S. Proletarian Fiction, 1929–1941*. Durham, NC: Duke University Press, 1993.
Foote, Stephanie. *Regional Fictions: Culture and Identity in Nineteenth-Century American Literature*. Madison: University of Wisconsin Press, 2001.
Ford, Lacy K. *Deliver Us from Evil: The Slavery Question in the Old South*. New York: Oxford University Press, 2009.
Forret, Jeff. *Race Relations at the Margins: Slaves and Poor Whites in the Antebellum Southern Countryside*. Baton Rouge: Louisiana State University Press, 2006.
Franklin, Tom. Preface to *Grit Lit: A Rough South Reader*, vii–viii. Edited by Brian Carpenter and Tom Franklin. Columbia: University of South Carolina Press, 2012.
Frost, William Goodell. "Our Contemporary Ancestors in the Southern Mountains." *Atlantic Monthly* 83, March 1899, 311–19.
Fryar, Cheryl D., Jeffery P. Hughes, Kirsten A. Herrick, and Namanjeet Ahluwalia. "Fast Food Consumption among Adults in the United States, 2013–2016." NCHS Data Brief no. 322, National Center for Health Statistics, October 2018. www.cdc.gov/nchs/products/databriefs/db322.htm.
Gandal, Keith. *The Virtues of the Vicious: Jacob Riis, Stephen Crane, and the Spectacle of the Slum*. New York: Oxford University Press, 1997.
Garrett, Matthew. *Episodic Poetics: Politics and Literary Form after the Constitution*. New York: Oxford University Press, 2014.
Genovese, Eugene D. "'Rather Be a Nigger Than a Poor White Man': Slave Perceptions of Southern Yeomen and Poor Whites." In *Toward a New View*

of America: Essays in Honor of Arthur C. Cole, edited by Hans L. Trefousse, 79–96. New York: Burt Franklin, 1977.
Gilligan, Heather Tirado. "Reading, Race, and Charles Chesnutt's 'Uncle Julius' Tales." *ELH* 74, no. 1 (Spring 2007): 195–215.
Gingher, Robert. "Grit Lit." In *The Companion to Southern Literature: Themes, Genres, Places, People, Movements, and Motifs,* edited by Joseph M. Flora and Lucinda H. MacKethan, 319–20. Baton Rouge: Louisiana State University Press, 2002.
Gladney, Margaret Rose. Introduction to *Killers of the Dream,* by Lillian Smith, n.p. New York: W. W. Norton, 1994.
Glazener, Nancy. *Reading for Realism: The History of a U.S. Literary Institution, 1850–1910.* Durham, NC: Duke University Press, 1997.
Gold, Mike. "Notes of the Month." *New Masses,* September 1930, 3–5.
Gordon, Leah. *From Power to Prejudice: The Rise of Racial Individualism in Midcentury America.* Chicago: University of Chicago Press, 2015.
Gordon, Robert. *It Came from Memphis.* New York: Pocket Books, 1995.
Grady, Henry W. "The South and Her Problem." In *Life of Henry W. Grady Including His Writings and Speeches: A Memorial Volume,* edited by Joel Chandler Harris, 94–120. New York: Cassell, 1890.
Grammer, John M. "Plantation Fiction." In *A Companion to the Literature and Culture of the American South,* edited by Richard Gray and Owen Robinson, 58–75. Malden, MA: Blackwell, 2004.
Green, John Patterson. *Recollections of the Inhabitants, Localities, Superstitions, and KuKlux Outrages of the Carolinas: By a "Carpet-Bagger" Who Was Born and Lived There.* Cleveland: n.p., 1880.
Greeson, Jennifer Rae. *Our South: Geographic Fantasy and the Rise of National Literature.* Cambridge, MA: Harvard University Press, 2010.
Guinier, Lani. *The Tyranny of the Meritocracy: Democratizing Higher Education in America.* Boston: Beacon, 2015.
Guinn, Matthew. *After Southern Modernism: Fiction of the Contemporary South.* Jackson: University Press of Mississippi, 2000.
Gustafson, Kaaryn S. *Cheating Welfare: Public Assistance and the Criminalization of Poverty.* New York: New York University Press, 2011.
Hagerman, Margaret A. *White Kids: Growing Up with Privilege in a Racially Divided America.* New York: New York University Press, 2018.
Hague, W. Grant. *The Eugenic Mother and Baby: A Complete Home Guide.* New York: Hague, 1913.
Hale, Dorothy J. "*As I Lay Dying*'s Heterogeneous Discourse." *NOVEL: A Forum on Fiction* 23, no. 1 (Autumn 1989): 5–23.
——— "Part I: Form and Function." In *The Novel: An Anthology of Criticism and Theory, 1900–2000,* edited by Dorothy J. Hale, 17–30. Oxford: Blackwell, 2006.
Hale, Grace Elizabeth. *Making Whiteness: The Culture of Segregation in the South, 1890–1940.* New York: Pantheon Books, 1998.
Hapke, Laura. *Labor's Text: The Worker in American Fiction.* New Brunswick, NJ: Rutgers University Press, 2001.

Harris, Joel Chandler. "Azalia." *Century Illustrated Monthly Magazine* 34, August–October 1887, 541+.
Uncle Remus: His Songs and His Sayings. New York: Penguin, 1982.
Hartigan, John, Jr. *Odd Tribes: Toward a Cultural Analysis of White People.* Durham, NC: Duke University Press, 2005.
Racial Situations: Class Predicaments of Whiteness in Detroit. Princeton, NJ: Princeton University Press, 1999.
"Who Are These White People? 'Rednecks,' 'Hillbillies,' and 'White Trash' as Marked Racial Subjects." In *White Out: The Continuing Significance of Racism,* edited by Ashley W. Doane and Eduardo Bonilla-Silva, 95–113. New York: Routledge, 2003.
Hemenway, Robert. "The Functions of Folklore in Charles Chesnutt's *The Conjure Woman.*" *Journal of the Folklore Institute* 13, no. 3 (1976): 283–309.
Introduction to *Uncle Remus: His Songs and His Sayings,* by Joel Chandler Harris, 7–32. New York: Penguin, 1982.
Henninger, Katherine. "'My Childhood Is Ruined!': Harper Lee and Racial Innocence." *American Literature* 88, no. 3 (2016): 597–626.
Hentz, Caroline Lee. *The Planter's Northern Bride.* Philadelphia, PA: T. B. Peterson, 1854.
Hicks, Granville. *The Great Tradition: An Interpretation of American Literature since the Civil War.* Rev. ed. New York: Macmillan, 1935.
Hoberek, Andrew. *The Twilight of the Middle Class: Post–World War II American Fiction and White-Collar Work.* Princeton, NJ: Princeton University Press, 2005.
Hochschild, Arlie Russell. *Strangers in Their Own Land: Anger and Mourning on the American Right.* New York: New Press, 2016.
"Strangers in Their Own Land: What Led to the Rise of Trump and What Now?" Sociology Department Colloquium, Stanford University, Palo Alto, CA, February 23, 2017.
Holcombe, Heather E. "Faulkner on Feminine Hygiene, or, How Margaret Sanger Sold Dewey Dell a Bad Abortion." *MFS: Modern Fiction Studies* 57, no. 2 (Summer 2011): 203–29.
Holland, Henry W. "Heredity." *Atlantic Monthly* 52, October 1883, 447–52.
Hollander, A. N. J. den. "The Tradition of 'Poor Whites.'" In *Culture in the South,* edited by William T. Couch, 403–31. Chapel Hill: University of North Carolina Press, 1934.
Holley, Marietta. *Samantha on the Race Problem.* New York: Dodd, Mead, 1892.
Holtsmark, Erling B. "The *Katabasis* Theme in Modern Cinema." In *Classical Myth and Culture in the Cinema,* edited by Martin M. Winkler, 23–50. New York: Oxford University Press, 2001.
Howard, Christopher. *The Hidden Welfare State: Tax Expenditures and Social Policy in the United States.* Princeton, NJ: Princeton University Press, 1997.
Hubbs, Nadine. *Rednecks, Queers, and Country Music.* Berkeley: University of California Press, 2014.

Hundley, Daniel R. *Social Relations in Our Southern States*. New York: Arno, 1973.

Hurwitz, Michael, and Jason Lee. "Grade Inflation and the Role of Standardized Testing." In *Measuring Success: Testing, Grades, and the Future of College Admissions*, edited by Jack Buckley, Lynn Letukas, and Ben Wildavsky, 64–93. Baltimore: Johns Hopkins University Press, 2018.

Inge, M. Thomas. "Literature." In *Literature*, vol. 9 of *The New Encyclopedia of Southern Culture*, edited by M. Thomas Inge, 1–18. Chapel Hill: University of North Carolina Press, 2008.

Jameson, Fredric. *Postmodernism, or, The Cultural Logic of Late Capitalism*. Durham, NC: Duke University Press, 1991.

Jetter, Alexis. "The Roseanne of Literature." *New York Times Magazine*, December 17, 1995, 54+.

Johnson, Charles J. *Patterns of Negro Segregation*. New York: Harper and Brothers, 1943.

Johnson, Claudia Durst. *"To Kill a Mockingbird": Threatening Boundaries*. New York: Twayne Publishers, 1994.

Johnson, Gregory R. "Pagan Virtue and Christian Charity: Flannery O'Connor on the Moral Contradictions of Western Culture." In *The Moral of the Story: Literature and Public Ethics*, edited by Henry T. Edmondson III, 237–54. Lanham, MD: Lexington Books, 2000.

Jones, Gavin. *American Hungers: The Problem of Poverty in U.S. Literature, 1840–1945*. Princeton, NJ: Princeton University Press, 2007.

Kaplan, Amy. "Nation, Region, and Empire." In *Columbia History of the American Novel*, edited by Emory Elliott, 240–66. New York: Columbia University Press, 1991.

Kartiganer, Donald M. "Modernism as Gesture: Faulkner's Missing Facts." *Renaissance and Modern Studies* 41 (1998): 13–28.

Kellogg, D. O. "The Pauper Question." *Atlantic Monthly* 51, May 1883, 638–52.

——— "The Principle and Advantage of Association in Charities." *Journal of Social Science* 12 (December 1880): 84–90.

Kemble, E. W. "Illustrating Huckleberry Finn." *Colophon: A Book Collectors' Quarterly* 1 (February 1930): n.p.

Kessler, Edward. *Flannery O'Connor and the Language of Apocalypse*. Princeton, NJ: Princeton University Press, 1986.

Khan, Shamus Rhaman. *Privilege: The Making of an Adolescent Elite at St. Paul's School*. Princeton, NJ: Princeton University Press, 2011.

Khan, Shamus, and Colin Jerolmack. "Saying Meritocracy and Doing Privilege." *Sociological Quarterly* 54, no. 1 (2013): 9–19.

King, Edward. "The Great South." *Scribner's Monthly* 8, August 1874, 385–412.

——— *The Great South: A Record of Journeys in Louisiana, Texas, the Indian Territory, Missouri, Arkansas, Mississippi, Alabama, Georgia, Florida, South Carolina, North Carolina, Kentucky, Tennessee, Virginia, West Virginia, and Maryland*. Hartford, CT: American, 1875.

Kirby, Jack Temple. *Rural Worlds Lost: The American South, 1920–1960*. Baton Rouge: Louisiana State University Press, 1987.
Kirke, Edmund [James R. Gilmore]. *Among the Pines; or, South in Secession-Time*. New York: J. R. Gilmore, 1862.
"John Jordan." *Atlantic Monthly* 16, October 1865, 434–45.
Kirstein, Lincoln. "Photographs of America: Walker Evans." In *American Photographs*, by Walker Evans, 189–98. New York: Museum of Modern Art, 1988.
Kline, Wendy. *Building a Better Race: Gender, Sexuality, and Eugenics from the Turn of the Century to the Baby Boom*. Berkeley: University of California Press, 2001.
Lang, Amy Schrager. *The Syntax of Class: Writing Inequality in Nineteenth-Century America*. Princeton, NJ: Princeton University Press, 2003.
Lange, Dorothea. "The Assignment I'll Never Forget: Migrant Mother." *Popular Photography*, February 1960, 42+.
Larson, Edward J. *Sex, Race, and Science: Eugenics in the Deep South*. Baltimore: Johns Hopkins University Press, 1995.
Laughlin, Harry Hamilton. *The Legal Status of Eugenical Sterilization: History and Analysis of Litigation under the Virginia Sterilization Statute, which Led to a Decision of the Supreme Court of the United States Upholding the Statute*. Chicago: Fred J. Ringley, 1930.
Lawler, Steph. *Identity: Sociological Perspectives*. Cambridge: Polity, 2008.
Lee, Harper. *To Kill a Mockingbird*. Philadelphia, PA: J. B. Lippincott, 1960.
Levine, Susan. *School Lunch Politics: The Surprising History of America's Favorite Welfare Program*. Princeton, NJ: Princeton University Press, 2008.
Lewis, Oscar. "The Culture of Poverty." *Trans-action* 1, November 1963, 17–19.
Leyda, Julia. "Reading White Trash: Class, Race, and Mobility in Faulkner and Le Sueur." *Arizona Quarterly* 56, no. 2 (Summer 2000): 37–64.
Lipsitz, George. *The Possessive Investment in Whiteness: How White People Profit from Identity Politics*. Philadelphia, PA: Temple University Press, 1998.
Logan, Rayford Whittingham. *The Negro in American Life and Thought: The Nadir, 1877–1901*. New York: Dial, 1954.
Lombardo, Paul A. *Three Generations, No Imbeciles: Eugenics, the Supreme Court, and Buck v. Bell*. Baltimore: Johns Hopkins University Press, 2008.
Longstreet, Augustus Baldwin. "The Fight." In *Georgia Scenes*, 53–64. Nashville: J. S. Sanders, 1992.
Ludmerer, Kenneth M. *Genetics and American Society: A Historical Appraisal*. Baltimore: Johns Hopkins University Press, 1972.
Lynn, Kenneth S. *Mark Twain and Southwestern Humor*. Boston: Little, Brown, 1959.
MacKenzie, Donald A. *Statistics in Britain, 1865–1930: The Social Construction of Scientific Knowledge*. Edinburgh: Edinburgh University Press, 1981.
MacKethan, Lucinda H. "Plantation Fiction, 1865–1900." In *The History of Southern Literature*, edited by Louis D. Rubin Jr., 209–18. Baton Rouge: Louisiana State University Press, 1985.

Maharidge, Dale, and Michael Williamson. *And Their Children after Them*. New York: Pantheon Books, 1989.
Manne, Kate. *Down Girl: The Logic of Misogyny*. New York: Oxford University Press, 2018.
Marable, Manning. *How Capitalism Underdeveloped Black America*. Boston: South End, 1983.
Massengill, Reed. *Portrait of a Racist: The Man Who Killed Medgar Evers?* New York: St. Martin's, 1994.
Matthews, John T. "*As I Lay Dying* in the Machine Age." In *National Identities and Post-Americanist Narratives*, edited by Donald E. Pease, 69–94. Durham, NC: Duke University Press, 1994.
— "Faulkner and Proletarian Literature." In *Faulkner in Cultural Context: Faulkner and Yoknapatawpha, 1995*, edited by Donald M. Kartiganer and Ann J. Abadie, 166–90. Jackson: University Press of Mississippi, 1997.
Maugham, W. Somerset. *On a Chinese Screen*. New York: George H. Doran, 1922.
McAdams, Richard H. "Empathy and Masculinity in Harper Lee's *To Kill a Mockingbird*." In *American Guy: Masculinity in American Law and Literature*, edited by Saul Levmore and Martha C. Nussbaum, 239–61. New York: Oxford University Press, 2014.
McAfee, Tierney. "Parents Change 14-Month-Old Son Atticus' Name After *Go Set a Watchman* Controversy." *People*, July 24, 2015. http://people.com/books/parents-change-son-atticus-name-after-go-set-a-watchman-controversy/.
McCarthy, Cormac. *Suttree*. New York: Random House, 1979.
McIlwaine, Shields. *The Southern Poor-White from Lubberland to Tobacco Road*. Norman: University of Oklahoma Press, 1939.
McIntosh, Peggy. "White Privilege and Male Privilege: A Personal Account of Coming to See Correspondences through Work in Women's Studies." In *Critical White Studies: Looking behind the Mirror*, edited by Richard Delgado and Jean Stefancic, 291–9. Philadelphia, PA: Temple University Press, 1997.
McLaurin, Tim. *The Acorn Plan*. New York: W. W. Norton, 1988.
Megan, Carolyn E. "Moving toward Truth: An Interview with Dorothy Allison." *Kenyon Review* 16, no. 4 (Autumn 1994): 71–83.
Merish, Lori. *Archives of Labor: Working-Class Women and Literary Culture in the Antebellum United States*. Durham, NC: Duke University Press, 2017.
Merritt, Keri Leigh. *Masterless Men: Poor Whites and Slavery in the Antebellum South*. New York: Cambridge University Press, 2017.
Michelmore, Molly C. *Tax and Spend: The Welfare State, Tax Politics, and the Limits of American Liberalism*. Philadelphia: University of Pennsylvania Press, 2012.
Mickler, Ernest Matthew. *White Trash Cooking*. Berkeley: Ten Speed, 1986.
Miller, Susan B. *Disgust: The Gatekeeper Emotion*. Hillsdale, NJ: Analytic, 2004.
Miller, William Ian. *The Anatomy of Disgust*. Cambridge, MA: Harvard University Press, 1997.

Millgate, Michael. *The Achievement of William Faulkner*. New York: Random House, 1966.
Mills, Marja. *The Mockingbird Next Door: Life with Harper Lee*. New York: Penguin, 2014.
Mitchell, Margaret. *Gone with the Wind*. New York: Macmillan, 1963.
Mitchell, W. J. T. *Picture Theory: Essays on Verbal and Visual Representation*. Chicago: University of Chicago Press, 1994.
Moody, Anne. *Coming of Age in Mississippi*. New York: Dial, 1968.
Moreland, Richard C. *Faulkner and Modernism: Rereading and Rewriting*. Madison: University of Wisconsin Press, 1990.
Moss, Barbara Robinette. *Change Me into Zeus's Daughter*. New York: Scribner, 2001.
Moss, Kirby. *The Color of Class: Poor Whites and the Paradox of Privilege*. Philadelphia: University of Pennsylvania Press, 2003.
Mott, Frank Luther. *A History of American Magazines*. Vol. 2. Cambridge, MA: Harvard University Press, 1938.
Napolin, Julie Beth. "'Ravel Out into the No-Wind, No-Sound': The Audiophonic Form of *As I Lay Dying*." In *Fifty Years after Faulkner*, edited by Jay Watson, 122–37. Jackson: University Press of Mississippi, 2016.
Nielsen, Paul S. "What Does Addie Bundren Mean, and How Does She Mean It?" *Southern Literary Journal* 25, no. 1 (Fall 1992): 33–9.
Nilon, Charles H. "The Ending of *Huckleberry Finn*: 'Freeing the Free Negro.'" *Mark Twain Journal* 22, no. 2 (Fall 1984): 21–7.
Nossiter, Adam. *Of Long Memory: Mississippi and the Murder of Medgar Evers*. Reading, MA: Addison-Wesley, 1994.
Nowatzki, Robert C. "'Passing' in a White Genre: Charles W. Chesnutt's Negotiations of the Plantation Tradition in *The Conjure Woman*." *American Literary Realism, 1870–1910* 27, no. 2 (Winter 1995): 20–36.
O'Connor, Flannery. *Everything That Rises Must Converge*. New York: Farrar, Straus and Giroux, 1965.
  A Good Man Is Hard to Find and Other Stories. San Diego: Harcourt Brace Jovanovich, 1983.
  The Habit of Being. New York: Farrar, Straus and Giroux, 1979.
Olmsted, Frederick Law. *A Journey in the Seaboard Slave States: With Remarks on Their Economy*. New York: Dix and Edwards, 1856.
Oney, Steve. "The Making of the Writer." *New York Times*, December 24, 1978, Sunday Book Review, 3+.
Opie, Frederick Douglass. "Molasses-Colored Glasses: WPA and Sundry Sources on Molasses and Southern Foodways." *Southern Cultures* 14, no. 1 (Spring 2008): 81–96.
Orvell, Miles. *The Real Thing: Imitation and Authenticity in American Culture, 1880–1940*. Chapel Hill: University of North Carolina Press, 1989.
Orwell, George. *The Road to Wigan Pier*. London: Secker and Warburg, 1986.
Ownby, Ted. "Three Agrarianisms and the Idea of a South without Poverty." In *Reading Southern Poverty between the Wars, 1918–1939*, edited by Richard

Godden and Martin Crawford, 1–24. Athens: University of Georgia Press, 2006.
Page, Thomas Nelson. *The Negro: The Southerner's Problem*. New York: Charles Scribner's Sons, 1904.
——. *In Ole Virginia; or, Marse Chan and Other Stories*. Nashville: J. S. Sanders, 1991.
Painter, Nell Irvin. *The Narrative of Hosea Hudson: The Life and Times of a Black Radical*. New York: W. W. Norton, 1994.
Parrish, Susan Scott. *The Flood Year 1927: A Cultural History*. Princeton, NJ: Princeton University Press, 2017.
Parsons, Willard. "The Story of the Fresh-Air Fund." *Scribner's Magazine* 9, April 1891, 515–24.
Payne, Charles M. *I've Got the Light of Freedom: The Organizing Tradition and the Mississippi Freedom Struggle*. Berkeley: University of California Press, 1995.
Peek, Charles A. "'A-laying There, Right Up to My Door': As American *As I Lay Dying*." In *Faulkner in America: Faulkner and Yoknapatawpha 1998*, edited by Joseph R. Urgo and Ann J. Abadie, 116–35. Jackson: University Press of Mississippi, 2001.
Percy, William Alexander. *Lanterns on the Levee: Recollections of a Planter's Son*. Baton Rouge: Louisiana State University Press, 2006.
Perdue, Charles L., Jr., Thomas E. Barden, and Robert K. Phillips, eds. *Weevils in the Wheat: Interviews with Virginia Ex-Slaves*. Charlottesville: University of Virginia Press, 1976.
Pew Research Center. "In Changing News Landscape, Even Television Is Vulnerable." September 27, 2012. www.pewresearch.org/politics/2012/09/27/in-changing-news-landscape-even-television-is-vulnerable/.
Pick, Daniel. *Faces of Degeneration: A European Disorder, c. 1848–c. 1918*. Cambridge: Cambridge University Press, 1989.
Poppendieck, Janet. *Free for All: Fixing School Food in America*. Berkeley: University of California Press, 2010.
Potts, Matthew. "'Their Ragged Biblical Forms': Materiality, Misogyny, and the Corporal Works of Mercy in *Suttree*." *Religion and Literature* 47, no. 2 (Summer 2015): 65–86.
Price, Kenneth M. "Charles Chesnutt, the *Atlantic Monthly*, and the Intersection of African-American Fiction and Elite Culture." In *Periodical Literature in Nineteenth-Century America*, edited by Kenneth M. Price and Susan Belasco Smith, 257–74. Charlottesville: University Press of Virginia, 1995.
Prown, Katherine Hemple. *Revising Flannery O'Connor: Southern Literary Culture and the Problem of Female Authorship*. Charlottesville: University Press of Virginia, 2001.
Pryal, Katie Rose Guest. "Walking in Another's Skin: Failure of Empathy in *To Kill a Mockingbird*." In *Harper Lee's "To Kill a Mockingbird": New Essays*, edited by Michael J. Meyer, 174–92. Lanham, MD: Scarecrow, 2010.
Rabinowitz, Paula. *Labor and Desire: Women's Revolutionary Fiction in Depression America*. Chapel Hill: University of North Carolina Press, 1991.

Rafter, Nicole Hahn. *Creating Born Criminals*. Urbana: University of Illinois Press, 1997.
White Trash: The Eugenic Family Studies, 1877–1919. Boston: Northeastern University Press, 1988.
"White Trash: Eugenics as Social Ideology." *Society* 26, no. 1 (November–December 1988): 43–9.
Ramsay, W. G. "The Physiological Differences between the European (or White Man) and the Negro." *Southern Agriculturist and Register of Rural Affairs: Adapted to the Southern Section of the United States* 12, no. 6 (June 1839): 286–94.
Reid, Whitelaw. *After the War: A Tour of the Southern States, 1865–1866*. New York: Harper and Row, 1965.
"The Reign of King Cotton." *Atlantic Monthly* 7, April 1861, 451–65.
Rembis, Michael A. "'Explaining Sexual Life to Your Daughter': Gender and Eugenic Education in the United States during the 1930s." In *Popular Eugenics: National Efficiency and American Mass Culture in the 1930s*, edited by Susan Currell and Christina Cogdell, 91–119. Athens: Ohio University Press, 2006.
Ring, Natalie J. *The Problem South: Region, Empire, and the New Liberal State, 1880–1930*. Athens: University of Georgia Press, 2012.
Robertson, Sarah. *Poverty Politics: Poor Whites in Contemporary Southern Writing*. Jackson: University Press of Mississippi, 2019.
Robert Wood Johnson Foundation. "Adult Obesity in the United States." State of Childhood Obesity. Accessed August 20, 2019. www.stateofobesity.org/adult-obesity/.
Roediger, David R. *The Wages of Whiteness: Race and the Making of the American Working Class*. London: Verso, 1991.
Romero, Lora. *Home Fronts: Domesticity and Its Critics in the Antebellum United States*. Durham, NC: Duke University Press, 1997.
Ross, Stephen M. "'Voice' in Narrative Texts: The Example of *As I Lay Dying*." *PMLA* 94, no. 2 (March 1979): 300–10.
Ruffin, Edmund. *The Political Economy of Slavery; or, The Institution Considered in Regard to its Influence on Public Wealth and the General Welfare*. Washington, DC: Lemuel Towers, 1857.
Satterwhite, Emily. *Dear Appalachia: Readers, Identity, and Popular Fiction since 1878*. Lexington: University Press of Kentucky, 2011.
Schocket, Eric. *Vanishing Moments: Class and American Literature*. Ann Arbor: University of Michigan Press, 2006.
Schryer, Stephen. *Fantasies of the New Class: Ideologies of Professionalism in Post–World War II American Fiction*. New York: Columbia University Press, 2011.
Seguin, Robert. *Around Quitting Time: Work and Middle-Class Fantasy in American Fiction*. Durham, NC: Duke University Press, 2001.
Shapiro, Joe. *The Illiberal Imagination: Class and the Rise of the U.S. Novel*. Charlottesville: University of Virginia Press, 2017.

Sharpless, Rebecca. *Cooking in Other Women's Kitchens: Domestic Workers in the South, 1865–1960*. Chapel Hill: University of North Carolina Press, 2010.

Sherman, Jennifer. *Those Who Work, Those Who Don't: Poverty, Morality, and Family in Rural America*. Minneapolis: University of Minnesota Press, 2009.

Sherrill, Robert. "A Son of the Hungry South." Review of *A Childhood: The Biography of a Place*, by Harry Crews. *New York Times*, December 24, 1978, Sunday Book Review, 3+.

Shloss, Carol. *In Visible Light: Photography and the American Writer, 1840–1940*. New York: Oxford University Press, 1987.

Simmel, Georg. *Simmel on Culture: Selected Writings*. Edited by David Frisby and Mike Featherstone. London: Sage Publications, 1997.

Singal, Daniel J. *The War Within: From Victorian to Modernist Thought in the South, 1919–1945*. Chapel Hill: University of North Carolina Press, 1982.

——. *William Faulkner: The Making of a Modernist*. Chapel Hill: University of North Carolina Press, 1997.

Skitt [Hardin E. Taliaferro]. "Ham Rachel, of Alabama." In *Fisher's River (North Carolina) Scenes and Characters*, 249–69. New York: Harper and Brothers, 1859.

Smedes, Susan Dabney. *Memorials of a Southern Planter*. Baltimore: Cushings and Bailey, 1887.

Smith, Dina. "Cultural Studies' Misfit: White Trash Studies." *Mississippi Quarterly* 57, no. 3 (Summer 2004): 369–87.

Smith, Lillian. *How Am I to Be Heard? Letters of Lillian Smith*. Edited by Margaret Rose Gladney. Chapel Hill: University of North Carolina Press, 1993.

——. *Killers of the Dream*. New York: W. W. Norton, 1994.

Social Security Administration. "Baby Names." Accessed June 20, 2021. www.ssa.gov/oact/babynames/.

Stafford, Jean. Review of *Naked in Garden Hills*, by Harry Crews. *New York Times*, April 13, 1969, Sunday Book Review, 4–5.

Stein, Sally. "Passing Likeness: Dorothea Lange's 'Migrant Mother' and the Paradox of Iconicity." In *Only Skin: Changing Visions of the American Self*, edited by Coco Fusco and Brian Wallis, 345–55. New York: International Center of Photography / Harry N. Abrams, 2003.

Stephens, C. Ralph, ed. *The Correspondence of Flannery O'Connor and the Brainard Cheneys*. Jackson: University Press of Mississippi, 2008.

Stern, Alexandra Minna. "'We Cannot Make a Silk Purse Out of a Sow's Ear': Eugenics in the Hoosier Heartland." *Indiana Magazine of History* 103, no. 1 (March 2007): 3–38.

Stockett, Kathryn. *The Help*. New York: Berkley Books, 2009.

Stoddard, Lothrop. *The Revolt against Civilization: The Menace of the Under Man*. New York: Charles Scribner's Sons, 1922.

Sullivan, Shannon. *Good White People: The Problem with Middle-Class White Anti-Racism*. Albany: State University of New York Press, 2014.

Sundquist, Eric J. *Faulkner: The House Divided*. Baltimore: Johns Hopkins University Press, 1983.

"Realism and Regionalism." In *Columbia Literary History of the United States*, edited by Emory Elliott, 501–24. New York: Columbia University Press, 1988.

To Wake the Nations: Race in the Making of American Literature. Cambridge, MA: Belknap Press of Harvard University Press, 1993.

Taylor, William R. *Cavalier and Yankee: The Old South and American National Character.* New York: Harper and Row, 1961.

Thanet, Octave [Alice French]. "The Indoor Pauper: A Study." *Atlantic Monthly* 47, June 1881, 749–64.

"Then and Now in the Old Dominion." *Atlantic Monthly* 9, April 1862, 493–502.

Thompson, E. P. *The Making of the English Working Class.* New York: Random House, 1963.

Titus, Mary. "The Dining Room Door Swings Both Ways: Food, Race, and Domestic Space in the Nineteenth-Century South." In *Haunted Bodies: Gender and Southern Texts*, edited by Anne Goodwyn Jones and Susan V. Donaldson, 243–56. Charlottesville: University of Virginia Press, 1997.

Trachtenberg, Alan. Foreword to *You Have Seen Their Faces*, by Erskine Caldwell and Margaret Bourke-White, v–viii. Athens: University of Georgia Press, 1995.

Tracy, Susan J. *In the Master's Eye: Representations of Women, Blacks, and Poor Whites in Antebellum Southern Literature.* Amherst: University of Massachusetts Press, 1995.

Trowbridge, J. T. *The South: A Tour of Its Battle-Fields and Ruined Cities.* New York: Arno, 1969.

Tucker, Robert C., ed. *The Marx-Engels Reader*, 2nd ed. New York: W. W. Norton, 1978.

Twain, Mark. *Adventures of Huckleberry Finn.* New York: W. W. Norton, 1999.

Autobiography of Mark Twain. Edited by Harriet Elinor Smith. Vol. 1. Berkeley: University of California Press, 2010.

Life on the Mississippi. Boston: James R. Osgood, 1883.

Twelve Southerners. *I'll Take My Stand: The South and the Agrarian Tradition.* Baton Rouge: Louisiana State University Press, 1977.

Twyman, Robert W. "The Clay Eater: A New Look at an Old Southern Enigma." *Journal of Southern History* 37, no. 3 (August 1971): 439–48.

United States Bureau of the Census. *Population 1920.* Vol. 1 of *Fourteenth Census of the United States Taken in the Year 1920.* Washington, DC: Government Printing Office, 1921.

Valentine, Victoria. "When Love Was a Crime." *Emerge*, June 1997, 60–2.

Vance, J. D. *Hillbilly Elegy: A Memoir of a Family and Culture in Crisis.* New York: HarperCollins, 2016.

Veblen, Thorstein. *The Theory of the Leisure Class: An Economic Study of Institutions.* New York: Macmillan, 1912.

Wadlington, Warwick. *"As I Lay Dying": Stories Out of Stories.* New York: Maxwell Macmillan International, 1992.

Walerstein, Rachel. "Recomposing the Self: Joyful Shame in Dorothy Allison's *Bastard Out of Carolina*." *Mosaic* 49, no. 4 (December 2016): 169–83.
Warner, Amos G. "Notes on the Statistical Determination of the Causes of Poverty." *Publications of the American Statistical Association* 1, no. 5 (March 1889): 183–205.
Warren, Kenneth W. *Black and White Strangers: Race and American Literary Realism*. Chicago: University of Chicago Press, 1993.
Washington, Booker T. "The Awakening of the Negro." *Atlantic Monthly* 78, September 1896, 322–8.
  Up from Slavery: An Autobiography. New York: Doubleday, 1901.
Watkins, Evan. *Throwaways: Work Culture and Consumer Education*. Stanford, CA: Stanford University Press, 1993.
Watson, Jay. "Genealogies of White Deviance: The Eugenic Family Studies, *Buck v. Bell*, and William Faulkner, 1926–1931." In *Faulkner and Whiteness*, edited by Jay Watson, 19–55. Jackson: University Press of Mississippi, 2011.
  "The Rhetoric of Exhaustion and the Exhaustion of Rhetoric: Erskine Caldwell in the Thirties." *Mississippi Quarterly* 46, no. 2 (Spring 1993): 215–29.
Watts, Trent A. *One Homogeneous People: Narratives of White Southern Identity, 1890–1920*. Knoxville: University of Tennessee Press, 2010.
Welty, Eudora. "The Art of Fiction XLVII." *Paris Review* 55 (Fall 1972): 72–97.
  One Writer's Beginnings. Cambridge, MA: Harvard University Press, 1983.
  "Where Is the Voice Coming From?" In *The Collected Stories of Eudora Welty*, 603–7. New York: Harcourt Brace Jovanovich, 1980.
Wendell, Evert Jansen. "Boys' Clubs in New York." In *The Poor in Great Cities*, 151–76. New York: Charles Scribner's Sons, 1895.
Whitt, Margaret Earley. "The Pivotal Year, 1963: Flannery O'Connor and the Civil Rights Movement." In *A Political Companion to Flannery O'Connor*, edited by Henry T. Edmondson III, 79–98. Lexington: University Press of Kentucky, 2017.
Williamson, Joel. *The Crucible of Race: Black/White Relations in the American South since Emancipation*. New York: Oxford University Press, 1984.
Willis, Susan. "Learning from the Banana." *American Quarterly* 39, no. 4 (Winter 1987): 586–600.
Wilson, Anthony. "Narrative and Counternarrative in *The Leopard's Spots* and *The Marrow of Tradition*." In *The Oxford Handbook of the Literature of the U.S. South*, edited by Fred Hobson and Barbara Ladd, 212–30. New York: Oxford University Press, 2016.
Wilson, Christopher P. *White Collar Fictions: Class and Social Representation in American Literature, 1885–1925*. Athens: University of Georgia Press, 1992.
Woo, Andrew, and Chris Salviati. "Imbalance in Housing Aid: Mortgage Interest Deduction vs. Section 8." Apartment List, October 17, 2017. www.apartmentlist.com/rentonomics/imbalance-housing-aid-mortgage-interest-deduction-vs-section-8/.

Wood, Ralph C. *The Comedy of Redemption: Christian Faith and Comic Vision in Four American Novelists*. Notre Dame, IN: University of Notre Dame Press, 1988.

Woodward, C. Vann. *The Burden of Southern History*. Baton Rouge: Louisiana State University Press, 2008.

Woolf, Steven H., Heidi Schoomaker, Latoya Hill, and Christine M. Orndahl. "The Social Determinants of Health and the Decline in U.S. Life Expectancy: Implications for Appalachia." *Journal of Appalachian Health* 1, no. 1 (Spring 2019): 6–14.

Wray, Matt. *Not Quite White: White Trash and the Boundaries of Whiteness*. Durham, NC: Duke University Press, 2006.

Wray, Virginia. "Flannery O'Connor and Lillian Smith: A Missed Opportunity?" *Flannery O'Connor Review* 5 (2007): 35–43.

Yellin, Jean Fagan. *The Intricate Knot: Black Figures in American Literature, 1776–1863*. New York: New York University Press, 1972.

Yukins, Elizabeth. "'Feeble-Minded' White Women and the Spectre of Proliferating Perversity in American Eugenics Narratives." In *Evolution and Eugenics in American Literature and Culture, 1880–1940: Essays on Ideological Conflict and Complicity*, edited by Lois A. Cuddy and Claire M. Roche, 164–86. Lewisburg, PA: Bucknell University Press, 2003.

Zandy, Janet. *Hands: Physical Labor, Class, and Cultural Work*. New Brunswick, NJ: Rutgers University Press, 2004.

Zoll, May Lou. "Susanna." *Peterson Magazine* 6, January 1896, 84–91.

Index

African Americans, 4, 23, 28, *see also* slavery
Agee, James
  Let Us Now Praise Famous Men, 13
Agrarian movements, 47–8, 51
alcohol consumption, 100, 118
Allison, Dorothy, 95, 109–10, 120–1, *see also*
  Bastard Out of Carolina (Allison)
  Skin: Talking about Sex, Class, and Literature,
  110
American dream, achievement of, 130–1
Andrews, Sidney, 23, 28
Appalachia, 25–6, 54, 127, 129
As I Lay Dying (Faulkner), 44–8, 50–67
  Bundren family in, 44–6, 50–3, 55–67
  farming community in, 58–9, 66
  funeral journey in, 44–6, 64–7
  intraracial conflict in, 44–6
  language of motherhood in, 62–3
  manuscript vs. typescript of, 44–6
  overview, 17
  poor whites as foil to modernness in, 17, 45–6,
    53, 55
  representational techniques in, 17, 46, 51
  social distinctions in, 55–67
  stasis and suspension in, 46, 51–3
  sweat as labor in, 50–1
  townspeople in, 44–6, 55–7, 64, 66
  urban/rural divide in, 53, 55–8
aspirational class, 125
Atkinson, Ted, 58
Atlanta Constitution, 39
Atlantic Monthly, 17, 21–8, 31, 54
autobiographies/memoirs, 101, 108–10, 123

Bastard Out of Carolina (Allison)
  Bone (character) in, 95, 101–2, 106–8, 114,
    117–18
  class consciousness in, 102–3
  first-person narration of, 109–10
  intertextual relationships in, 95, 100,
    102–3

portrayal of hunger in, 18, 95, 100, 105–8,
  121
as response to peckeresque works, 112,
  114–18
Beckwith, Byron De La, 72
Bedient, Calvin, 50
Bledsoe, Eric, 110
Bleikasten, André, 45
bodies, female, 113, 117–18
Bonilla-Silva, Eduardo, 80
boundaries, social, 66
Bourdieu, Pierre, 10
Bourke-White, Margaret
  You Have Seen Their Faces, 121
Bragg, Rick, 11
Brodhead, Richard H., 5, 19–20, 22, 32
Brooks, Cleanth, 45, 58
Brown, Emma E.
  "Children's Labor: A Problem," 26
Brown, Larry, 112
  Joe, 112, 115–16, 119
Brundage, William Fitzhugh, 81
Buck v. Bell, 59
Burwell, Letitia M., 104
Byrd, William, 96
  History of the Dividing Line, 96

Cable, George Washington, 33
Caldwell, Erskine
  Tobacco Road, 48, 52
  You Have Seen Their Faces, 48, 121
Carpenter, Brian (editor)
  Grit Lit: A Rough South Reader, 111
Carroll, Lewis
  Alice's Adventures in Wonderland, 101
  Through the Looking-Glass, 102
Case, Anne, 127
Cash, Jean W., 110
Century Illustrated Monthly Magazine, 1–3, 15,
  26, 97, 123
Change Me into Zeus's Daughter (Moss)

184

Index

class consciousness in, 103
first-person narration of, 109–10
intertextual relationships in, 18, 95, 100–2
portrayal of hunger in, 18, 100–3, 105–8, 117
as response to peckeresque works, 112, 116–19
change vs. stasis, 33–9, 51–3, 85, 87, 89
Chesnutt, Charles W., 28
Colonel's Dream, The, 7
conjure stories of, 21, 28–30, 32–3, 38–40, 131
"Deep Sleeper, A," 30
disruption of stereotypes by, 13, 17, 21, 28–33, 38–43
"Goophered Grapevine, The," 29, 39
"Marked Tree, The," 31
"Mars Jeems's Nightmare," 29–30
children, socialization of white, 88
citizenship rights in South, 20
civil rights era, *see* literature of civil rights era
Civil War, essays on, 22–3
class consciousness, literature and, 100–3
class distinctions, *see also* poor white characters as foils for middle class
anxiety over changes in, 33, 35, 37, 40
in college admissions, 130
in communication, 82–4
corpse as embodiment of, 64–7
definition of, 10
food as marker of, 86, 94–100, 104–8, 126–7
with government assistance, 128
in grit lit, 111
health as marker of, 74, 87, 94–8, 126–7
in homogeneous population, 58
in literary structures, 8, 10–11, 17, 40–1, 46, 51, 64, 95
in photographs, 15–16, 120
between poor whites, 7, 85, 89, 99
racism and, 17, 71–3, 76–8, 80, 86
shared norms as marker of, 86, 89, 125–6
shoes as marker of, 86–7
social mobility/immobility and, 9, 33–9, 51–3
with urban/rural divide, 44–6, 50, 53, 55–8
clay eaters, 28, 31, 96
college admissions, 130
Cook, Sylvia Jenkins, 54
Cowart, David, 119
Crews, Harry
Childhood: The Biography of a Place, A, 102, 108–10
grit lit by, 110, 112
"Grits" (*Esquire*), 110
Scar Lover, 112, 116
Crisis, The (NAACP magazine), 31
cross-class racism, 76–7, 80
culture of poverty thesis, 129
Currid-Halkett, Elizabeth, 125–6

Daniel, Pete, 72
Davis, David A., 104
De Forest, J. W.
"Drawing Bureau Rations," 23
de Graffenried, Clare, 97, 123
Deaton, Angus, 127
dialogues vs. monologues, 82–4
discursive poverty, 52
disgust, social boundaries and, 66
Douglas, Mary
Purity and Danger, 63
Douglass, Frederick
"Race Problem, The," 1, 4
Du Bois, W. E. B.
Black Reconstruction, 79
Duck, Leigh Anne, 52
Dugdale, Richard L.
"*Jukes, The*," 24
"Origin of Crime in Society," 24
Durr, Virginia Foster, 98

economic downturns, 16
economic inequality, middle-class explanation for, 95, 97, 99
economic mobility, 9, 33
education, 4, 22, 24, 31, 130
Edwards, Harry Stillwell, 3, 19, 25
empathy, 86–7
Esquire, 108, 110
essays
in Gilded Age, 22–7, 31, 97
modernist, 54, 64
in 1930s, 48
eugenics
fictional rebuttals to, 4, 61–3
heredity as explanation in, 4, 25, 60
as justification for erasing poor whites, 20, 27, 55
and sterilization, 7, 59–60
Evans, Walker, 13–16
Evers, Medgar, 69, 71–2, 75

family farms, food on, 106–7
famineways, 95, 108, 121
fast food consumption, 127
Faulkner, William
Absalom, Absalom!, 15, 40, 49, 51
As I Lay Dying, see *As I Lay Dying* (Faulkner)
"Barn Burning," 49
critical reviews on fiction of, 47, 50, 52, 58, 61
disruption of stereotypes by, 17, 45–51, 54, 57–8, 61–3, 65–7, 131

Faulkner, William (cont.)
  and modernism, 45–6, 53, 67
  Sound and the Fury, The, 47–8
Faust, Drew Gilpin, 34
first-person narratives, 10, 71–2, 78–84, 109–10, 116
Fishkin, Shelley Fisher
  Was Huck Black?, 6
food, *see also* hunger of poor whites
  Allison's and Moss's challenges to stereotypes about, 18, 95, 100–8, 121
  on family farms, 106–7
  grit lit's portrayal of women with, 113–15, 117–18
  as marker of class distinctions, 86, 94–100, 104–8, 126–7
  plantation life and, 104–6
  in works by Carroll, Lewis, 102
food fantasies, writing about, 105–6
Foote, Stephanie, 19
Fortune, 13
frame narrative structure, 17, 29–30, 33, 35, 39–40, *see also* plantation literature
Franklin, Tom, 111
French, Alice (pseud. Octave Thanet), 25
  "Indoor Pauper, The," 27
Frost, William Goodell
  "Our Contemporary Ancestors in the Southern Mountains," 54

Garrett, George, 120
Gilmore, James R., 98
Gold, Mike, 48
government assistance, 128
Grady, Henry W., 39
Great Depression, 8, 67
Greeson, Jennifer Rae, 6
grit lit
  female response to male themes in, 18, 95, 110, 114–19
  as insider account, 110, 128
  male and female traditions in, 110–12
  male friendships in, 119
  male vs. female trajectories in, 119–20
  as peckeresque, 112, 115–19
  selfishness of male characters in, 115–19
  sexuality in, 113–19
  women and food in, 113–15, 117–18
  women as human givers in, 112–15, 119–20
Guinn, Matthew, 103

Hagerman, Margaret A., 130
Hale, Dorothy J., 50, 73
ham as symbol, 99–100
Harper's New Monthly Magazine, 23

Harris, Joel Chandler
  depiction of poor whites by, 3, 19
  "Mr. Bear Catches Old Mr. Bull-Frog," 36
  Uncle Remus, 35–7, 40, 42
  "Why Mr. Possum Has No Hair on his Tail," 37
Hartigan, John, Jr., 71, 73, 86
health as class marker, 74, 87, 94–8, 126–7
Hemenway, Robert, 35, 37
Hentz, Caroline Lee
  Planter's Northern Bride, The, 34, 105
Here Comes Honey Boo Boo (TV show), 94
heredity vs. environment, poverty and, 4, 22–5, 87
Hicks, Granville, 47
Hochschild, Arlie
  feels-as-if stories by, 124, 131
  Strangers in Their Own Land, 18, 123–7, 129, 132
Holland, Henry W., 27
Hollander, A. N. J. den
  Culture in the South contribution by, 55
Holley, Marietta
  Samantha on the Race Problem, 1, 4
Hubbs, Nadine, 71
human givers, women as, 112–15, 119–20
Hundley, Daniel R.
  Social Relations in Our Southern States, 22, 97
hunger of poor whites
  Allison's and Moss's challenges to stereotypes about, 18, 95, 100–8, 121
  literature as sustenance for, 100–3
  middle-class denial of, 98, 104–8
  unhealthy appetites as cause of, 94–100
  and writing about food fantasies, 105–6
hypocrisy, exposure of, 13, 32

immigrants, 5, 19, 43
inferiority complexes, 70, 92
intelligence of poor whites
  refutation of stereotypes about, 46, 81–4, 91, 100–3
  stereotypes about, 3, 23, 27, 59–60, 79, 99
intelligence tests, 59–60
intertextual relationships in Allison and Moss, 18, 95, 100–3
intraracial class conflict, 10, 34–5, 40–1, 43–5, 73, 85

Jameson, Fredric, 46

Kaplan, Amy, 19
katabasis (journey to underworld), 127, 132
Kellogg, D. O.
  "Pauper Question, The," 27

Index

Kemble, E. W., 1–4, 132
Kennedy, John Pendleton
   Swallow Barn, 33
Khan, Shamus, 131
King, Edward, 97
   "Great South, The," 26
Kirby, Jack Temple, 97
Kline, Wendy, 62

labor
   disruptions of stereotypes about, 29–32, 49–51
   Faulkner's portrayal of, 46–51
   stereotypes about, 28, 34
lack, rhetoric of, 125
Lange, Dorothea
   "Migrant Mother" (photograph), 120
language of motherhood, 62–3
language, stereotyping of poor whites with, 69
Lawler, Steph, 125
laziness, poor whites and, 11, 131
   in literature of civil rights era, 70, 74
   in literature of Gilded Age, 23, 27–32
   in literature of modern era, 46–51, 58, 61
   in literature of 2000s, 129–31
   in narratives of 1700s, 96
Lee, Harper, 68, 84–90, 92, 99–100
   Go Set a Watchman, 68
   To Kill a Mockingbird, see *To Kill a Mockingbird* (Lee)
leisure-class life, 30–2, 49–51
Levine, Susan, 104
Lewis, Oscar
   "Culture of Poverty, The," 129
Leyda, Julia, 58
literary devices, see narrative structures
literary disruptions of poor white stereotypes
   by Allison and Moss on false class identities, 102–3
   by Allison and Moss on food, 18, 95, 100–8, 121
   by Allison and Moss on grit lit, 18, 95, 110, 112, 114–19
   by Chesnutt, Charles, 13, 21, 28–33, 38–43
   by Crews, Harry, 108–10
   by Faulkner, William, 17, 45–51, 54, 57–8, 61–3, 65–7
   by O'Connor, Flannery, 18, 69, 73–8, 81–4, 88–93
   overview of, 8, 11, 17–18, 131
literature as sustenance, 100–3
literature of civil rights era
   classism and racism in, 17, 71–3, 76–8, 80, 86
   hunger in, 108
   individual racist villains in, 18, 68, 70–3, 92
   of Lee, Harper, 68, 84–90, 92, 99–100
   middle-class assumed authority in, 71–3, 75, 78–9, 81
   misrepresentations in, 71–3, 75, 80
   of O'Connor, Flannery, 18, 69, 73–8, 81–4, 88–93
   overview of, 8, 17, 68–9
   poor whites as foils for middle class in, 71–3, 77, 79–80, 98–100
   poor whites as lazy in, 70, 74
   of Smith, Lillian, 10, 69, 78–81, 99, 103
   of Welty, Eudora, 68, 70–3, 75–6, 78
literature of Gilded Age (late 1800s), see also local color/regional writers
   Chesnutt's disruption of stereotypes in, 13, 17, 21, 28–33, 38–43
   essays, 22–7, 31
   overview of, 5, 8, 17, 123
   poor whites as degenerate in, 22–7, 37
   poor whites as foils for middle class in, 19, 21, 33, 37, 39, 43
   poor whites as lazy in, 23, 27–32
   regional texts, 19–22
literature of modern era
   of Faulkner, William, 45–6, 53, 67, see also Faulkner, William
   Faulkner's disruption of stereotypes in, 17, 45–51, 54, 61–3, 65–7
   narrative devices of, 17, 46
   overview of, 17
   poor whites as antiquated in, 17, 45–6, 54–7
   poor whites as country people in, 44–6, 53, 55–8
   poor whites as foils for middle class in, 17, 43, 45–6, 50, 53, 58, 67
   poor whites as lazy in, 46–51, 58, 61
   poor whites as trash in, 55, 64–7
literature of 1990s
   of Allison, Dorothy, 95, 110, 120–1, see also *Bastard Out of Carolina* (Allison)
   of Crews, Harry, 102, 108–10, 112, 116
   grit lit, see grit lit
   hunger in, see hunger of poor whites
   literary devices in, 18, 95, 100–3
   memoirs, 101, 108–10
   of Moss, Barbara Robinette, 95, see also *Change Me into Zeus's Daughter* (Moss)
   overview of, 8, 18, 95
literature of 2000s, see recent (2010s) works depicting poor whites
local color/regional writers, 3, 19–22, 25, 28, 32, 133
Longstreet, Augustus Baldwin, 9, 96
Louisiana, 123, 125–6, 132
Loving v. Virginia, 93

Loving, Richard, 93
lynching, 81, 86
Lytle, Andrew
  I'll Take My Stand, essay in, 49, 106–7

male-oriented grit lit, 110–12
malnutrition, *see* hunger of poor whites
Manne, Kate, 112, 114
Marable, Manning, 80
Matthews, John T., 48, 51, 53, 57
Maugham, W. Somerset, 64
McCarthy, Cormac
  Suttree, 112–13, 115–20
McLaurin, Tim, 112
  Acorn Plan, The, 112–16, 119
memoirs/autobiographies, 101, 108–10, 123
Mickler, Ernest Matthew
  White Trash Cooking, 94
middle-class monologic, 79–84
middle-class whites, *see also* poor white characters
  as foils for middle class
  assumed authority of, 71–3, 75, 78–9, 81, 120–1, 123
  characterizations of ignorance of, 82–4, 90–2
  as creators of black narrators, 32, 35
  as creators of poor white images, 10–11, 13–16, 54, 70–3, 75, 78–9, 102–3, 120–1, 123, 132
  with cultural capital of modernism, 46, 53, 55
  ethics/morals and, 58–9, 77, 86
  O'Connor's exposure of, 73–8, 81–4, 88–93
  and poor white hunger, 94–100, 104–8
  racism of, 18, 71–3, 76–8, 80
  and rhetoric of lack, 125
  self-satisfaction of, 78
  with shared norms, 86, 89, 125–6
  work as basis of identity for, 12, 130
Miller, William Ian, 66
Millgate, Michael, 45
Miss Minerva and William Green Hill (Calhoun), 88
Mississippi, 60, 67
Mitchell, C. D., 60
Mitchell, Margaret
  Gone with the Wind, 9, 102
Mitchell, W. J. T.
  Picture Theory, 16
modern era, *see* literature of modern era
monologues, 10, 71–2, 78–84
Monroe, Sputnik, 92
Moody, Anne
  Coming of Age in Mississippi, 108
mortality, theme of, 126–8
mortgage interest deduction, 128

Moss, Barbara Robinette, 95, 104, 109–10, *see also Change Me into Zeus's Daughter* (Moss)
motherhood, language of, 62–3
Mott, Frank Luther, 21
Murfree, Mary Noailles (pseud. Charles Egbert Craddock), 3, 12, 19, 25
  "A-Playin' of Old Sledge at the Settlemint," 28
  "'Harnt' that Walks Chilhowee, The," 27
  "Over on the T'other Mounting," 27

narrative structures
  class distinctions in, 8, 10–11, 17, 40–1, 46, 51, 95
  famineways as, 95, 108, 121
  with first-person, 10, 71–2, 78–84, 109–10, 116
  frame, 17, 29–30, 33, 35, 39–40
  with intertextual relationships, 18, 95, 100–3
  monologues, 10, 71–2, 78–84
  of plantation fiction, 32, 35, 38–43
  with pronouns in place of proper nouns, 119
  with repetition, 52
  reveries, 57–8
  with single character point of view, 73–4, 79
  stream-of-consciousness, 17, 46
  suspension, 46, 51
  with third-person, 12, 73, 116
  unreliability in, 75
Nashville Agrarians (Twelve Southerners), 47–8, 50–1
  I'll Take My Stand, 47–8, 106–7
New Masses, 48
New York Times Magazine, 120
New Yorker, 11, 69, 72
norms, shared, 86, 89, 125–6
Nossiter, Adam, 72
nostalgia of plantation fiction, 35, 38, 41–2

O'Connor, Flannery, 73, 81, 92–3
  "Circle in the Fire, A," 82–4
  "Displaced Person, The," 82
  disruption of stereotypes by, 18, 69, 73–8, 81–4, 88–93, 131
  "Good Country People," 89–92
  "Greenleaf," 82
  "Revelation," 73–8
  Turpin, Ruby (character), 73–8
obsolescence, poor whites and, 54–7
opioid epidemic, 127
oral sex in grit lit, 115–16
organic foods, 126
Orwell, George, 64
Ownby, Ted, 106
Owsley, Frank Lawrence, 49

Index

Page, Thomas Nelson, 29
  "Marse Chan," 36
  "Meh Lady: A Story of the War," 41
  "Ole 'Stracted," 37
  plantation stories of, 32, 36–7, 40–2
  scholarly interpretations of, 43
Parsons, Willard, 6
"Pauper Question, The," 24
peckeresque works, 112, 115–19
Percy, William Alexander
  Lanterns on the Levee, 43
photographs, poor white imagery in, 13–16, 120
plantation literature, 17
  anxiety over social change and, 33, 37, 40, 43
  black narrators in, 32, 35, 37, 39–43, 105
  Chesnutt's reworking of, 32–3, 38–43
  classism of, 40–1
  disparaging of poor whites by, 34–5, 37–9, 41
  paternalism in, 38, 40
  polyvocality in, 41–3
  portrayal of food in, 104–6
  relations between formerly enlaved people and enslavers in, 35, 37–9, 41–2
  social mobility in, 35–9
point of view, single character, 73–4, 79
polyvocality in plantation fiction, 39–43
poor white characters as foils for middle class
  in civil rights era, 71–3, 77, 79–80, 98–100
  in late 1800s, 19, 21, 33, 37, 39, 43
  in mid-1900s, 43
  in modernism, 17, 45–6, 50, 53, 55, 58, 67
  overview, 7, 10–11, 13–17, 123, 133
  in 2000s, 124–7, 130–1
  with unhealthy habits as cause of hunger, 94–100
poor whites, *see also* literary disruptions of poor white stereotypes
  hunger and, *see* hunger of poor whites
  literary experiences of, 100–3
  literary importance of, 7, 16
  in literature, overview, 7, 16–18
  marginalizing of, 5, 12, 20, 34–6
  memoirs by, 101, 108–10, 123
  middle-class ignorance of, 82–4, 90–2, 132
  vs. poor and white, 7, 85, 89, 99
  as "race problem," 1–3, 133
  as racial group, 26
  scholarship on fiction about, 5, 19, 43, 45, 133
  self-definition by, 110
  stereotyping of, *see* stereotypes of poor whites
  vs. working-class whites, 11
Poppendieck, Janet, 107
Potts, Matthew, 113

poverty
  first-person accounts of, 95, 108–10, 116
  heredity vs. environment and, 4, 22–5, 87
  Hollywood versions of, 108
  hunger and, 107–8
  as personal failing, 74, 97, 99, 129–31
  relief efforts for, 6, 23, 25
  representational techniques for, 52
  slavery and, 24
  of southern US, 6
Powell, Tara, 104
Price, Kenneth M., 32
proletarian fiction, 47–8
pronouns, objectification with, 119

"race problem," 1–3
racial degeneration, 26–7, 37
racial hierarchies, 33, 35, 37
racism
  as cross-class, 76–7, 80
  individual vs. institutional, 68–9, 72–3, 80
  of middle class, 18, 71–3, 76–7, 80
  poor white stereotypes and, 69, 71–3, 76, 79–81, 86, 98
  as sustenance for poor whites, 98
Rafter, Nicole Hahn, 4
Ransom, John Crowe, 49
recent (2010s) works depicting poor whites
  feels-as-if stories in, 124, 131
  by Hochschild, Arlie, 18, 123–7, 129, 132
  poor whites as foils for middle class in, 124–7, 130–1
  poor whites as lazy in, 129–31
  poor whites as unalive in, 18, 123–4, 126–8, 132
  by Vance, J. D., 18, 123–4, 126–30, 132
regional/local color writers, 3, 19–22, 25, 28, 32, 133, *see also* plantation literature
restaurant workers in grit lit, 111, 113–14
Ring, Natalie J., 21
Romero, Lora, 69
rural/urban divide, 44–6, 50, 53, 55–8

sandhillers, 28
Scientific American, 97
Scribner's Monthly, 6, 26
Sewanee Review, 73
sexuality in grit lit, 113–19
sharecropping, 48
shoes as marker of social class, 86–7
Simmel, Georg
  "Sociology of the Senses," 64
Singal, Daniel J., 49, 58

slavery
    in Chesnutt's "Mars Jeems's Nightmare," 29–30
    in plantation fiction, 33–8, 41, 105
    and white poverty, 24
Smedes, Susan Dabney
    Memorials of a Southern Planter, 105
smell, social status and, 64–7
Smith, Lillian, 78, 81
    Killers of the Dream, 10, 69, 78–81, 99, 103
snuff dipping, 97
social class, *see* class distinctions
social hierarchies, 9, 37, 44, 76–8, 85–8
social mobility/immobility, 9, 33–9, 51–3, 85, 87, 89, 131
social status, 9–10, 30, 44, 64–7, 73, 77, 87–90, 125–6
social stigma, 65–6, 85–8, 92
South, US
    food and cooking in, 94, 104–8
    historic revisionism of, 47, 49
    Jim Crow system in, 79–80
    in 1960s, 85
    optimism about social mobility in, 131
    poor whites in, 26, 55, *see also* poor whites
    post-Reconstruction fragmentation of, 20
    poverty of, 6
    White Citizens' Councils in, 72
    women writers of, *see* literature of civil rights era
southwestern humor, 1, 7–8, 96
standardized tests, 130
stasis vs. change, 33–9, 51–3, 85, 87, 89
stereotypes of poor whites, *see also* literary disruptions of poor white stereotypes
    as backward and obsolete, 17, 45–6, 54–7
    as country people, 44–6, 54–8, 90–2
    as degenerate, 26–7, 37
    as dirty, 64, 74
    as diseased, 24–5, 74, 87, 94–8
    embodiment of, 64–7
    as helpless, 129
    with hunger as personal pathology, 94–100
    as ignorant and feebleminded, 3, 23, 27, 59–60, 79, 99
    as jealous, 70
    with language, 69
    as lazy, *see* laziness, poor whites and
    minimal or contrary evidence for, 74–5
    as racists, 69, 71–3, 76, 79–81, 86, 98
    with sense of inferiority, 70, 92
    as trash/waste, 55, 64–7, 77, 85, 90, 100, 102
    as unalive, 18, 123–4, 126–8, 132
    as unimprovable, 4, 7, 9, 22–5, 87, 89
sterilization, 7, 59–60, 62

Stern, Alexandra Minna, 7
Stockett, Kathryn
    Help, The, 108
Stoddard, Lothrop
    Revolt Against Civilization, The, 54
stream-of-consciousness narration, 17, 46
Sundquist, Eric J., 20, 37, 40
sweat economics, 49–51
syntax, class distinctions with, 10

tax exemptions, 128
third-person narration, 12, 73, 116
Thompson, E. P., 10
Thompson, Florence, 120
Titus, Mary, 104
To Kill a Mockingbird (Lee)
    Atticus Finch (character), 68, 85
    change agents vs. stasis in, 85, 87, 89
    food and class distinctions in, 99–100
    influence of, 84
    middle-class norms in, 85, 89
    O'Connor's reaction to, 88–93
    racism of poor whites in, 68, 86
    reconsideration of, 68
    socialization of white children in, 88
    stigma of poor whites in, 85–8, 92
tobacco use, 97
Tourgée, Albion, 33
Trachtenberg, Alan, 121
Tracy, Susan J., 34
trash, poor whites as, 26–7, 37, 55, 64–7, 77, 85, 90, 100, 102
Twain, Mark
    Adventures of Huckleberry Finn, 4
    Huckleberry Finn (character), 1, 6
Twelve Southerners, *see* Nashville Agrarians (Twelve Southerners)

unalive, stereotype of poor whites as, 18, 123–4, 126–8, 132
unreliable narration, 75
urban/rural divide, 44–6, 50, 53, 55–8
US Supreme Court, 59
us/them dichotomies, 10

Vance, J. D.
    Hillbilly Elegy, 18, 123–4, 126–30, 132
Veblen, Thorstein
    Theory of the Leisure Class, The, 30
Virginia, sterilization laws in, 59
voting rights, 4

Warner, Amos G., 94
Warren, Kenneth W., 35
Washington, Booker T., 31

Up From Slavery, 31
waste, poor whites as, 26–7, 37, 55, 64–7, 77, 85, 90, 100, 102
Watson, Jay, 52, 60
welfare fraud, 128
wellness culture, 123–4, 127
Welty, Eudora, 71, 78
   "Where Is the Voice Coming From?," 10, 68, 70–3, 75–6, 78
White Citizens' Councils, 72
white southerners, *see also* poor whites, *see also* middle-class whites
   leisure-class life of, 30–2, 49–51
   with social capital, 46, 53, 55–7
white supremacy, 72, 79–81
Williamson, Joel, 11
Willis, Susan, 52
women, poor white
   bodies of, 95, 113, 117–18
   as feebleminded, 56, 59
   and food in grit lit, 113–15, 117–18
   as grit lit authors, 110–12
   as human givers in grit lit, 112–15, 119–20
   and sex in grit lit, 113–19
   sterilization of, 7, 59–60, 62
   visual signifiers of, 3, 15
Wood, Ralph C., 78
Woodward, C. Vann, 6
   Burden of Southern History, The, 85
   "Search for Southern Identity, The," 107
work, *see* labor
work ethic, 11, 130–1
working-class whites, 11, 64, 71
writing "naked," 109

Zandy, Janet, 12

Recent books in this series (*continued from page ii*)

181. ROB TURNER
 Counterfeit Culture
180. KATE STANLEY
 Practices of Surprise in American Literature after Emerson
179. JOHANNES VOELZ
 The Poetics of Insecurity
178. JOHN HAY
 Postapocalyptic Fantasies in Antebellum American Literature
177. PAUL JAUSSEN
 Writing in Real Time
176. CINDY WEINSTEIN
 Time, Tense, and American Literature
175. CODY MARS
 Nineteenth-Century American Literature and the Long Civil War
174. STACEY MARGOLIS
 Fictions of Mass Democracy in Nineteenth-Century America
173. PAUL DOWNES
 Hobbes, Sovereignty, and Early American Literature
172. DAVID BERGMAN
 Poetry of Disturbance
171. MARK NOBLE
 American Poetic Materialism from Whitman to Stevens
170. JOANNA FREER
 Thomas Pynchon and American Counterculture
169. DOMINIC MASTROIANNI
 Politics and Skepticism in Antebellum American Literature
168. GAVIN JONES
 Failure and the American Writer
167. LENA HILL
 Visualizing Blackness and the Creation of the African American Literary Tradition
166. MICHAEL ZISER
 Environmental Practice and Early American Literature
165. ANDREW HEBARD
 The Poetics of Sovereignty in American Literature, 1885–1910
164. CHRISTOPHER FREEBURG
 Melville and the Idea of Blackness
163. TIM ARMSTRONG
 The Logic of Slavery
162. JUSTINE MURISON
 The Politics of Anxiety in Nineteenth-Century American Literature

161. HSUAN L. HSU
    Geography and the Production of Space in Nineteenth-Century American Literature
160. DORRI BEAM
    Style, Gender, and Fantasy in Nineteenth-Century American Women's Writing
159. YOGITA GOYAL
    Romance, Diaspora, and Black Atlantic Literature
158. MICHAEL CLUNE
    American Literature and the Free Market, 1945–2000
157. KERRY LARSON
    Imagining Equality in Nineteenth-Century American Literature
156. LAWRENCE ROSENWALD
    Multilingual America: Language and the Making of American Literature
155. ANITA PATTERSON
    Race, American Literature, and Transnational Modernism
154. ELIZABETH RENKER
    The Origins of American Literature Studies: An Institutional History
153. THEO DAVIS
    Formalism, Experience, and the Making of American Literature in the Nineteenth Century
152. JOAN RICHARDSON
    A Natural History of Pragmatism: The Fact of Feeling from Jonathan Edwards to Gertrude Stein
151. EZRA TAWIL
    The Making of Racial Sentiment: Slavery and the Birth of the Frontier Romance
150. ARTHUR RISS
    Race, Slavery, and Liberalism in Nineteenth-Century American Literature
149. JENNIFER ASHTON
    From Modernism to Postmodernism: American Poetry and Theory in the Twentieth Century
148. MAURICE S. LEE
    Slavery, Philosophy, and American Literature, 1830–1860
147. CINDY WEINSTEIN
    Family, Kinship, and Sympathy in Nineteenth-Century American Literature
146. ELIZABETH HEWITT
    Correspondence and American Literature, 1770–1865
145. ANNA BRICKHOUSE
    Transamerican Literary Relations and the Nineteenth-Century Public Sphere
144. ELIZA RICHARDS
    Gender and the Poetics of Reception in Poe's Circle
143. JENNIE A. KASSANOFF
    Edith Wharton and the Politics of Race

142. JOHN MCWILLIAMS
New England's Crises and Cultural Memory: Literature, Politics, History, Religion, 1620–1860

141. SUSAN M. GRIFFIN
Anti-Catholicism and Nineteenth-Century Fiction

140. ROBERT E. ABRAMS
Landscape and Ideology in American Renaissance Literature

139. JOHN D. KERKERING
The Poetics of National and Racial Identity in Nineteenth-Century American Literature

138. MICHELE BIRNBAUM
Race, Work, and Desire in American Literature, 1860–1930

137. RICHARD GRUSIN
Culture, Technology, and the Creation of America's National Parks

136. RALPH BAUER
The Cultural Geography of Colonial American Literatures: Empire, Travel, Modernity

135. MARY ESTEVE
The Aesthetics and Politics of the Crowd in American Literature

For EU product safety concerns, contact us at Calle de José Abascal, 56–1º,
28003 Madrid, Spain or eugpsr@cambridge.org.

www.ingramcontent.com/pod-product-compliance
Lightning Source LLC
LaVergne TN
LVHW041632060526
838200LV00040B/1552